Human Judgment
and Decision Making

Human Judgment and Decision Making

Theories, Methods, and Procedures

Kenneth R. Hammond
Gary H. McClelland
Jeryl Mumpower
University of Colorado at Boulder

PRAEGER

PRAEGER SPECIAL STUDIES • PRAEGER SCIENTIFIC

●HEMISPHERE PUBLISHING CORPORATION

Published in 1980 by Praeger Publishers
CBS Educational and Professional Publishing
A Division of CBS, Inc.
521 Fifth Avenue, New York, New York 10017 U.S.A.

0123456789   056   987654321
BCBC

Library of Congress Cataloging in Publication Data

Hammond, Kenneth R.
    Human judgment and decision making.

    Report presented at the 12th annual Conference on
Human Judgment, held Apr. 28-30, 1978 in Boulder, Colo.
    Bibliography: p.
    Includes index.
    1. Decision-making. I. McClelland, Gary H.,
date   joint author. II. Mumpower, Jeryl, date
joint author. III. Conference on Human Judgment, 12th,
Boulder, Colo., 1978. IV. Title.
HD30.23.H35   658.4'03   79-27566
ISBN 0-03-057567-2

Printed in the United States of America

Contents

THEORY

METHOD

Preface

We undertook this book in the hope that it would help integrate the numerous approaches to judgment and decision making that have evolved over the past few decades. More immediately, the book was to provide a point of departure for a conference that we hoped would mark the start of such integration, the Twelfth Annual Conference on Human Judgment (held April 28-30, 1978, in Boulder, Colorado). Twenty-five prominent researchers and theoreticians in the field of judgment and decision making were invited. All but one accepted the invitation, and only one other was unable to attend, a remarkable indication of the interest in integration. A draft of the present book was distributed to all participants prior to the conference; with some revisions, the same report appears here.

Work on the integration effort continues. We wish to take this opportunity to thank all those who have helped us make whatever progress we have achieved to date. Among them are Martin Tolcott, director of engineering psychology programs at the Office of Naval Research, who provided inspiration and assistance both before and after the conference; a number of conference participants; and our colleagues and staff at the Center for

Research on Judgment and Policy, Institute of Behavioral Science, University
of Colorado at Boulder. We are particularly grateful to Donald Deane for his
critical editorial review of our manuscript and to Lois Stroh, Mary Luhring,
Barbara Marvin, Susan Cohen, and Judy Fukuhara, without whose help neither
the book nor the conference would have succeeded.

Kenneth R. Hammond
Gary H. McClelland
Jeryl Mumpower

Chapter 1

Introduction

Contemporary students of human judgment and decision making include operations researchers, management scientists, statisticians, mathematical psychologists and economists as well as others; a wide variety of disciplines have converged on a single topic. What brings these disciplines together is a new vigor in the belief that this critical cognitive activity—judging, deciding, choosing—can be brought under scientific, empirical scrutiny and that as a result of such scrutiny, it cannot only be understood but improved. But the scientific approach to the study of human judgment and decision making is not universally held, or even widely held, to be a method appropriate for this problem; by no means is everyone convinced that science will enable us to understand our cognitive processes. Moreover, the sharp division of opinion as to whether the scientific method is applicable to this problem is age-old, as Raphael shows us in his famous Renaissance painting, in which he arranges the peripatetic philosophers of Athens from right to left in terms of whether they took a quantitative, scientific approach, or an intuitive approach, to understanding nature, including human perception, judgment and thinking.

Even by mid 19th century, these two approaches were still\ equal contenders for recognition as the proper epistemological method. Note, for example, how Isaiah Berlin (1978) describes the state of these "rival types of knowledge," in the mid 19th century and how familiar the terms of the dispute will seem today:

> The quarrel between these rival types of knowledge—that which results from methodical inquiry, and the more impalpable kind that consists in the 'sense of reality', in 'wisdom'—is very old. And the claims of both have generally been recognised to have some validity: the bitterest clashes have been concerned with the precise line which marks the frontier between their territories. Those who made large claims for non-scientific knowledge have been accused by their adversaries of irrationalism and obscurantism, of the deliberate rejection, in favour of the emotions of blind prejudice, of reliable public standards of ascertainable truth; and have, in their turn, charged their opponents, the ambitious champions of science, with making absurd claims, promising the impossible, issuing false prospectuses, of undertaking to explain history or the arts or the states of the individual soul (and to change them too) when quite plainly they do not begin to understand what they are; when the results of their labours, even when they are not nugatory, tend to take unpredicted, often catastrophic directions—and all this because they will not, being vain and headstrong, admit that too many factors in too many situations are always unknown, and not discoverable by the methods of natural science. Better, surely, not to pretend to calculate the incalculable, not to pretend that there is an Archimedean point outside the world whence everything is measurable and alterable; better to use in each context the methods that seem to fit it best, that give the (pragmatically) best results; to resist the temptations of Procrustes; above all to distinguish what is isolable, classifiable and capable of objective study and sometimes of precise measurement and manipulation, from the most permanent, ubiquitous, inescapable, intimately present features of our world, which, if anything, are over-familiar, so that their 'inexorable' pressures, being too much with us, is scarcely felt, hardly noticed, and cannot conceivably be observed in perspective, be an object of study. This is the distinction that permeates the thought of Pascal and Blake, Rousseau and Schelling, Goethe and Coleridge, Chateaubriand and Carlyle; of all those who speak of the reasons of the heart, or of men's moral or spiritual nature, of sublimity and depth, of the 'profounder' insight of poets and prophets, of special kinds of understanding, of inwardly comprehending, or being at one with, the world. (pp. 78-79)*

Any judgment or decision analyst who reads that passage will recognize that Berlin has caught the essence of the antinomy between the scientific approach to this topic and the "rival type of knowledge," known as common

*Copyright 1978, Viking Press. Reprinted by Permission of Viking Penguin Inc.

sense or wisdom, so often put forth as superior by the "man on the street." The persistence of the sharp division that Berlin draws between these claims to the correct path to truth that was characteristic of the mid 19th century can clearly be seen in a parallel description of the present rivalry between "common sense" and "refined knowledge" drawn by Stephen Pepper in 1948:

> *Tension between common sense and refined knowledge.*—This is a strange set of traits for an important mass of cognitive material [common sense]—to be not definitely cognizable, to be not cognitively responsible and so irritable, and yet to be cognitively secure. The first two traits in the order just indicated are negative in the eyes of knowledge; only the last is positive. The first two traits are, in fact, so displeasing to experts of cognition that the material of common sense has very frequently been ignored as a respectable factor in cognition. And so, on this side, we find common sense, the opinions of the man in the street, disparaged and ridiculed in comparison with the definite and responsible knowledge of science and philosophy. Yet, on the other side, the security of common sense does not wholly escape the attention of men, nor can men wholly ignore an insecurity in the abstract concepts, the hairsplitting definitions, the speculative hypotheses of expert critical knowledge. So, on this score, common sense becomes an object of praise for its simple homespun wisdom and plain practical sense.
>
> This tension between common sense and expert knowledge, between cognitive security without responsibility and cognitive responsibility without full security, is the interior dynamcis of the knowledge situation. The indefiniteness of much detail in common sense, its contradictions, its lack of established grounds, drive thought to seek definitiveness, consistency, and reasons. Thought finds these in the criticized and refined knowledge of mathematics, science, and philosophy, only to discover that these tend to thin out into arbitrary definitions, pointer readings, and tentative hypotheses. Astounded at the thinness and hollowness of these culminating achievements of conscientiously responsible cognition, thought seeks matter for its definitions, significance for its pointer readings, and support for its wobbling hypotheses. Responsible cognition finds itself insecure as a result of the very earnestness of its virtues. But where shall it turn? It does, in fact, turn back to common sense, that indefinite and irresponsible source which it so lately scorned. But it does so, generally, with a bad grace. After filling its empty definitions and pointer readings and hypotheses with meanings out of the rich confusion of common sense, it generally turns its head away, shuts its eyes to what it has been doing, and affirms dogmatically the self-evidence and certainty of the common-sense significance it has drawn into its concepts. Then it pretends to be securely based on self-evident principles or indubitable facts. If our recent criticism of dogmatism is correct, however, this security in self-evidence and indubitability has proved questionable. And critical knowledge hangs over a vacuum unless it

acknowledges openly the actual, though strange, source of its significance and security in the uncriticized material of common sense. Thus the circle is completed. Common sense continually demands the responsible criticism of refined knowledge, and refined knowledge sooner or later requires the security of common-sense support.

Why cannot the two merge? No doubt, that is the inherent aim of cognition. For what the question amounts to is, Why is there any ignorance? It is clear that the answer to such a question can only be given with any specificity in terms of refined knowledge ... it seems fairly obvious that as long as refined knowledge is not complete, so long at least will there be a discrepancy between the material of common sense and that of critical cognition. For, considering the situation at its worst, even the extremest efforts of dictatorial propaganda cannot stop those insistent questionings that well up in the most innocent as also in the most sophisticated minds.

Whence do these questionings well up, which are the signs of the obstinate security of common sense? For though man reason himself into a machine, into a solipsism of the present moment, into Nirvana, or into Nothing, life still breaks out in hunger and craving, and nature affirms itself in the strong pressure of the ground and the heat of the sun. There is no doubt of these common-sense insistencies, but if we seek the reasons for them we can find them only in refined critical knowledge ... But until ignorance completely disappears we cannot expect a specific and fully adequate answer.

Such, then, is the basic polarity of cognition, which we may expect to continue as long as we fall short of omniscience. On the one side, irresponsible but secure common sense; on the other, responsible but insecure critical cognition. (pp. 44-47)

These passages from students of the history of thought are quoted at length because, despite their difference in style, they will convey to the reader a perspective not ordinarily encountered; they illustrate the fact that the study of human judgment and decision making is not a new idea, that the rivalry between different views of what knowledge is has a long history, and that this rivalry may be expected to persist "as long as we fall short of omniscience," as Pepper puts it. Moreover, these passages should serve to indicate to the reader that the pursuit of the study of human judgment and decision making will lead one to encounter one of the fundamental problems of mankind: How do we know our world and choose what to do? And by what method shall we find the answer?

The longer view aside, however, it will be noted that Pepper's remarks were made in 1948; the reader will now want to know: is the situation no different in 1978? Has the scientific approach not filled out to any significant degree the "thinness and hollowness of conscientiously responsible cognition"? Not yet "found matter for its definitions"? Nor "significance for its pointer readings"? "Nor support for its wobbling hypotheses"? In short, does critical cognition not yet offer a sense of security as well as responsibility?

The modern, quantitatively oriented descendants of those on the right of Rapheal's painting who study human judgment and decision making will answer in the affirmative: they will say that responsible cognition, refined knowledge, has indeed become more secure, if not fully so. The greatest source of increased security comes from the increased reliance on the use of the logic of mathematics and the resort to empirical test of hypotheses; greater rigor in thought, method, and empirical research has led to more cognitive security. As a result, even though they are aware of how "thin" and "hollow" the results of their efforts can be, and even though the security of common sense is not altogether despised, common sense is under sharper scrutiny (and sharper attack) than ever before by the advocates of responsible cognition. It has been the (slow and uneven) *cumulative* growth of hard-won empirical knowledge and skill that has increased the security that responsible cognition has sought, and found, for its "wobbling hypotheses." For while the mid 19th-century philosophers were continuing to pursue the nuances of meaning in the verbal struggle between "rival types of knowledge," mid 19th-century scientists, little known then and now, were successfully making quantitative analyses of judgments for the first time, and were thus preparing the way for the mid 20th-century judgment and decision analysts. The fact that judgments *can* be quantified, *can* be refined in a responsible way, and *can* be analyzed and understood in quantitative terms, can no longer be doubted.

And that brings us to the reasons for this monograph. Awareness of the possibility of mathematically oriented, empirically based methods for analyzing and perhaps improving common sense has led to a proliferation of quantitative concepts and techniques, and these are now so numerous and diverse they constitute a threat to the cumulative nature of the scientific study of judgment and decision making; the proliferation of effort is so large and so scattered over the academic and nonacademic terrain that its very profuseness is a danger to its future. It will, therefore, be our purpose to attempt to organize and integrate contemporary approaches to this topic in order to assist in the continuance of the cumulative growth of what may, because of its central function, become a separate, identifiable scientific discipline.

1.1 EFFORTS TOWARD INTEGRATION

The present need for integration is reflected in the fact that at least three sponsored conferences and at least nine articles (not counting review articles) have recently addressed themselves to the problem of the proper study of judgment and decision making.

The following two paragraphs from the introduction to one recent conference indicate the breadth of the academic interests of the participants:

> The search for theories, concepts, and techniques applicable to decision-making processes under multiple criteria has steadily been intensified during the past few years. We feel that the time has come to review the results, to compare them, and to outline possible future directions. As far as we know, the seminar at which the papers in this volume were read was the first meeting of this nature in the United States. To assure the highest quality of this meeting, we have sought participation of leading researchers and practitioners in this field. Since the problem is highly general, the participants represent many areas of applied decision making. Most are from *business and economics, but a number of engineers, psychologists, sociologists, behavioral scientists, mathematicians, statisticians,* and *political scientists* also contributed (italics ours).
>
> The important part of the discussions explored the relation between formalized decision-making techniques (utilizing computer and mathematical analysis) and of human judgment, based on intuition, experience, and "professional insight." Rejuvenation of the role of human judgment seems to be one of the main aspects of the literature on multiple criteria decision making but many participants seem to be skeptical about man's ability to choose among multiattributed alternatives. (Cochrane & Zeleny, 1973, p. xiv)*

There are few signs, however, that paper-reading conferences lead to integration. And although it is too soon to appraise the result of the most recent integrative efforts (Fischhoff's "Attribution Theory and Judgment Under Uncertainty," 1976, and Shanteau & Phelps's "Judgment and Swine: Approaches and Issues in Applied Judgment Analysis," 1977), the results of similar articles are discouraging; progress seems not to have occurred. For example, Anderson's effort in 1974 to integrate the approaches of Information Integration Theory and Attribution Theory can only be described as heroic, yet in a recent compendium on Attribution Theory (Harvey, Ickes, & Kidd, 1976) that includes 26 authors, Anderson's article is mentioned only once, and that reference ignores his attempt at integration. Similarly, Kukla's effort (1972) to combine "concepts of decision theory with those of attribution theory" (p. 454) is not mentioned in that compendium by a single author (except Fischhoff).

Nor is there any evidence that the other efforts at integration have achieved recognition, or have changed anyone's approach to the study of judgment and decision making. Typically, related work carried out by a member of a different discipline is given an academic "nod." Keeney and Raiffa's (1976) footnote (p. 8) regarding the contributions of psychologists provides a good example, thus: "Clearly there is much overlap of interest

*Copyright © 1973 by University of South Carolina Press.

between the prescriptive and descriptive viewpoints. Over the past 25 years, the contributions of many people concerned with descriptive aspects of decision making has had a significant impact on prescriptive decision analysis." Keeney and Raiffa then refer to four "excellent reviews." But they fail to indicate what these "significant impacts" are, and reading Keeney and Raiffa did not enable us to discern them; even Edwards' work on Bayesian decision making is given only passing mention. The only hopeful note we find is in (alas!) another footnote (p. 212) in which Keeney and Raiffa acknowledge that "Tversky (1975) and other experimental psychologists working in descriptive decision theory indicate that assessors inadvertently bias responses by the forms of questions they pose," an acknowledgement that can hardly be said to capture the full spirit of the work done so far.

Not to be one-sided, we must also note that the academic "nod" relationship is symmetrical. While psychologists studying judgment and decision making sometimes cite the precursors of modern decision theory (e.g., von Neuman & Morgenstern and Savage), one must look hard to find any serious consideration by psychologists of recent work in decision theory. In short, it is not that bridges need to be built between different approaches, rather, a *kinship system* must be found within which each approach can determine its relationship to every other approach.

1.2 THE PRESENT APPROACH TO INTEGRATION

We shall, therefore, try to provide a *broad, theoretically neutral, systematic* framework that will permit, indeed, encourage the discovery of that "kinship system" rather than to compare pairs of approaches in detail. Our framework will be *broad* because the contributions to the study of judgment and decision making come from a wide range of theoretical approaches. Only a broad framework that encompasses these apparently disparate approaches can help us to determine whether there is a common core of concepts, methods and procedures within them, and what the boundaries of that common core might be.

Our framework will attempt to achieve *theoretical neutrality* by comparing each approach on a set of neutral dimensions that will be indicated below. Theoretically neutral description should make systematic comparison possible and, we hope, acceptable as well. Systematic treatment of several approaches over a series of dimensions has the virtue of demanding completeness from the author and providing it for the reader. But just as we have learned that it requires a patient, even pedestrian, diligence on the part of the authors, the reader will learn that she or he will have to be patient, too. Good organization of what is generally known about various approaches, accuracy and completeness of description of these approaches—these are our aims, not the overwhelming insight that produces yet one more new approach, or that declares that only one of the present approaches is on the narrow road to truth (which, we admit, remains indistinct to us).

Our work is *programmatic* as well as systematic. We have no illusions that our overview will be the end of this project; it is clearly only the beginning. We shall take full responsibility for providing a good organizational framework that can be used, if only to be used to develop a better one. Failure here will be wholly our failure. We do not take full responsibility for accuracy, however; we shall simply do the best we can. The knowledge that our descriptions and interpretations of the work of others will be reviewed and criticized by them, however, gives us full confidence that few inaccuracies will fail to be detected and corrected with precision, perhaps even enthusiasm.

Completeness, of course, is far beyond our capacity: it is a goal that can only be approximated more closely over time. That is why our work is programmatic. Our resources permitted us to do no more than rely on a few major sources, although these are generally original ones. Here again we rely on the personal interests of the proponents of various approaches to provide the materials as well as the guidance to make certain that first things are dealt with first. But the reverse is true as well; conceptual boundaries must be drawn; not everything that a proponent of a given approach has done or written is relevant to this project. Therefore, while errors of fact and interpretation can be corrected rather quickly, incompleteness can be remedied only through contributions to a programmatic effort by all concerned.

It is precisely this programmatic aim that most significantly marks off the present method for achieving integration from previous ones. We shall present a framework for integration that invites various researchers in the field of judgment and decision making to participate in the persistent reconstruction of that framework and the continuous alteration of its content. Thus we invite researchers to reconstruct that framework in a form that brings integration closer.

Our approach, then, will be to provide a broad, systematic descriptive framework for the reader to improve, in addition to a report to contemplate. We hope that our readers will find our report to be sufficiently well organized and accurate to be worthy of their efforts to complete and improve it, and thus to participate in the initial step toward the development of a cumulative scientific discipline of judgment and decision making.

1.3 DEVELOPING A DESCRIPTIVE FRAMEWORK

Theoretical approaches cannot be integrated without describing and comparing them, and, therefore some means must be found for making comparative description possible, as well as palatable.

Because we chose to develop a broad descriptive framework ours encompasses approaches from decision theory (as it is developed and applied in the field of management science) to attribution theory (as it is developed and applied in psychology). Six approaches were included within that range:

Decision Theory (DT)
Behavioral Decision Theory (BDT)
Psychological Decision Theory (PDT)
Social Judgment Theory (SJT)
Information Integration Theory (IIT)
Attribution Theory (AT)

It will be immediately apparent to students of judgment and decision making that we took some liberties with the names we assigned to the second and third approaches. We have deliberately and (somewhat) arbitrarily assigned the name of Behavioral Decision Theory to the work of Edwards and his colleagues, and the name Psychological Decision Theory to the work of Kahneman and Tversky and their colleagues (among whom we include Fischhoff, Lichtenstein, and Slovic). Our defense is simply that we believed the distinction to be necessary, a defense the reader will have an opportunity to evaluate below.

Although others may well have chosen to consider other, or more, approaches, we believe that an effort to integrate these six approaches should satisfy the requirements of an initial effort. True, we have cast a net with a very broad mesh. But the use of a finer mesh, the inclusion of more approaches, would have meant a long postponement of this report and criticism of it. As it is, the reader may well wish that we had cast even a broader net, for then we could have more nearly completed our work.

1.4 SIX APPROACHES

The six approaches to be described in this monograph include three whose origins lie primarily in economics (Decision Theory, Behavioral Decision Theory, Psychological Decision Theory) and three whose origins lie primarily in psychology (Social Judgment Theory, Information Integration Theory, and Attribution Theory). Each is discussed very briefly below.

1.4.1 Decision Theory (DT)

Of a number of possible approaches within Decision Theory we chose to describe the work of Ralph Keeney and Howard Raiffa not only because of their steady series of contributions to this problem, but because of the recent organization of their work into a well-recognized book (Keeny & Raiffa, 1976) that provides a highly accessible reference work. When we refer to DT in the remainder of the text, therefore, we shall be referring to that version of

DT that is contained in their book, a version often referred to as "Multi-attribute Utility Theory."

Main topic. The main topic for DT is the problem of choosing among alternatives with multiple attributes. According to DT, the principal parameters of the process of choosing this alternative over that one are (a) the *probability* of the occurrence of the alternative and (b) its *utility* to the decider. This formulation of the decision process lends itself to formal, mathematical analysis, thus enabling the decision theorist to address a fundamental question: does the decision process of this (or any other) decision maker conform with the formal axioms of choice, as set forth by the logic of the mathematics of choice? Having found evidence that the cognitive activity of decision making often does not meet this criterion, decision theorists have developed means to assist decision makers to achieve rationality by bringing their cognitive activity in conformity with the demands of logic. DT is, then, essentially a means for *prescribing* what the decision process should be, if it is to be rational. Decision analysis, the art of assisting decision makers, as well as research on decision theory, are now thriving activities.

1.4.2 Behavioral Decision Theory (BDT)

The discovery that human decision making falls short of meeting the demands of rationality was hardly a new idea, and it was not greeted, inside or outside the academic world, with astonishment, or even doubt. But a new vigor was given to the study of the cognitive aspects of decision making when a psychologist—Ward Edwards—observed the progress that had been made by economists, noted the parallel interests of psychologists in the topic of decision making, showed how the work of psychologists and economists could supplement one another, and, most important, showed how supplementation could produce a systematic empirical program of research.

Main topic. In particular, Edwards focused on the question of how to *describe* the less-than-optimal behavior of the decision maker, and offered a theory of what the behavior of the decision maker *is* (as compared with the decision theorists' interest in showing what it is *not*). Edwards' effort to document the value of Bayesian statistics as a descriptive point of reference led to a number of similar efforts by others, nearly all of which were tested in the psychological laboratory, within the general framework of psychological research methodology, as well as with due regard for the theory of psychological measurement that had begun over a century earlier. In addition, Behavioral Decision Theorists have also investigated the value of Multiattribute Utility Theory as a method for assisting decision makers, in a manner analogous to that of Keeney and Raiffa.

1.4.3 Psychological Decision Theory (PDT)

Roughly 20 years after Edwards' classical 1954 paper, two psychologists, Daniel Kahneman and Amos Tversky, took the psychological approach further; they developed a theory of decision making that moved beyond description to explanation and prediction of decision behavior.

Main topic. The main interest of these researchers is to find the cognitive sources of the departure from the criteria of rationality. Specifically, they seek the manner in which the processes of memory, perception and specific varieties of experience lead decision makers to develop systematic errors in their estimates of the probabilities and utilities that are the key parameters in decision theory.

1.4.4 Transition

In short, DT is largely if not entirely *prescriptive* in its efforts, whereas the latter two approaches are descriptive—and explanatory. That is, whereas DT indicates how the decision maker *should* arrive at rational decisions, the latter approaches describe how and why they *depart* from DT's rational prescription for cognition that include judgments of probability and utility. The approaches we shall next describe, however, are wholly concerned with the description of the process of judgment, without significant regard for prescription. And that is because they are primarily concerned with how people *know,* rather than how they *choose,* a distinction that is important, not only because it specifies differences in aims, but because it carries implications for the methodology that researchers use.

1.4.5 Social Judgment Theory (SJT)

This approach has its origins in the field of perception, and takes its general theory and method from the work of Egon Brunswik (1903-1955). Kenneth Hammond extended this approach to the study of judgment and decision making, and, in doing so, continued to emphasize the cognitive difficulties created by the probabilistic, interdependent relation among variables in the world (i.e., the causal texture of the natural environment) as it is experienced by the person attempting to understand it. SJT is thus related to the approaches described above because it shares their emphasis on the uncertainty inherent in the physical, biological and social environment.

Main topic. SJT gives considerable attention to the manner in which the formal properties ("causal texture") of the environment create significant difficulties for human beings to learn to make accurate judgments about environmental events (multiple cue probability learning) including the behavior of other people (interpersonal learning). Interpersonal conflict arising from different judgments is also a topic to which SJT gives considerable attention. In general, SJT emphasizes the interaction between environmental and cognitive systems.

1.4.6 Information Integration Theory (IIT)

There is a direct line from the work of the psychophysicists mentioned earlier to the approach taken by Norman Anderson in his development of IIT. For in their efforts to understand the cognitive process of integrating information, IIT theorists place considerable emphasis on measuring, in a precise metric sense, the social as well as physical judgments of persons.

Main topic. IIT emphasizes and provides for the analysis of the cognitive integration of multiple pieces of information that are measured subjectively, and for which subjective importance is also measured. A person's method of integrating such information is indicated in terms of the "cognitive algebra" employed. The principal aim of IIT is to discover the form of cognitive algebra human beings employ in various cognitive activities required by various tasks. For example, is the information in one set of conditions integrated or combined by one form of cognitive algebra (e.g., averaging), while information in other conditions is integrated by a different algebraic form (e.g., multiplying)?

1.4.7 Attribution Theory (AT)

The psychology of knowing in social as well as physical circumstances was emphasized by Fritz Heider, Brunswik's contemporary. Just as Brunswik emphasized the "causal texture" of the environment, Heider emphasized the cognitive difficulties of attributing causes when they are buried in the structural interdependency of the variables in the environmental context.

Main topic. Causal attribution has been the principal topic of interest to researchers following Heider's general approach to inference. Under what conditions will a person be seen as a causal agent in contrast to an environmental circumstance? When will a person rather than circumstances be blamed (or rewarded) for outcomes of events? Causal attribution is of course, a central feature of "the psychology of common sense" and, therefore, Attribution Theory addresses directly the "tension between common sense and refined knowledge" of which Pepper wrote. Edward Jones and Harold Kelley, as well as many others, have pursued these questions primarily by means of the experimental approach.

1.5 A COMMON THEME

For those on the left of Raphael's Renaissance painting, the wisdom of common sense is a combination of rationality tempered by experience, a powerful form of cognition not to be destroyed by putatively scientific methods of anlysis that decompose it into artificial and "hollow" fragments. For those quantitatively oriented philosophers on the right, however, human cognition is not beyond analysis, nor does analysis necessarily destroy it. Since cognition is a natural activity, it requires scientific understanding, and should be susceptible to the empirical method that is basic to all science. But those who intend to bring the scientific method to bear on the process of human judgment and decision making know that their work will be protested (even by scientists), not merely because of its boldness, but because of its arrogance. For by asserting their premise—that human cognition can and should be studied by scientific methods—they imply that they expect not only to *understand* one of nature's most mysterious processes, but expect to *control* it as well. And therein lies the protest of the 20th century against the effort to "calculate the incalculable," as Berlin phrased it. But as the remainder of this monograph indicates, that protest has failed to discourage scientific efforts to understand human judgment and decision processes. We turn now to the development of a systematic, descriptive framework for comparing and integrating these scientific efforts.

1.6   A DESCRIPTIVE FRAMEWORK

In our effort to be systematic, we began with fundamentals; we divided our work into three major sections, *theory, method,* and *procedure,* and examined the six approaches mentioned above accordingly.

The theory section deals with the six approaches in terms of their origins, scope, intended function, principal concepts, loci of concepts, and their intended use. The method section examines each approach's basic methodology with respect to idiographic versus nomothetic analysis, sampling domains, object decomposition, judgment decomposition, aids for decision makers, and methodological claims. The procedure section focuses on description and comparison of the operational definitions that each approach provides for the important concepts identified in the theory section.

Having indicated the purpose of integration—the development of a cumulative scientific discipline—and the general method we employ in order to initiate this effort, we turn to the question of what integration could possibly mean. We take it that integration requires the following steps:

1 Denotation of similarities and differences;

2 Denotation of gaps and redundancies in the coverage of judgment and decision-making issues;

3 Denotation of antinomies that point to the need for empirical test (crucial experiments) and/or logical or conceptual reconciliation;

4 Logical and conceptual reconciliation whenever possible, as well as

suggestions for empirical reconciliation, although we hasten to add that integration does not mean "amalgamation," "coalescence," or even "unification." Our purpose is not to eliminate differences, providing that they are not merely verbal, or trivial in other ways.

And what if these steps were accomplished to some detectable degree? What would have been accomplished? First, a strong move would have been made toward the intellectual coherence that is now lacking; second, a clearer understanding of what various approaches add to the growth of scientific knowledge in the area of cognition would have been achieved, and third, a greater appreciation of the ability of various approaches to contribute to the judgment and decision-making capacity of human beings.

Are these important tasks? To ask that question of our readers may be analogous to asking the workers in Newcastle if coal is important. But it may not be superfluous to point out just how far we have already come in our own judgments of the validity and significance of our work. Consider these remarks made by Paul Slovic in the context of an article addressed to laymen: "This work [on judgment and decision making] . . . has led to the sobering conclusion that, in the face of uncertainty, man may be an *intellectual cripple* (italics ours), whose intuitive judgments and decisions violate many of the fundamental principles of optimal behavior" (1976). If there was tentativeness in this "sobering conclusion" conveyed by the word "may," that tentativeness was obliterated in the next sentence: "These intellectual deficiencies underscore the need for decision-making techniques" (p. 222). Slovic's views are undoubtedly shared by other scientifically-oriented students of judgment and decision making. Are these the conclusions that the philosophers on the right of Raphael's painting would have anticipated?

Theory

Chapter 2

Introduction to Theory

This section addresses itself to two problems: (a) describing and comparing the theoretical content of the six approaches to judgment and decision theory, and (b) attempting to integrate those approaches.

We begin our description and comparison of the six approaches by ordering them along a continuum as indicated in Fig. 2-1.

Any such single-dimensional ordering will of course be unsatisfactory. The above ordering will, however, serve the purpose of indicating the origins, or point of departure, of the six approaches. It represents roughly the largely economic reference of the approaches on the right, a reference that gradually diminishes as we move to the left on the continuum, and concomitantly represents the gradual increase in emphasis on psychology. This change of emphasis is also reflected in the fact that in all of the three approaches on the right (DT, BDT, and PDT), concepts of probability, utility and aggregation are taken to be major ones, whereas the three approaches on the left (SJT, IIT, and AT) treat these concepts as subvarieties of larger concepts of interest. Consequently, we shall categorize the first three approaches as Group I, and the second as Group II. As we shall see, however, integration is as likely to be needed within these groups as between them.

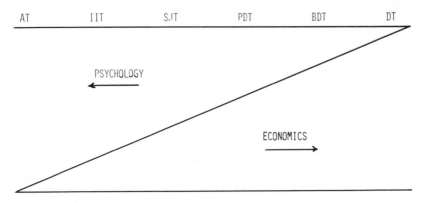

Figure 2-1 Differences in origins and reference groups among the six approaches. The area between the horizontal and diagonal lines provides a very rough approximation of the relative contribution of psychology and economics to each approach.

The separation of the six approaches into two major groups can be seen in Fig. 2-2(a).

Separation of these approaches into the above two groups not only indicates our point of departure, it also indicates differences in the reference groups that evaluate the work each group undertakes, the differences in the academic

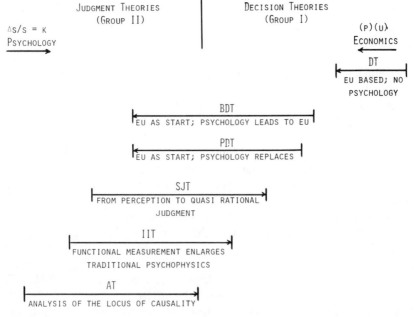

Figure 2-2 (a) Origins, overlapping interests, and direction of research among the six approaches and two groups.

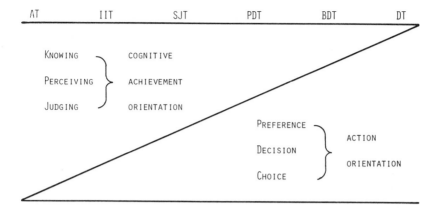

AT   IIT   SJT   PDT   BDT   DT

KNOWING   COGNITIVE

PERCEIVING   ACHIEVEMENT

JUDGING   ORIENTATION

PREFERENCE

DECISION   ACTION

CHOICE   ORIENTATION

Figure 2-2 (b)   Relative differences in orientation among the six groups.

background of those who read the work and cite it and thus make the work a prominent (or obscure) part of the literature.

Having indicated the manner in which the six approaches were ordered and categorized we now attempt to describe them in terms of the following theoretically neutral dimensions:

3   *Origins of approaches* (e.g., economics, psychology);
4   *Scope of approaches* (e.g., single person decisions, interpersonal learning);
5   *Intended functions of the theories* (e.g., descriptive, explanatory);
6   *Principal concepts employed* (e.g., probability, causal attribution);
7   *Loci of concepts* (e.g., peripheral, mediating, central);
8   *Intended uses of research results* (e.g., as building blocks for psychologic laws, or for use in real-life circumstances, or both).

The general development of the work may be seen in Fig. 2-3.

Thus, each of the six approaches (1-6) is described in terms of the six categories (3-8) indicated above. Each of the six approaches is discussed *within* each category. That is, the discussion proceeds down successive columns of the table, thus providing a discussion of DT in terms of its origins, the names of its primary concepts, its scope, etc. BDT is then discussed in terms of the same six categories, followed by a similar discussion of the remaining four approaches. Admittedly far more general than previous efforts at integration, we believe the loss in specificity is compensated for by the gain in systematization. Systematic treatment of the six approaches makes comparison as well as description possible, and thus brings integration within our reach, if not our grasp. Future work can bring more specificity to the comparisons.

Integration is attempted by two means: first, a "Transition" section appears between the discussions of the Group I and Group II approaches. The

		CATEGORIES					
		ORIGINS	SCOPE	INTENDED FUNCTION	PRINCIPAL CONCEPTS	LOCI OF CONCEPTS	INTENDED USES
		CHAPTER 3	CHAPTER 4	CHAPTER 5	CHAPTER 6	CHAPTER 7	CHAPTER 8
APPROACHES	DT (1)						
	BDT (2)						
	PDT (3)						
	SJT (4)						
	IIT (5)						
	AT (6)						

Figure 2-3 Neutral categories for describing and comparing the six approaches.

purpose of the Transition section is to remedy to some extent the inaccuracy we create by the division of the six approaches into two groups, when there are, in fact, many similarities between them (as suggested in Fig. 2-2 (*a*) and (*b*). That is, the Transition section describes the conceptual *watershed,* not the conceptual *barrier,* that lies between these two general approaches and thus indicates the diffuse rather than sharp differences between approaches on either side of the division.

The second means for achieving integration is more direct; a section at the end of each of the six descriptive categories (origins, intended function, etc.) is entitled "Integration." It is this section, of course, that is the most important, because it is here that we attempt to integrate the material from the six approaches with regard to each of the categories indicated above.

The reader may accept our definition of the task of integration yet still be curious about our conception of a theory, conspicuously absent so far. We have not attempted to present a set of criteria that must be met before an "approach" could achieve the status of a theory because we are not analytical philosophers. Nor do we believe that the approaches to judgment and decision making have progressed to the point where such analytical treatment would prove useful. Rather, we simply describe each approach in terms of the categories indicated above. We recognize that clear and concise definitions of "similarities," "differences," and "antinomies" require an analytical treatment of the question of what the form and substance of a theory in the field of judgment and decision behavior should consist of. All in good time.

We turn now to a discussion of each of the six approaches in terms of the six descriptive categories indicated in Fig. 2-3.

Chapter 3

Origins

Why should a work directed toward the integration of different approaches to the study of judgment and decision making begin with comments on the origins of these approaches? Because (a) the theories, methods and procedures used by different approaches, (b) the judgment and decision aids they offer to those who want them, and (c) the criteria by which all of these are evaluated as "right," and "wrong," "competent," "useless," "correct," "misguided" stem directly from their origins. And unless the story of the development of standards as well as approaches is unraveled, there is little likelihood of the development of a cumulative scientific discipline.

Obviously, we cannot even begin to write the complete history of the development of these approaches. We should, however, at least point to the different origins of different approaches; otherwise integration would be impossible.

The study of judgment and decision making has two primary sources—economics and psychology. And mathematics hovers above, beyond, or around them, thus providing the logical context for the study of judgment and decision. In economics, people are believed to decide on a rational course of action (to buy, to sell, in general to accept or not accept an alternative) because they have values (utilities) and beliefs about the likely occurrence of events (probabilities), a view that gave rise to what was labelled the "rational man" theory of consumer choice. That was enough for (at least some) economists who then explored the consequences of the choices and actions that follow from various sets of utilities and beliefs. Psychologists (and philosophers), on the other hand, have wanted to know what are the *sources* of beliefs, expectancies and preferences rather than merely to explore the consequences of holding them.

We do not, of course, recount here the history of the growth of the interaction and gradual merging (and dim but certain recognition of the merging) of these general approaches (nor the acknowledgment by modern philosophers of advances in judgment and decision analysis, as for example, in Rawls, 1971, or Hawkins, 1977), but readers will be aided if they keep these different origins in mind. For not only do different concepts emerge from these different origins, but different aims, methods and procedures emerge as well.

3.1 DECISION THEORY

The mathematical terms of DT (probabilities, utilities, and methods of aggregation) were taken from the "behavioral-mathematical" theory called "expected utility theory" constructed by economists (Morgenstern) and mathematicians (von Neumann). Expected utility theory is itself a derivative of an earlier utility theory (the value theory of the 19th-century economists), and can also be traced to the famous Bernouli expression that indicates that the worth of a deicsion is determined by the probability of events and their associated utilities.

In short, the major concepts of DT are a legacy from the 19th-century economists, the principal modifications being (a) the acknowledgement in the 20th century of the presence of uncertainty in the mind of the decision maker, and (b) the effort to deal with it directly. The implications of these concepts have been refined by the mathematical logic of the 20th century and made available to decision makers by the work of such decision theorists as Keeney and Raiffa and others. A guide to the development of Multiple Criteria Decision Making (not to be confused with Multi Attribute Utility Theory) can be found in Starr and Zeleny (1977).

3.2 BEHAVIORAL DECISION THEORY

Behavioral decision theory (BDT) is the brainchild of Ward Edwards, who coined this term as well as "Subjective Expected Utility" (SEU). The origin of BDT is clearly set forth in his landmark article "The Theory of Decision

Making," (reprinted in Edwards' and Tversky's *Decision Making*, Penguin, 1967, to which page numbers in this book will refer). Although Edwards was not the first psychologist to become interested in this topic, his article gave it a coherence that enabled psychologists to see that an important type of behavior needed their attention, and that its study could be interesting and rewarding. There is little doubt that this article and his later one in the *Annual Review of Psychology* in 1961 are classics in the history of research on judgment and decision making. These seminal articles include numerous references to economic theory, (economic) decision theory, game theory, clinical psychology, psychophysics, probability and statistics, and psychometrics. From this point of departure, Edwards developed an interest in the Bayesian theory of statistics, an interest that led to a large number of studies by Edwards and, very soon, his numerous colleagues, including Peterson, Phillips, Beach and others. Bayesian research then led to an interest in multi-attribute utility theory (MAUT) in the 1960s and thence to Edwards's most recent technique for aiding public policy decision makers—SMART (simple multi-attribute rating technique; see Gardiner & Edwards in Kaplan & Schwartz, 1975).

BDT now encompasses more than Edwards work, of course, and as may be seen from the chapter on "Behavioral Decision Theory" in the 1977 *Annual Review of Psychology,* work in this area has grown considerably. The 319 references cited by Slovic, Fischhoff and Lichtenstein (the authors of the review) in 1977 probably constitute much less than one half of the articles and books written on the general topic within the period considered. In general, research in this area has moved toward increasing the role of explanatory psychological concepts. And that effort has developed such a large momentum that we have grouped these studies under the separate heading of Psychological Decision Theory (*PDT*).

3.3 PSYCHOLOGICAL DECISION THEORY

Although Slovic and Lichtenstein were in 1971 able to review a few information-processing studies of judgment and decision making, the recent interest in PDT clearly originated in the studies of Amos Tversky and Daniel Kahneman—regarding the "law of small numbers" (1971), "representativeness" (1972), and "availability" (1973), in which the concept of "heuristics" was introduced as a major concept. These studies marked a sharp change from previous investigations of judgments of uncertainty. Earlier students (mostly within BDT) had concentrated on descriptions of subjects' judgment and decision behavior in terms of (or as deviations from) basic normative models. Tversky and Kahneman rejected further "baseline" descriptions of judgment and emphasized the search for the psychological (mainly cognitive) mechanisms which people use to evaluate frequencies and likelihoods. The reason for the change in emphasis (from *behavioral* to *psychological* DT) was apparently that there had accumulated sufficient empirical generalizations (indicating that deviations of subjective from objective probability were reliable, systematic, and difficult to eliminate) to demand a "systematic theory about the psychology of uncertainty" (Kahneman & Tversky, 1972, p. 430).

Before concluding this section, we should note that the uninitiated (and others) may be excused if they should become confused about the use of terms such as SEU and MAUT. The origin of the term SEU is clear enough; Edwards in 1961 stated that: "Work since [1954] has focused on the model which asserts that people maximize the product of utility and subjective probability; I have named this the subjectively expected utility maximization model (SEU model)" (Edwards & Tversky, 1967, p. 67). But it appears that this appellation has not been accepted by those to whom it was intended to apply. It was not mentioned by Raiffa in 1968, by Fishburn in 1972, nor by Keeney and Raiffa in 1976. Milti-attribute utility theory was, however, discussed by Raiffa in 1968 and the reader is referred to several sources, mainly in the 1960s, for further reading.

The use by Edwards of both Bayesian concepts and MAUT can be seen in his article in a book edited by Hammond in 1978 entitled "Judgment and Decision in Public Policy Formation."

3.4 TRANSITION

Moving from Group I approaches to Group II approaches shifts the origins of theoretical concepts. As noted above, Group I has its origins in the concepts introduced by economics (primarily in the theory of consumer choice), but Group II has its origins in psychology (largely in the psychology of perception).

The general theme of Group II ignores the motivational component so central to Group I (people try to "maximize something"). Although Group II retains the concept of "intention," this concept has a meaning more nearly akin to "focus" than to "getting." Thus, the study of "knowing" rather than "getting" is the main theme of Group II.

Although the origin of the concepts employed by Group II is markedly different than that of Group I, the differences between the aims of the approaches that are adjacent to the conceptual watershed are not sharp in this regard, probably because most of the people adjacent to the watershed were trained as psychologists.

3.5 SOCIAL JUDGMENT THEORY

SJT has its origins in Brunswik's theory of perception (probabilistic functionalism), as may be seen from the prominent role played by such concepts as "ecological validity of cues," "utilization of cues," etc. Probabilistic function-alism gave great emphasis to the question of the accuracy of perceptual judgments about, for example, the sizes of objects under various environ-mental conditions outside the laboratory (thus marking it off from laboratory work in psychophysics) and thus giving it a strongly Darwinian tone; there is much emphasis on achievement and adaptation.

Brunswik's untimely death occurred as he was shifting his interest from perception proper to quasi-rational judgment. Hammond continued this devel-opment and extended it to interpersonal learning and interpersonal conflict in the '60s and '70s, and named this approach "Social Judgment Theory" (see Kaplan & Schwartz, 1975).

The probabilism that forms the major point of departure for SJT provides a conceptual link to the probabilism of all the approaches from economics. A major difference, however, is that whereas the probabilism of the approaches from economics requires explicit procedures for *inquiring* about a subject's probabilities regarding the occurrence of various conditions, events, or outcomes, SJT *observes* probabilistic behavior in those making judgments. Thus, while the SEU approach requires that the subjects directly "measure" their own uncertainty by, for example, choosing between lotteries, or other means, SJT measures the subjects' uncertainty (not their subjective probabilities) in terms of their *performance* on judgment tasks, including interpersonal learning and interpersonal conflict. That difference grows out of the difference in the original aims of different approaches.

3.6 INFORMATION INTEGRATION THEORY

IIT was developed by Norman Anderson in the early 1960s. IIT has its origin in psychophysics; measurement of the subjective counterpart of physical *and* social stimuli is the point of departure for IIT. There is no history of a special interest in uncertainty in IIT; it is not a probabilistic theory. Rather, IIT sees the logic of psychophysical measurement as the essential foundation for the competence of psychological measurement, in more complex circumstances involving social circumstances as well as physical ones. Indeed, one of the strong attractions of IIT lies in its demonstrated ability to apply its basic measurement theory (*functional measurement*) to traditional psychophysical problems and to traditional sociopsychological problems. The breadth of this effort may be seen in Anderson's chapter in Berkowitz (1974).

3.7 ATTRIBUTION THEORY

AT has its origins in the theoretical work of Fritz Heider who moved from Gestalt psychology to a more functionally oriented psychology (see Heider, 1959) by focusing his attention on what he called "naive psychology" or "common-sense psychology." Heider's theoretical work described the cognitive strategies of persons who were required to make inferences, or judgments, about circumstances (e.g., causes) not immediately given in the midst of the ambiguities of life outside the laboratory.

Heider's book (1958) was highly influential and gave rise to several empirical and theoretical efforts to explore its utility. The most prominent and effective of these is AT. Among the most frequently cited papers are those by Jones and Davis (1965), and Kelley (1967, 1973). These authors, among others, laid the groundwork for what became the most prominent theory in social psychology during the 1970s. AT has drawn a large number of participants who have carried out a large number of empirical studies. We include AT in our attempt at the integration of judgment and decision theory because AT is also a theory of judgment—the most psychological, and least mathematical, of all the theories to be discussed.

3.8 INTEGRATION

3.8.1 Group I Approaches

DT, BDT, and PDT clearly have a common origin—the economic theory of choice. DT has pursued the logical, mathematical aspects of those theories, BDT and PDT have pursued the behavioral and psychological aspects. Prior to 1954, there does not seem to have been much intellectual contact between economics and the psychological approach to this subject matter. As Edwards observed at that time: the "voluminous . . . literature" in economics regarding "the theory of consumer's choice . . . is almost unknown to psychologists in spite of sporadic pleas in both psychological . . . and economic . . . literature for greater communication between the disciplines" (Edwards & Tversky, p. 13). Edwards further noted that he "could not find any thorough bibliography on the theory of choice in the economic literature" and as a result he included "a rather extensive bibliography of the literature since 1930" (Edwards & Tversky, p. 13). He did not mention that there was no "thorough bibliography" of the psychological literature regarding probabilistic approaches to judgment and decision in psychology in 1954. Brunswik's 1952 monograph on "The Conceptual Framework of Psychology," which gave some theoretical attention to probabilism, was known to him, but he did not refer to it, an omission that was symptomatic of the intellectual gap between Group I and Group II approaches. Edwards' main effort was in a different direction, namely, to *construct* the bases for a conceptual and empirical link between work in decision making in economics and in psychology, which he did.

3.8.2 Group II Approaches

The origins of two of these approaches (SJT and AT) are close. Both Brunswik and Heider were Europeans who departed from the Gestalt point of view; Heider most notably in 1926 with the publication of "Ding und Medium," Brunswik in 1934 with "Wahrnehmung und Gegenstandswelt." Both could also be said to have reacted against conventional psychology, especially toward traditional psychophysics. Both could thus be said to have an "ecological" approach in contrast to a "physical" one. (Note: Brunswik and Konrad Lorenz were contemporary graduate students (and friends) in Karl Buhler's laboratory in Vienna; it is not unlikely that both were attracted to a biological point of view as a result of Buhler's influence; personal communication from K. Lorenz to K. R. Hammond. Karl Popper also mentions Bühler's influence on him). It was probably Brunswik's training as an engineer that turned him toward quantification and empirical work, whereas it may have been Heider's philosophical interests that moved him toward more theoretical work. The two arrived in the United States about the same time and were close intellectual companions, however, who referred to one another's work frequently and with enthusiasm, both in print and in their lectures.

Hammond's "Psychology of Egon Brunswik" (1966) includes a chapter from Heider's book which illustrates a similarity in outlook, and a recent "Introduction to Attribution Processes" by Shaver (1975) includes a slightly abridged version of Brunswik's well-known lens model to explain the nature of Heider's approach to social perception. The interested reader should turn to Brunswik's (1952) development of "The Conceptual Framework of Psychology" for a description of the development of both approaches in the history of psychology, particularly with regard to their departure from both Gestalt psychology and psychophysics. And it should be noted that in 1958 Heider refers several times to the fact that Brunswik was making arguments similar to his as early as 1934 (see p. 56, for example). In fact, Heider's first reference to attribution, on whether failure will be "attributed" to the person or the environment (p. 56) includes a reference to Brunswik (p. 220, 1934). But if AT and probabilistic functionalism were closely related in 1958, that close relation has virtually disappeared.

The one point that separated these two original thinkers during their lifetimes and still separates their intellectual offspring is probabilism (cf. Fischhoff, 1976); Brunswik enthusiastically incorporated the concept of uncertainty (in fact, was the first psychologist to do so), Heider minimized it, and one may guess (personal communication: K. R. Hammond) that he found it distasteful. (See Holton, 1973, for a detailed account of the role of personal taste in the history of science; see also Brunswik, 1955 and Krech, 1955, for a frank discussion (and contrast) of preference for scientific style in psychology.)

IIT is an off-shoot of the psychophysical tradition which Brunswik and Heider rejected. Anderson's interest in psychophysical matters has always been strong (but clearly different from Edwards') because he saw the possibility not only of expanding the psychophysical approach to a multi-dimensional psychophysics (already underway by the 1950s) but also of extending it to social "stimuli," which he did. This step is particularly evident in his applications of "functional measurement" to "impression formation" (from the Gestalt psychologist Asch), as well as to a wide variety of substantive problems of interest to those working in quantitative psychology as well as those in social psychology. Be that as it may, there is no doubt that the origins of IIT are very different from those of SJT and AT, and attempts to integrate their present work will be superficial unless the fundamental metatheoretical positions taken by these approaches are somehow reconciled.

If more is to be written at this point, we should, ideally, now describe a series of "constructive crises" in the history of judgment and decision making that result in the convergence of these six approaches into a cumulative, scientific discipline. Since those constructive crises have not yet occurred, this section will, we hope, be written in the next edition; the readers of that edition should be able to enjoy the comparison with the blank space in this section in this edition. In the present development of convergence, we note only one constructive series of events which clustered themselves in the 1950s:

1954: Edwards's article on the Theory of Decision Making
1954: Thrall, Coombs and Davis's book on Decision Processes
1952, 1956: Publication of Brunswik's major works.
1955: Hammond's application of Brunswik's probabilistic functionalism to judgment
1958: Publication of Heider's major work

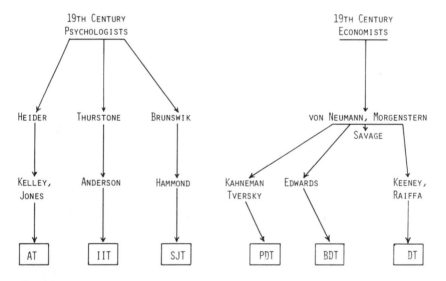

Figure 3-1 First and second generation theorists.

In short, probabilism became a respectable idea, and judgment and decision making, including attributions, became respectable fields of study in the 1950s, flourished, and continue to flourish, in contrast to many other enterprises that began during that period.

The independent and interdependent lines of development will provide a rich source for the historians of social science, and the results of organizing the material should be valuable for understanding how the field of judgment and decision making became a cumulative scientific discipline. As a start, we offer the outline in Fig. 3-1.

Chapter 4

Scope

Judgment and decision theorists have cut out a large domain of behavior to be studied; this is particularly true if and when they recommend that the results of their research should be used. Indeed, Fischhoff (1976) has suggested that judgment and decision researchers stand in much the same scientist/practitioner role that clinical psychologists do. It is, therefore, highly important for judgment and decision making researchers to specify the scope of their theories, their empirical work, and their applications. That means disavowing competence in certain areas as well as claiming it in others. It also means acknowledging the fact that research tends to produce fragments of information, for such fragmentation makes it difficult for the judgment and decision analyst to bring all the bits and pieces of knowledge that have been accumulated from piece-meal studies of part-processes to bear on problems involving application—which do not present themselves in pieces. As a result, efforts at application will always run the risk of requiring generalizations across gaps in our knowledge. It is, in short, essential that the scope of various theories be somehow described, even though it is not in the nature of theorists to delimit and to disavow competence.

We shall use four broad descriptive categories in order to indicate differences in scope among different approaches, namely, the *single*-system case, the *double*-system case, the *triple*-system case, and the *n*-system case (see Figs. 4-1, 4-2, and 4-3). A brief digression is required in order to explain what is meant by these terms. Briefly, the term *single-system case* refers to the situation in which judgment processes are the only phenomena of interest. No information about the relations among variables (e.g., ecological validities of cues) in the task is considered; cue intercorrelations are a possible exception. No criterion is available for evaluating the accuracy of the judgments and therefore there are no right or wrong judgments. The single-system case is the case most often studied by judgment and decision theorists. (For example, see Anderson, 1974; Keeney and Raiffa, 1976; Kelley, 1973.)

The *double-system* case refers to the situation where task characteristics are known, task outcomes are known, and therefore judgments can be evaluated with respect to their accuracy. The double-system case is the one in which Phillips and Edwards (1966) can discover "conservatism," (posterior odds are not revised as much as they should be) because the correct revision for a given task is provided by Bayes' Theorem, or in which Kahneman and Tversky (1973) can discover that sample size is ignored because the correct answer is provided by the logic of sampling theory, or in which Hammond (1971) could discover that "cognitive feedback" (i.e., feedback about task

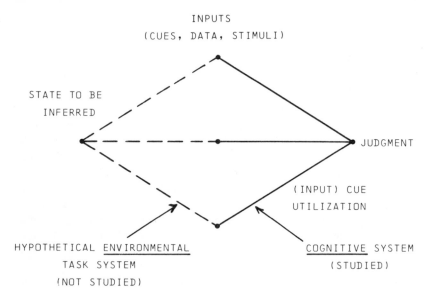

Figure 4-1 Diagram of the single-system case.

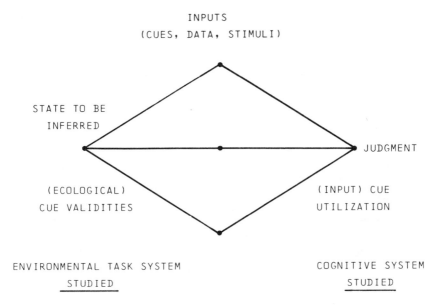

Figure 4-2   Diagram of the double-system case.

characteristics) could lead to rapid learning of judgment tasks, and Hammond, Summers and Deane (1973) could discover that outcome feedback (providing the right answer on each trial) can lead to a *decrement* in performance in relation to cognitive feedback.

The *triple-system* case is that in which there are two persons making judgments about a known task system. This situation has been the site for the studies of interpersonal learning and interpersonal conflict studied by SJT, in which Hammond and Brehmer (1973) and Brehmer and Hammond (1977) found that interpersonal learning is poor and interpersonal conflict reduction is slow when cognitive differences exist. (See also Brehmer, 1974, and Mumpower & Hammond, 1974, for studies of the effect of "entangled task dimensions" on interpersonal learning.)

The *n-system* case refers to the cases that involve group decision making. Examples can be found in Stewart, Joyce, and Lindell (1975), Balke, Hammond and Meyer (1973) and Hammond, Rohrbaugh, Mumpower, and Adelman (1977).

We return now to our discussion of the *scope* of various approaches in terms of these four general cases described above.

4.1   DECISION THEORY

DT restricts its theoretical interest to the single-system case, which involves one person making decisions without full knowledge of the task situation and

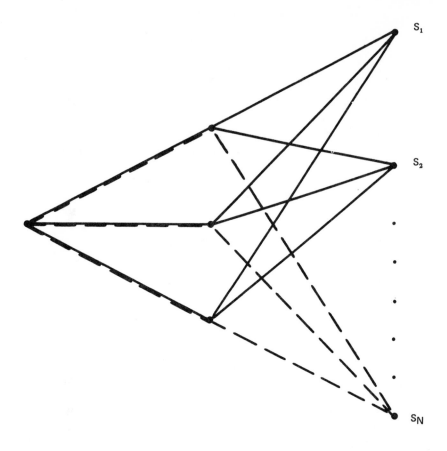

Figure 4-3 The double-system case expanded to include two or more subjects—with or without study of the environmental (task) system.

without feedback about the effect of the decision. Since decision theorists do not theorize (systematically) about psychological processes or states, the scope of DT is limited to those circumstances in which one person exercises his or her rational powers to the utmost under the guidance provided by a specialist in DT. But no analytical effort is devoted to the relation between the specialist and the client although it is often described in the language of popular psychology (see Fischhoff's analogy, 1977, with clinical psychology for more).

   Since game theory also follows from von Neumann and Morgenstern's (1947) classical work, it can be seen as an approach to the n-system case in parallel with the development of DT. Keeney and Raiffa (1976) make little use of game theory of the Luce and Raiffa (1957) variety or that pursued by

Anatol Rapoport (1974) with his special emphasis on the Prisoner's Dilemma game that captured the interest of psychologists for at least a decade (1955-65). And although Keeney and Raiffa indicate an interest in group decision making they treat the matter of interaction largely on a "clinical" level.

DT work on social welfare functions and group decision making (Chapter 10 of Keeney & Raiffa, 1976) might also be viewed as studies of the n-system case. However, the basic approach to such problems is to reduce the group decision to an individual decision of a supra decision maker (see also, Harsanyi, 1974); in effect, the n-system case is converted into the single-system case so that existing DT can be directly applied to the group situation.

An interesting extension of the SEU model has recently been provided by McClintock (1977) who applies the model to the n-system case and studies interpersonal conflict (and introduces new concepts). This extension is discussed below in connection with BDT.

4.2 BEHAVIORAL DECISION THEORY

Because BDT is directed toward construction of SEU theory in light of the experimental analysis of decision and choice behavior, BDT theorists found it necessary and useful to do experiments. The primary reason for doing experiments was to increase our understanding of how closely human information processing approximated the Bayesian process; to discover, for example, the impact of information on the revision of subjective probabilities. Thus external conditions were manipulated in order to test hypotheses regarding internal conditions; that is, objective (external) probabilities were manipulated to examine the extent to which the Bayesian model could account for revision of subjective probabilities. Manipulations of objective probabilities (including conditional probabilities) could thus lead to observing, for example, the *impact of a datum* (information) on the revision of a probability of an event. In order to do this, the investigators had to construct task systems (the properties of which would be fully known to the investigators). Comparisons could be made between the properties of various decision tasks (e.g., their unconditional probabilities and conditional probabilities) and the properties of the cognitive (decision) systems brought to bear on the tasks (e.g., the parallel probabilities). BDT theorists could thus examine the relations between external and internal unconditional probabilities, *describe* the differences between them, and possibly *explain* why such differences occurred.

Probabilities are again treated as judgments, as in the case of DT, but they are now related to objective probabilities and the relation between the two is treated as if it were a scaling problem in psychophysics. The theoretical examination of the relation between the two includes concepts taken from psychophysics, as for example, anchoring, etc. In addition to *unconditional probabilities,* BDT theorists found it useful to compare the *conditional probabilities* in the cognitive systems of the decision maker with those in the task. The conditional probabilities typically concern the probability of a distal event given the occurrence of some proximal event. But inter-event conditionality is considered as well.

BDT research that included decision *tasks* with known properties meant that BDT theorists not only were interested in the single-system case but the double-system case as well (Hammond, Stewart, Brehmer, Steinmann, 1975, erroneously described BDT as interested only in the single-system case). The shift from the single-system case to the double-system case marks an important distinction between the scope of the theoretical effort of DT and BDT. (This distinction is also illustrated by Shanteau's diagram; see Fig. 6-2.)

Introducing an independently real second system into the analysis requires BDT theorists to be specific about the properties of the decision task system. That requirement meant that some set of terms must be employed to describe the task. The terms chosen by the BDT theorist are *statistical* terms (unconditional and conditional probabilities, states of the system, dependencies, etc.). Note that the terms used by BDT to describe cognitive activity are *parallel* to the terms used to describe the environmental task.

BDT has not, however, so far extended its theoretical or empirical hypothesis-testing research efforts to include interpersonal conflict (or interpersonal learning) with regard to decisions although it has extended its application to that situation (the n-system case).

4.3 PSYCHOLOGICAL DECISION THEORY

This approach was developed in the context of the single-system case, and some extensions have been made to the double-system case (see for example, Kahneman and Tversky's work on "illusory correlation," (1972). Generally, however, a comparison is made between (a) inferences justified by statistical logic and (b) inferences made by persons from the same data, rather than in connection with tasks involving independently real events. So far no work has been done with regard to the n-system case.

4.4 TRANSITION

Moving from Group I approaches to Group II approaches enlarges the scope of the behavior covered by both theory and research. For whereas the Group I approaches considered here intensively focus on measurement problems related to subject probabilities, utilities, and their combinations with respect to such matters as transitivity of choices, etc., the conceptual framework that applies to more than one decider bears an uncertain relation to DT, BDT, and PDT. (The substantial amount of theory and research that flows from game theory and social welfare function theory, however, needs eventually to be considered in detail here, for it considerably enlarges the scope of the work within Group I approaches.)

Group II theories have produced a substantial amount of research involving two or more persons involved in judgments, decisions, and inferences. These approaches have, to various degrees, also developed theoretical concepts intended to apply to the interaction between persons. As we shall see, SJT has extended the original lens model to include cases involving two or more persons, IIT has inspired at least a few studies involving groups, and AT has been applied to a wide variety of individual and group circumstances.

4.5 SOCIAL JUDGMENT THEORY

This approach includes within its scope the single-system case as well as all other cases, and Brehmer in particular has carried out a large number of multiple-cue probability studies (double-system case) and a large number of studies on interpersonal learning and interpersonal conflict (n-system case). The latter studies are fundamental insofar as SJT is concerned, and provide the basis for generalization to the analysis of the single-system case. Thus SJT intends to include within its scope the following topics: (a) learning under uncertainty (MCPL), (b) interpersonal learning, (c) interpersonal conflict, and (d) group judgments and decisions. The work that has been done in these areas is intended to provide the basis for conflict resolution in situations involving policy disputes.

4.6 INFORMATION INTEGRATION THEORY

This approach was developed to deal with the single-system case, although it has been applied to both the double-system case (involving learning) as well as the n-system case (involving group judgments). There is no reason in principle why IIT should not be or cannot be applied to the study of interpersonal learning or interpersonal conflict.

4.7 ATTRIBUTION THEORY

This approach is highly general in its aim. It covers not only the case of a single person making judgments about causal locus, but interpersonal relations between two or more people. Its intended scope is large and includes references to interpersonal learning and conflict. No boundaries are implied in AT.

4.8 INTEGRATION

4.8.1 Group I Approaches

Proponents of the three approaches within Group I are restricted in scope. DT gives virtually no attention to empirical research carried out within the double-system case by BDT theorists, such as Edwards and his colleagues, other than to provide footnote acknowledgments of the existence of such work (see p. 8 and p. 212 of Keeney & Raiffa, 1976). And although there is mathematical work within the general framework of SEU theory on coalitions and interpersonal comparisons of utilities, it does not seem to appear relevant to DT as described by Keeney and Raiffa, 1976; neither topic is indexed by them. Nor is there any significant reference in Keeney and Raiffa to work on conflict resolution by theorists such as Anatol Rapoport or to the psychological research on interpersonal conflict by SJT, although the analytical work by Luce and Raiffa, Arrow, and Harsanyi is mentioned. One might guess that work by DT in this area will be more likely to extend in the direction of welfare functions than game theory.

But what if decision theorists like Keeney and Raiffa (or Zeleny) become more clinical? Psychologists are certain to find the remarks of Keeney and Raiffa (and DT generally) regarding conflict resolution to be naive, however sophisticated they may be from a logical viewpoint. Keeney and Raiffa do refer to the use of sensitivity analysis as a conflict-reduction technique, but that is about as far as they go. And although Edwards observed in 1961 that the early work on group decisions "had a substantial resemblance to the SEU model," (p. 487) there has been no systematic theoretical unification of individual decision making and conflict behavior by BDT. Moreover, the increasing challenge to the basic premises of the traditional SEU model from PDT and other approaches (e.g., IIT), suggests that the extension of SEU theory to group decision making is likely to be challenged by the other approaches.

There are psychologists within the BDT approach who are now attempting to extend the SEU approach to the n-system case and thus to study interpersonal conflict. McClintock's (1977) recent article in Druckman provides an excellent example.

> Proposition 5. In situations of social interdependence, one's access to one's own valued outcomes is dependent upon the values assigned by others to their possible outcomes (and vice versa). Furthermore, the attractiveness of outcomes for one actor may be influenced not only by the outcomes he receives but also by the outcomes he judges the other(s) will receive. (p. 54)*

4.8.2 Group II Approaches

The three approaches grouped here appear to be highly similar in intended scope. SJT has been explicit in its efforts to study all four cases mentioned

---

*This excerpt is reprinted from "Social Motivation in Settings of Outcome Interdependence" by Charles G. McClintock in *Negotiations: Social-Psychological Perspectives,* Daniel Druckman, Editor, © 1977, P. 54 by permission of the publisher, Sage Publications, Inc. (Beverly Hills/London).

above, and thus intends to contribute to the literature regarding judgments, learning regarding a physical environment, learning in a social environment (e.g., interpersonal learning from and about another person) and interpersonal conflict; research in all of these areas applies the same systematic framework; work on the n-system case has continued since about 1965; work with other cases began earlier. But there has been no attempt to relate this work to IIT or AT or incorporate any of the concepts from either into SJT research. (See Mumpower, 1976, for a detailed analysis of the similarities and differences between SJT and AT.) The same is true for IIT and AT with regard to SJT.

There have been attempts by Anderson (1974) to integrate IIT and AT within the framework of the single-system case, and to some extent, the n-system case as well. The reverse is also true; Jones, Kanouse, Kelley, Nisbett, Valins and Weiner (1972) make use of certain IIT concepts and measurement techniques in (primarily) the single-system case. There is no reason, in principle, why the techniques employed by SJT to study interpersonal conflict could not be employed by IIT. The effects of different subjective scale values and/or weights could be studied in exactly the same way. Most important, the approach could readily examine the differential effect of various integrative mechanisms (adding, averaging, multiplying, etc.) on interpersonal conflict just as, for example, Brehmer and Hammond (1973) examined the differential effect of the use of various function forms in interpersonal conflict, and as Brehmer has examined similar effects on interpersonal learning. This is perhaps the easiest situation for integration and potential cumulative information we shall encounter. In addition, interest in the n-system case could lead to the evaluation of the role of equal weights in conflict reduction.

4.8.3 The Single-System Case:
Producing Cohesion or Confusion?

In this case there is no environmental task "out there," the characteristics of which are independently known. Do you choose to merge your company with this one *or* that one? Choose one· or the other course of action and you will never discover what the outcome of the action not chosen would have been. In this case, the "right" choice will never be empirically known because taking one action ordinarily precludes the possibility of discovering what a different action might have accomplished. Einhorn and Hogarth (1978) have considered the psychological implications of this situation in detail. (Contrast the single-system case with the double-system case, in which the right answer can be ascertained more or less readily; for example, predicting the weather or the activity of the stock market or a horse race.) But all six approaches share a common interest in the single-system case. Indeed, it is because of the shared interest in this specific case that this attempt at integration is being made; this case provides the link between Group I and II as well as within Groups. And it is here that confusion is likely to arise over the intended scope (and function) of various approaches. Therefore, at the risk of repetition, we offer what appear to us to be important distinctions in scope (and aim) with regard to this case.

1. DT offers descriptions of what *ought* to be taking place, not of what *is* taking place, and offers assistance in reducing the gap between the two. DT declares that its intentions are to help their clients "get their heads (or preferences) straight," or something similar. Careful delineation of probabilities and utilities aggregated by the decision analyst provide the remedy (see, Keeney, 1977, for a detailed, worked out example). Although probability assessments are treated with some sophistication and steps are often taken to straighten out logical flaws, no specific remedies other than those based on "clinical" experience are offered. (This is particularly true with regard to interpersonal dispute over probabilities and utilities, in regard to which discussion (!) is offered as remedy.)

2. BDT is prepared to offer similar assistance for similar reasons. The distinction between the two is that BDT believes it has learned what the deviations from logic are, knows what errors will be made, and thus offers specific remedies.

3. PDT is primarily interested in explaining why departure from rational choice occurs in situations where probability assessment is pivotal, and on the basis of these explanations offering remedies (debiasing techniques) for the biases observed. Note that PDT offers remedies based directly on its empirical research. Thus it offers specific debiasing remedies for the specific biases it discovers in the single-system case. PDT does not, however, address the double-system case in which answers are *empirically* produced. (Answers are produced through calculations based on statistical logic.) Nor does PDT address the n-system case, although it would not find it difficult to do so. Indeed, its psychological orientation and concepts (availability, etc.) offer strong suggestions as to the source of difficulties in interpersonal learning and interpersonal conflict. Thus, the potential scope of PDT does include the n-system case. And if one recalls the work in the area already carried out by SJT and the similar potential for work by IIT, a strong case could be made for the argument that such work should be pursued because of the complementary character of that work. This opportunity for cumulativeness should not be overlooked; moreover, it is precisely in this same situation that, as we noted above, there is a strong potential for integration between IIT and SJT.

4.8.4 Domains of Behavior of Theoretical Interest

There is one further question that can be addressed to the intended scope of various approaches: insofar as they intend to be descriptive or explanatory, what is it they intend *not* to describe and/or explain? Do these approaches intend to limit their descriptions and/or explanations in any way? Although these approaches seem to be limited to certain domains of behavior and in the breadth of their intentions, they are not specific about their boundaries. For example, with the exception of AT none of these approaches include concepts that apply to domains of behavior other than cognition (although there is certainly room for Group I approaches to *claim* an interest in motivation). No approach includes theoretical concepts that apply to states other than normal ones. Thus, for example, stress, affect, specific need-oriented states are generally ignored, as are other processes (e.g., memory; but see Hamilos & Pitz's, 1977, research on memory and judgment; see also Tversky & Kahneman for references to memory in their work). Gillis (1975) and Hammond and Joyce (1975) have shown how SJT can be profitably extended to the study of the effects of psychoactive drugs on judgment in the single-system, double-system and n-system cases in populations of psychotic patients. It may well be that the limits of applicability of judgment and decision theories are broad indeed.

Chapter 5

Intended Functions

What are the current theories of judgment and decision making supposed to do? What are their intended functions? Prescribe? Describe? Explain? Predict? Without knowledge of their intended function, theories can hardly be compared. Unfortunately, judgment and decision theorists have not always made their theoretical aims entirely explicit. And they are also apt to be vague with regard to the limits of competence of their theories. In this section, therefore we address the question of what the intended functions of the six approaches are.

5.1 DECISION THEORY

This approach focuses on decision-making from a *prescriptive* point of view only. Its prescriptions are based on the utility theory developed by the mathematician von Neumann and the economists Morgenstern and Arrow, among others. In its recent development, Keeney and Raiffa (1976) emphasize the point that the aim of DT is to elaborate the logical entailments of the subjective probability and utility theory and extend them to a variety of circumstances by means of mathematics. The criterion for the validity of the theory is its logical, mathematical consistency. Once developed, the theory stands as a logical structure for decision making; decision makers may then use it in order to achieve the logical consistency provided by this theory. Aiding decision makers to achieve logical consistency is, therefore, a major reason for the use of DT in the real world, and the provision of such aid is a primary activity of the practitioners of DT.

DT makes no claim that it represents or describes the cognitive activity (or information processing) of human decision makers. Indeed, it is precisely because of the presumed departure of decision making from the logic of decision theory that decision theorists such as Keeney and Raiffa insist that people, especially policy makers, should change their decision making behavior to make it conform with the precepts of DT. Accusations, therefore, that DT does not represent the cognitive activity of any person do not deter decision theorists from developing new applications or pursuing the implications of a theorem. The emphasis is not on what decision makers do, but what they *should* do.

Explanations of *why* human decision makers deviate from the logic of DT is a matter left to psychologists. And although many decision makers remain indifferent to discrepancies between what unaided reason suggests and what logical consistency demands, an increasing number are employing decision analysts to find such discrepancies. Although that point has been made many times, we repeat it here because current criticism by psychologists of SEU theory is directed precisely at its intended function, not its logical structure. That is, critics of SEU theory argue that however satisfying SEU theory might be from a mathematical point of view, it is not useful as a guide to decision making because human beings do not behave in accordance with the fundamental assumptions of the theory. When, for example, empirical evidence indicates that the premises of SEU theory do not represent actual choice *behavior,* the validity of the postulates of the SEU theory is denied, and the validity of the behavioral entailments of the theory is denied.

One might expect decision theorists to find such criticisms to be misdirected, on the grounds that it is based on a faulty interpretation of the intended function of the theory. DT argues that (a) if one must decide or choose, then an additive or multiplicative combination of expectations and utilities is an appropriate basis for decision or choice and (b) the logic of DT, as articulated by mathematical analysis, provides the best guide for reaching defensible decisions. Therefore, as far as DT is concerned, it is irrelevant whether (unguided) behavior is in accord with the axioms of SEU theory. What is important is that decision making behavior *should* be in accord with these axioms. Decision theorists further believe that once the axioms are carefully explained, any reasonably intelligent person would want to change his behavior to be in accord with these axioms. As a result, if and when psychologists (or others) find behavioral violations of the axioms, decision theorists dismiss such discoveries as irrelevant to their purposes. Thus, for example, Raiffa (1968, p. 77) states: "The following example will help to illustrate how intransitivies may arise in *descriptive* choice behavior and why in a *prescriptive* theory of choice this type of behavior should be discouraged." In short, DT considers its axioms to be reasonable and desirable rules for decision making behavior that everyone would want to follow, once they understood them. DT thus disavows any intention to provide explanations for why decision making takes the form others claim it does, for it has only prescriptions for improving it. And that, they appear to be saying, is enough. As a result, empirical (in contrast to mathematical) challenges to the basic postulates of DT have been ignored by Keeney and Raiffa, and management scientists in general.

5.2 BEHAVIORAL DECISION THEORY

This approach intends (a) to *describe* departures from optimal decision-making in empirical detail (in contrast to DT) and (b) it also intends to *explain* such departures in terms of both external (task) and internal (psychological) conditions. Perhaps the best-known description of a departure from optimal decision-making is *conservatism*. This term signifies the putative failure of decision makers to revise their posterior subjective probabilities as much as they should (as determined by Bayes' rule for aggregation of conditional probabilities in relation to hypotheses) upon the receipt of new information, a (disputed) finding that led BDT theorists to describe decision makers as "Conservative Bayesians."

Edwards made it clear in his landmark article of 1954 that he considered the economists' theory of value and choice to be a valuable guide for the empirical work of psychologists, and that psychologists should carry out empirical tests of the implications of the theory rather than dispute its assumptions (Edwards & Tversky, 1967, p. 16). By 1967 Edwards was still of this persuasion: "All these topics represent a new ... field for psychologists in which a theoretical structure has already been elaborately worked out [by economists] and in which many experiments need to be performed" (Edwards & Tversky, 1967, p. 55). That is, psychologists should discover to what extent deductions from theories of choice and preference are empirically true. Therefore, the intended function of BDT is to reconstruct, if, as, and when need be, the already worked out theory of decision or choice behavior, on the apparent assumption that such theories intend to be and should be a true description of the behavior of persons making decisions.

Such a confirmation or reconstruction of theories of choice would place a powerful prescription for decision making in the hands of decision analysts who could then provide "tools" for decision makers. The culmination of the effort can be seen in Edwards' paper presented during the 1977 meetings of the American Association for the Advancement of Science at a symposium entitled "Judgment and Decision in Public Policy Formation" ("Technology for Director Dubious: Evaluation and Decision in Public Contexts," 1978). Here Edwards refers to "... relatively simple tools ... currently in use, in contexts in which they obviously bear on public policy, and could be used by public policy makers, but so far have not been" (p. 73). (The final phrase is surprising in view of Keeney & Raiffa's work with these same "tools.")

It now appears that Edwards and his colleagues intend to pursue the study of choice behavior through experimental analysis within the Bayesian framework, and to pursue application of their findings in conjunction with SMART–a simplified version of MAUT.

5.3 PSYCHOLOGICAL DECISION THEORY

PDT intends not only to describe but to *explain* the discrepancies between human decision behavior and the fundamental premises upon which DT is based. Indeed, the proponents of PDT have made it clear that they believe that they, among others, have already shown the basic premises of SEU theory of decision behavior to be empirically false, and, therefore, that a different description of human decision behavior should replace it (see Kahneman & Tversky's *Prospect Theory,* 1979), also Slovic, Fischhoff & Lichtenstein, 1977). The proponents of the PDT approach have carried out empirical research that, in their view, and in the view of many others, not only *shows* that people do not make decisions and choices in conformity with the precepts of SEU that support DT and BDT, but *explains* why people do not. This research has been a fruitful combination of theory and empirical work in that new theoretical concepts have been introduced and their explanatory value tested empirically.

The approach of PDT is one psychologists would expect to (a) identify some important behavioral phenomenon (e.g., departure from optimal choice), (b) adduce some psychological concepts (e.g., availability, representativeness) to account for or explain why the discrepancy should occur, (c) conduct experiments to test the validity of the explanatory concepts. Thus, it might be said that if (a) the intended function of BDT is to shift the study of decision behavior from a *logical* path of research (that led to EU theory) to a *behavioral* path that led to SEU theory, then the intended function of PDT is to move us from a sheerly *behavioral* path to a *psychological* path that explains why decision makers behave the way they do. Have we now reached a different point from that described by Edwards when he indicated that "a theoretical structure has already been worked out"?

Not only does PDT offer to explain *why* "people replace the laws of chance by heuristics" they are now prepared to indicate *when* people are apt to make this replacement. Although Slovic, Fischhoff, and Lichtenstein observed in 1977 that "heuristics [PDT] may be faulted as a general theory of judgment because of the difficulty of knowing which will be applied in any particular instance" (p. 6), a recent paper ("Causal Schemas in Judgments under Uncertainty," Tversky & Kahneman, 1979) takes steps toward removing that "fault," thus: "Distributional data affect predictions *when* (italics ours) they induce a causal model which i) explains the base rate, and ii) applies to the individual case." And conditional statements are made, thus: "Distributional information which is not incorporated into a causal schema, either because it is not interpretable as an indication of propensity or because it conflicts with an established schema, is given little or no weight in the presence of singular data."

Certain predictions can also be found in earlier papers. Thus, in 1972; "the representativeness heuristic is more likely to be employed *when* events are characterized in terms of their general properties; whereas the availability heuristic is more likely to be employed *when* events are more naturally thought of in terms of specific occurrences. *When* the generic features of an event as well as its specific instances are considered, both heuristics are likely to enter into the evaluation" (Kahneman & Tversky, 1972, p. 452; italics ours). In short, PDT is clearly working toward the goal of prediction as well as explanation.

The clear aim of PDT to enter upon the enterprise of providing psychological explanations of probability (and utility) judgments has led to the sharp challenge of the validity and thus utility of DT (a challenge that has been ignored on the premise that it is irrelevant, as we mentioned earlier). In short, PDT argues that the logical path taken by DT, whatever its value in other fields (e.g., operations research), does not lead to a defensible prescriptive theory of decision making behavior.

It is important to note that PDT is rooted in *decision theory,* for it still includes probabilities and utilities among its central descriptive terms, and that one of its intended functions is to *evaluate,* as well as to describe, the decision making behavior of subjects in terms of optimality prescribed by a mathematical (statistical) model. As noted above, evaluation largely takes place with regard to the manner in which subjects assign probabilities to events. Thus, PDT intends to discover whether *biases* occur in this type of cognitive activity. Since PDT claims to have found that biases are highly prevalent, it offers suggestions as to how specific biases might be removed, an aim that has received the name of *debiasing.* Debiasing, it should be noted, is a far different type of assistance than that offered by DT and BDT, in that debiasing is intended to rectify errors of *input* to decisions whereas DT and BDT decision aids are intended to rectify errors of information *aggregation,* taking the inputs as given.

The intended function of PDT with regard to aiding the decision maker is perhaps best summarized by Slovic (1976) as follows:

> Subjective judgments of probability and value are essential inputs to decision analyses. We still do not know the best ways to elicit these judgments. Now that we understand many of the biases to which judgments are susceptible, we need to develop debiasing techniques to minimize their destructive effects. (p. 238)

The complexity of that task is also indicated, however;

> Simply warning a judge about a bias may prove ineffective. Like perceptual illusions, many biases do not disappear upon being identified. (p. 238)

And, indeed, Lichtenstein, Slovic, Fischhoff, Layman and Combs (1978), have shown that debiasing is not a simple matter, and Kahneman and Tversky's own work (1978) has not offered empirical proof of the efficacy of their debiasing efforts. However, Shanteau and Phelps (1977), working within the framework of IIT, have shown that some debiasing techniques may be carried out effectively, albeit unwittingly, by laymen.

5.4 TRANSITION

As noted in the sections on origins, moving from the PDT approach to SJT marks a move from three theories that have their origins in economics to three theories that have their origins in psychology. (Note: The academic origins of theories are not to be confused with the academic origins of the authors.) And although the first psychological approach (SJT) to be encoun-tered on the other side of the conceptual watershed includes probabilism in both environment and organism as a basic premise (which links it to SEU theories) neither it nor the other two psychologically-oriented theories include either probability or utility as basic descriptive terms or as basic units of analysis that require measurement. Neither probability nor utility are, as Slovic put it with regard to decision theory, "*essential* (italics ours) inputs to decision analyses," once the conceptual watershed is crossed, although proba-bilities and utilities are *acceptable* as "inputs" because any such "input" is acceptable. As might be expected, therefore, the intended function of the three theories to be discussed next is different from the previous three. Just how different is unclear and the reader should anticipate transitions rather than abrupt changes in the conceptual terrain.

Generally, the three psychological theories are theories of inductive knowing; that is, they are directed toward the question of how human beings acquire or apply knowledge under circumstances of *ambiguity* in the task.

Ambiguity is always present in the studies of problems that Group II theorists study, for it is ambiguity that creates the knowledge problem. Ambiguity, however, is described in different ways by different theorists. Indeed, as we shall see, identification and description of the sources of ambiguity is one main topic that differentiates these theories. Group I approaches, on the other hand are generally indifferent to analyzing, or theorizing about, the sources of ambiguity in environmental tasks (although PDT frequently points to them).

5.5 SOCIAL JUDGMENT THEORY

The primary intended function of this theory is to describe, but not explain, human judgment processes. In its formative stages (1955-1970) of applying Brunswikian concepts to judgment tasks its efforts were directed toward social perception (see e.g., Hammond & Kern, 1959; Crow & Hammond, 1957). Since 1970 its efforts have been directed less toward establishing the *accuracy* of its descriptions than toward the *usefulness* of its descriptions for the policy maker, within, of course, certain boundaries of accuracy (see Hammond, Stewart, Brehmer, & Steinman, 1975). In addition, SJT intends to provide guides toward the development of judgment (and decision) aids. At least one SJT researcher (Brehmer) does direct his efforts toward explanations, however, in the cases of multiple cue probability learning as well as interpersonal learning and interpersonal conflict, and offers and tests hypotheses that are explanatory in nature (see e.g., Brehmer, 1975).

There is no such thing as description without theory, of course, and therefore there is an explicit theoretical as well as metatheoretical basis for the descriptions provided by SJT. The strong emphasis placed on the problem of knowing (in contrast to choice) and the explicit theoretical attention given to the environment can be seen in the following quotation from Hammond, Stewart, Brehmer, and Steinmann (1975):

WHY IS JUDGMENT REQUIRED?

Knowledge of the environment is difficult to acquire because of causal ambiguity—because of the probabilistic, entangled relations among environmental variables. Tolman and Brunswik called attention to the critical role of causal ambiguity in their article "The Organism and the Causal Texture of the Environment" (1935), in which they emphasized the fact that the organism in its normal intercourse with its environment must cope with *numerous, interdependent, multiformal relations* among variables which are *partly relevant* and *partly irrelevant* to its purpose, which carry only a *limited amount of dependability,* and which are *organized in a variety of ways.* The problem for the organism, therefore, is to know its environment under these complex circumstances. In the effort to do so, the organism brings a variety of processes (generally labeled *cognitive*), such as perception, learning, and thinking, to bear on the problem of reducing causal ambiguity. As a part of this effort, human beings often attempt to manipulate variables (by experiments, for example) and sometimes succeed—in such a manner as to eliminate ambiguity. But when the variables in question *cannot* be manipulated, human beings must use their cognitive resources unaided by manipulation or experiment. They must do the best they can by passive rather than active means to arrive at a conclusion regarding a state of affairs clouded by causal ambiguity. They must, in short, exercise their judgment. Human judgment is a cognitive activity of last resort.

It may seem odd to remind the readers of this volume of the circumstances which require human judgment, yet it is essential that we do so, for it is precisely these circumstances which are so often omitted from studies of human judgment. If we are to understand how human beings cope with judgment tasks, however, not only must such ambiguity be present in the conditions under which human judgment is studied, but causal ambiguity must itself be represented within the framework of a theory of human judgment (Brunswik, 1952, 1956; Hammond, 1955). (p. 272)

The absence of the terms subjective probability, utility, worth, choice, preference, that are essential to theoretical discussions within the Group I approaches is apparent.

5.6 INFORMATION INTEGRATION THEORY

IIT is a psychological theory that intends to discover (cognitive) psychological laws that intervene between stimulus and response and thus explain, or at least account for, the relation between S and R. IIT intends to describe human cognitive activity (of which decision, judgment, and attribution are merely special cases) in quantitative terms; specifically, to account for such activity in terms of "cognitive algebra" (see Anderson, 1974, p. 84). That is, IIT focuses on the organization or integration of information by describing the adherence to (or departure from) various algebraic formulations such as additive equations, averaging equations, etc., that are treated as "models" of cognitive functioning. Therefore, a major part of the descriptive effort lies in discovering which model "best fits" the relation between S and R. Does a model that adds, or averages, or multiplies its term "best fit," i.e., best describe, best account for, the cognitive activity of integrating information of *any* kind that takes place under specified circumstances? Which, of such models, generally "fail" as descriptive devices?

But if it is clear that IIT is a law-seeking endeavor, it is unclear what generality it seeks. It surely is not in the *scale values* assigned to the stimuli in any task-situation, nor is it in the *weights* which subjects might assign to specific stimuli, nor does it seem even to lie in the generality of the *organizing principle* (integration rule) discovered—since Anderson and others are prepared to find persons adding, averaging or multiplying virtually any set of weighted, scaled stimuli. We do not find predictions of the appearance of any specific organizing principle other than on the grounds of a precedent. Rather, the search for generality seems to focus on a more genral level. Thus, for example, in Berkowitz (1974, p. 84) Anderson says: "The present survey has yielded considerable support for the operation of a *general cognitive algebra* in social judgment. Cognitive integration seems to follow simple averaging, subtracting and multiplying rules far more commonly than has been recognized" (italics ours). (Was "adding" intentionally omitted?)

We draw the conclusion therefore that for IIT, explanation and mathematical description converge, and from that convergence emerges a psychological law—precisely as in physics. Thus, if

Force = mass X acceleration

is a mathematical description of a relationship that can be applied to the behavior of a wide variety of objects under a wide variety of conditions, it is also explanation, and it is also physical law. And in parallel form, if a specific form of cognitive algebra is regularly found to describe with precision the cognitive activity of a wide variety of people under a wide variety of circumstances, then, just as in physics, that specific form of cognitive algebra is explanation enough. And if enough regularity is achieved over enough conditions, lawfulness is achieved.

Theory and a specific form of methodology are so tightly interwoven in IIT that it is difficult to separate them. One can hardly escape the conclusion that at least one intended function of IIT is methodological prescription, namely, to convince judgment and decision researchers on methodological grounds that the problem itself requires a certain method, namely, functional measurement.

Functional measurement is strongly related to psychophysical measurement. Indeed, the intended function of IIT appears to be that of applying a new and more complex form of the psychophysical method of measurement to (somewhat) complex social, rather than physical, data. (The SJT or Brunswikian approach, for example, is dismissed by IIT as applying only to subjects' use of physical stimuli; see Anderson, 1974.) Many of the conditions examined by IIT for their effect on cognitive activity include those employed in traditional psychophysics (e.g., serial effects, anchoring, contrast, etc.). And, of course, the large emphasis on stimulus scaling, response scaling, the concern with the correctness of the "Power Law," and the general respect for precision reflect the intended function of this approach to discover the laws of "information integration" that include not only traditional psychophysics but social data or stimuli as well.

The close tie that Anderson has established between methodology and theory is surely commendable, and it is to be regretted that it is not more frequently observed. But as we also noted in connection with SJT, strong ties between theory and method lead to resistance; investigators may be able to accept the results of empirical research carried out within a given approach, and may concede that such results lend support to the truth-value of the theory, but still refuse to carry out *their* research in the form demanded by the theory. This is not to say that theories do not require validation across *procedures* (see, for example, the classic admonition in this regard by Campbell and Fiske, 1959), they do. But theory and *methodology* should be congruent; and they are, in the case of IIT.

Admonitions that reflect the intended function of IIT can also be found with regard to theoretical style, e.g., "Those who work with models ... find that they impose a far tighter conceptual discipline than the more verbal formulations. Indeed, the attractiveness of verbal theories sometimes seem to reflect the verbal glitter of surplus meaning in the theoretical terms rather than any implicational power in the theoretical structure. Balance theory is a good example of unfilled promise ... and recent work on social attribution often seems to place undue weight on a clever theoretical story" (Anderson, 1974, pp. 85-86).

5.7 ATTRIBUTION THEORY

The general aim of Attribution Theory is to describe and explain the cognitive activity of persons as *they* attempt to describe and explain the behavior of objects and events in their customary habitat. Thus, AT is intended to be the psychology of "common sense." And therefore, the *locus* of its intended function is virtually the same as in the case of SJT, although its aim is more ambitious in that it attempts explanation as well as description.

More specific aims have been developed by Kelley and Jones; they intend to explain why persons attribute the causes of other persons' behavior to forces internal or external to them. That is, if person A fails a test, is the cause external (a very difficult test) or internal (lack of ability)? AT differs from the two previous theories in that it is largely indifferent to quantification of the data used as the basis of attribution, although this is not a formal position and there are some exceptions (mostly related to IIT or Bayesian work; see Fishbein & Ajzen, 1975, for an extended example of the latter).

Despite AT's recent (c. 1970) emphasis on the attribution of internal vs. external causality, the general theory developed by Heider (1958) is indeed a *general* theory; it disavows little competence in the domain of social behavior. Because it shares much of its aims with SJT, further discussion of the intended function of AT is deferred to the integration section.

5.8 INTEGRATION

5.8.1 Group I Approaches

Among these theories we find several aims: (a) to *describe,* (b) to *explain* choices of action and preferences for various states of the world, and (c) to *provide decision aids* for persons making such choices and preferences. Although different emphases are placed upon (a), (b), and (c) by different Group I approaches, it is not these differences in general aim that create the sharp division among them. Rather, it is differences at a more specific level. For example, although DT is content to accept the notion that unaided decision makers are less than rational, BDT intends to locate precisely where in the decision process those putative departures from rationality occur. "Conservatism," of course, is the classical example. Note that BDT (Edwards) is strongly committed to the Bayesian model of probability estimates, and therefore intends to describe choice or decision behavior in terms of the degree or form of departures from the Bayesian model, rather than in terms of a model that fits the behavior itself.

The PDT approach is not satisfied with that aim. It goes further in its explanatory effort than BDT in that it not only is concerned with departures from optimality, or rational choice, but is concerned with describing and explaining the psychological process that accounts for the subject's decision. Indeed, as we noted above, the results of PDT research challenge the validity of the premises upon which DT and Bayesian BDT research rests. That is, the results of PDT research indicate that the probability estimates obtained from decision makers are subject to persistent systematic biases and therefore the "essential inputs" (Slovic, Fischhoff, & Lichtenstein, 1977) to the decision process are biased. And insofar as these challenges find empirical support they may well result in the development of an entirely new "decision theory," one that is based on research carried out in the psychological laboratory. In short, the *prescribed* decision process may be inapplicable because human decision makers provide it with biased "inputs." (See Slovic, Fischhoff, & Lichtenstein for a review of empirical studies that contest the validity of the "staggering SEU model" [1977, p. 11].)

In sum, there is a progression in intended function from (a) DT which concerns itself only with the "best process," (b) BDT which examines and describes departures from the "best process," and (c) PDT which not only describes departures, but substitutes new explanatory models or theories of how subjects make decisions in place of the SEU or Bayesian model from which the subjects' decision making behavior departs. Integration of these approaches within Group I will require more specificity with regard to aims if *complementarity* of approaches is to be achieved.

5.8.2 Group II Approaches

None of these approaches are prescriptive. And although differences in intended function (to be discussed below) exist, it appears as if they are complementary. Thus, for example:

(a) AT intends to explain the direction and locus of causality (the distal variable of interest) in terms of the *substantive* aspects of the person-environment interaction. (One indication of this can be seen in Fig. 5-1, which reproduces the first page of the subject index of *New Directions in Attribution Research,* Harvey, Ickes, Kidd, 1976.)

(b) IIT intends to find the rules, or the cognitive algebra, whereby information regarding persons and circumstances are organized (or integrated) into an impression or judgment regarding a distal variable (see, for example, Anderson, 1974, p. 2), thus offering a *formal* mathematical description that

---

A

Ability and knowledge, 413–416
Ability/effort/chance attributions
  and helping behavior, 320–331
  and male–female performance, 339–341,
    343–351
  and reinforcement, 105–108, 113–114,
    117
Achievement motivation, 345
Action sequences in behavior perception,
  236–239
Actor–observer differences, 41–43, 61–62,
  88–89, 186–189, 294–297, 401–402
Actor–partner differences, 362–365
Affiliation, 209–210
Aggression
  and reciprocity, 250–254
  and social influence, 304–307
Altruism, *see* Helping behavior
ANOVA cube, 406–417, 431
  and correspondent inference theory,
    411–447
Anxiety, 148–154, 158–161, 405
Arousal
  and dissonance, 200–215
  effect of, on task performance, 234–235
  and emotional states, 143–164
  of reactance, 249–250
Attention, theory of, 179–182
Attitudes
  attribution of, and correspondent
    inferences, 394–398, 406

Attitudes (*contd.*)
  change of, 203–204, 206–214
  and dissonance, 201–204
  effect of feelings states on, 271–289
  and perceived freedom, 75–76
  and social influence, 292 ff.
Attribution, Heider's definition of, 4

B

Balance principle
  and attitude inference, 271–287
  and relation to attribution, 10, 13–14,
    16–17
Behavior modification, *see* Reinforcement
Bias, attributional, 322–323, 428–429, 438
Blame, *see* Responsibility
Bogus feedback, *see* Feedback, false
Break points in behavior sequences,
  227–231, 238, *see also* Unitization of
  behavior

C

Category-based expectancies, *see* Expectancies
Causal schemata, 271–272, 427
Causal taxonomies, 259, 312–316, 337,
  358–362, 383–385, 406–408
Causal unit formation, *see* Unit formation
Chance outcomes
  explanations for, 105

Figure 5-1 First page of subject index of Harvey, Ickes, and Kidd, *New Directions in Attribution Research,* 1976.

provides the explanation of the cognitive process involved in person-environment interaction. And Anderson finds at least some verbal formulations of AT to be confirmed by empirical test.

(c) Since SJT intends to describe the behavioral consequences (e.g., conflict) that follow from the *formal* characteristics of judgment tasks or situations (without imputing a lawful character to them), its aims are not challenged by the other approaches.

In short, whatever differences in aim might exist among Group II theorists, they do not charge that any one of the other approaches cannot possibly fulfill its intended aim, nor that any other theory is grounded in logically false or empirically untrue premises. There even seems to be a certain recognition of complementarity of aim, if disparity in method, among Group II approaches. Yet it must be said that the present coexistence is only that, and that the relations among these approaches might best be described by "aloofness," with the major exception of Anderson's effort (and Mumpower, 1976).

5.8.3 Groups I and II

There is no mistaking the fact that there are differences between Group I and II with regard to intended function. The critical question is: Are these differences *complementary?* And if they are, do they serve to *extend* the domain of behavior covered by judgment and decision research? Or do these differences in intended function mean that these two groups are involved in wholly unrelated activities, and, therefore, have no need to communicate with one another?

The possibility of complementarity is raised by the persistent use of different, yet closely related, terminology by Group I and II approaches. Even a cursory glance at the language of Group I and Group II theorists shows that there is a far greater use of the terms "decision," "choice," and "preference" in Group I and a much greater use of "judgment" and "inference" in Group II. Does this difference imply Group I and Group II theorists intend to study the same aspects of cognition? Different, but complementary aspects? or wholly unrelated aspects of cognition? The key to answering these questions may well lie in the distinction between *knowing* and *choosing*.

Knowing and Choosing No distinction between the aims of "decision theorists" and "judgment analysts" has ever been drawn, so far as we know, although Bock and Jones (1968) did approximate such a distinction, thus:

> Traditionally, the concept of a sensory continuum applies to the subject's experience of a continuously variable physical event which is called the

stimulus. The subject's response in comparing two such stimuli is usually called a *judgment* rather than a *choice.* This implies that the subject has no personal preference towards the outcome of the trial, but is merely an objective observer. This terminology carries into applied work when, for example, we call the expert sensory tester a "judge." (p. 4)

But this effort toward discrimination was obviously doomed because of its arbitrariness; why couldn't a response comparing two stimuli be called a *choice,* rather than a *judgment?* The need for the distinction occurred to Slovic and Lichtenstein in 1971, but they rejected it as "tenuous." In the second sentence of their well-known article they state that the "distinction between judgments and decisions ... will not be maintained here; we shall use these terms interchangeably" (p. 16 in Rappoport & Summers). And in their subsequent review, Slovic, Fischhoff, and Lichtenstein (1977) did not address the distinction between the two terms at all. Zeleny, a decision theorist, went further than ignoring the distinction; he argued that "It is *misleading* (italics ours) to maintain the customary differentiation between human judgment and decision making." Although Zeleny (1976) does not indicate why he believes the distinction is "customary," he indicates that it "leads to unhealthy separation and inbreeding in both disciplines where an interaction would lead to mutual enrichment and rejuvenation" (pp. 58-59).

Zeleny thus appears to believe that there is some form of difference that is associated with different disciplines. This difference should be reduced, he argues, because "the difference between judgments and decisions is purely terminological—they both represent a process of making a *choice* (italics ours) among available alternatives" (p. 59). But if Zeleny was prepared to find the distinction between judgment and decision to be "misleading" and reduce them both to *choice,* he and Starr thought it to be important to distinguish between the terms "decision" and "choice" (Starr & Zeleny, 1977). Thus: "When mostly attributes are involved we tend to refer to such situations as those of a *theory of choice,* while the cases dealing mostly with objectives may be referred to as a *theory of decision making*" (all italics in original, p. 14). But these distinctions in turn disappear because "In reality both the attributes and the objectives are often involved in a mixed fashion." It is hard to see how this distinction improves matters.

The title of R. N. Shepard's talk at the AAAS meetings in 1962 ("Use of judgments in making optimal decisions") provides a further illustration of the uncertain status of the distinction between these terms: Could that title have just as well read: "Use of decisions in making optimal judgments"? And it is indeed curious to find Anderson (1974, p. 2) explaining that greater inter-action has not occurred between IIT and AT because "much of the work on integration theory has been outside of social psychology, in *decision-making* (italics ours)."

These quotations indicate that however convenient Slovic and Lichten-stein (1971, 1973) might have found it to dismiss the distinction between these terms as "tenuous," the question of their different referents needs to be examined more closely. We shall not make that attempt here, but we *shall* make the distinction. We do so because we believe that the cause of the development of a cumulative scientific discipline will best be served by indicating that the work of researchers on both sides of the conceptual watershed may very well be complementary. Specifically, we believe that integration will be better served by *instituting* that distinction because it will be useful in identifying the complementary nature of the intended functions of the theories. For example, theories of choice, decision and preference DT, BDT and PDT aim at describing and explaining decisions to select, choose or to prefer one alternative (an object, an action, etc.) rather than another as a function of one's interests or goals. More specifically, DT aims at discovering the "nondominated" (i.e., best) alternative(s) in a set of many alternatives. DT thus intends to identify and then eliminate dominated (less than optimal) alternatives from consideration. Once identified, dominated alternatives are of little or no further interest to decision analysts. The intended function of the theory, then, is to prescribe, and to aid in, the choice of the non-dominated object (or course of action, etc.) that follows from the expression of the decision maker's probabilities and utilities. When the choice is made, the task is finished; DT is not curious about *why* persons should be less than rational.

BDT research, on the other hand, does have this curiosity, and it intends to show that decision makers often select, choose or prefer the alternative they shouldn't prefer, if their probabilities and utilities are what the decision maker says they are. BDT offers explanations for this; for example, people fail to use the appropriate likelihood ratio, or fail to revise posterior odds as much as they should upon the receipt of new information. Although BDT is clearly different from DT in its effort to describe the degree and general form of departures from accurate probability estimates, it does not pursue the investigation of inductive knowing beyond this interest. And therefore it can hardly make strong claims to function as a general theory of *knowing,* as against its strong claims to function as a theory of *decision* or *choice* or *preference*—unless, of course, it is prepared to argue that *all* forms of cognition can be reduced to estimations of probabilities, an argument not yet explicitly advanced, so far as we know.

PDT can make a stronger claim to being a general theory of knowing as well as a theory of choice, simply because of the wider scope of its theoretical, explanatory concepts. Additionally, PDT studies a wider range of judgment problems than one observes in BDT. Nonetheless, it is true that PDT studies knowing only within the context of the biases in probability estimates of the correct state of affairs "out there." And although such estimates can be involved in knowing what's "out there," such biases can hardly claim to exhaust the cognitive activity involved in knowing.

When the watershed is crossed to the Group II approaches it is clear that we are now dealing with approaches that emphasize knowing or learning about the character of the environment in contrast to making choices between alternatives or preferences. For judgment theorists see problems of choice, action, and preferences for various outcomes of the world as subproblems of the more general problem of knowing. The study of knowing is thus *propaedeutic* (that is, prior) to the study of choice. Group II theorists intend to develop a theory of knowing from which a theory of decision is produced. This highly general aim can clearly be seen in all three approaches within Group II, none of which ascertain probability estimates from their subjects because they do not regard such estimates of special interest, and none of which are primarily interested in utilities or rewards, although all are perfectly prepared to accept or request probability estimates or utility estimates in any special case. The primary goal of judgment analysis, in short, is to describe and to understand *inductive knowing,* rather than *choice* or *preference.* And as we shall see below, this difference in aim leads directly to a difference in the manner in which researchers carry out their work.

To summarize, one strong reason for maintaining the distinction between the terms decision and judgment is that it raises the possibility that the different approaches associated with these terms may *complement* one another, and may thus provide a broader scope than either approach taken alone. Moreover, understanding the nature of the complementary contribution of each approach may lead to a *cumulative* development of an integrated discipline. Although we cannot consider that possibility in depth here, it certainly should be pursued with care in future work. Moreover, as we turn to the matter of the evaluation of subjects' behavior, we shall see that differentiating the contributions of the Group I approach and Group II approach also points to the possibility of complementarity.*

Evaluating the Subjects' Behavior Differences in the intended function of Group I and Group II theories become apparent when we observe their attitudes toward the evaluation of behavior. In Group I, evaluation of the subjects' decision behavior is carried out with reference to the decision behavior of a mathematical model of rationality; the model is used to evaluate

---

*"The limited evidence on the lack of such strategies in judgment tasks (Goldberg, 1975), suggests that the distinction between judgment and choice be maintained and sharpened. Specifically, the distinction between diagnosis/prognosis and choice of therapy in the clinical area, for example, seems a useful analogy. In any event, more work is necessary to clearly distinguish judgment from choice and the processes that may be invoked by each" (Einhorn, Kleinmuntz, & Kleinmuntz, 1979).

logical correctness, or *subjective* optimality. This is also true for BDT's MAUT; no empirically correct answer need be available in order to evaluate the subjects' behavior with respect to optimality.

Bayesian research and PDT research move one step closer to empirical, as against logical, evaluation of the subjects' performance by calculating the correct answer to a decision problem through the use of a statistical model (Bayesian in the first case, and both Bayesian and frequentist in the second). Because the results of evaluating the subjects' behavior have almost invariably indicated sub-optimal performance, all three groups have recommended the use of decision aids of some kind. Most recently, "debiasing" of incorrect probability estimates has been attempted, in the hope that if such biases can be removed in cognitive probability assessments, then more nearly correct probability estimates (i.e., answers that are more nearly compatible with those produced by statistical models with strong logical and empirical claims to truth) will be produced by decision makers. Thus, the ultimate aim of ascertaining and evaluating the correctness of human performance includes the provision of a remedy for the inadequacy of that performance.

In contrast, on the other side of the conceptual watershed, when SJT and AT evaluate subjects' performance in judgment tasks they do so in terms of the subjects' achievement of an *empirical* criterion. (IIT foregoes evaluation as a general practice, see Shanteau and Phelps, 1977). Thus, the intended aim of SJT is to study the acquisition and use of empirical *knowledge* (under conditions of environmental ambiguity, including uncertainty), rather than to study the approximation of human probability assessment to logically optimal probability assessment, as in the case of BDT and PDT. SJT's intended function, then, is to study cognitive adaptation to an ambiguous (uncertain) environment. Thus, for example, SJT studies multiple-cue probability learning in which the evaluation of a subject's achievement of an empirically correct answer is the critical component of performance. To be sure, that performance is analyzed and often described in terms of various statistical concepts; nonetheless the correct answer with which the subject's answer is compared is a tangible, empirical one; not one provided through calculation as in the case of Group I approaches.

This point can be seen more clearly in SJT's studies of interpersonal learning and interpersonal conflict; the evaluation of performance is in terms of empirical achievement of an outcome (a second subject's response which is not under the control of the experimenter). But this does not mean that statistical analysis cannot be employed after the fact in order to analyze the components of the subject's achievement.

The same is true for AT; there is no reference here to optimal choices, preferences, or probability estimates, although the experiments do evaluate the performance of subjects. Although empirical correctness is not always empha-sized, it may be used as a reference point when criteria for correctness are available. The performance of subjects can thus be evaluated by showing that empirically incorrect attributions (or inferences) are made under certain conditions of social structure. It is the relation between (social) structural conditions and attributions (inferences) that form the basic materials from which laws of attributional behavior are to be constructed.

In short, the employment of different methods for evaluating the subjects' performance in SJT and AT on the one hand and in DT, BDT, and PDT on the other follows from the distinction between choosing and knowing made above, and thus leads to further support for the hypothesis that the Group I and II approaches may be complementary.

But what about IIT? Is it not also complementary in form to Group I approaches? Possibly, but it is more difficult to be clear about IIT in this context, for IIT is sharply different from SJT and AT in relation to evalution of its subjects' behavior.

IIT has indicated little, if any, interest in evaluating the fit of various models of *optimal* behavior to empirical behavior. As indicated above, IIT is wholly disinterested in the model or process that the subject departs *from* and is solely interested in the model that "fits," or accounts *for,* the subject's response. Anderson (1974, p. 66) makes this distinction clear when he states: "In the case of the Bayesian model, there is no doubt that it is wrong," and although "various attempts have been made to 'explain' [conservatism] . . . it is doubtful that there is anything to be explained, since the effect exists only by reference to an admittedly incorrect model." In short, since the Bayesian model is putatively "wrong" in its *description* of cognitive activity, it should be abandoned as a contender in what Anderson believes should be an effort to find the correct description or explanation of human cognitive activity (however much interest rational models might have for decision theorists). It should be added that IIT gives no significant attention to the evaluation of subjects' performance in terms of the achievement of empirically correct judgments. In short, with the absence of an evaluative component regarding subjects' behavior in IIT, this approach appears to *supplement,* rather than *complement,* either of the Group I of Group II approaches described above.

The distinction may well be important and useful, and therefore we quote from the Random House Dictionary College Edition (1968):

> COMPLEMENT, SUPPLEMENT both mean to make an addition or additions to something. To COMPLEMENT is to provide something felt to be lacking or needed; it is often applied to putting together two things, each of which supplied what is lacking in the other, to make a complete whole: *Two statements from different points of view may complement each other.* To SUPPLEMENT is merely to add to; no definite lack or deficiency is implied nor is there an idea of a definite relationship between parts: *Some additional remarks may supplement either statement or both.* (p. 275)*

*The Random House College Dictionary, Revised Edition, © 1975, 1979 by Random House, Inc.

Therefore, we offer, *as a hypothesis,* the suggestion that IIT provides valuable information that supplements and thus *adds* to the cumulative character of the new discipline, whereas other approaches complement and thus tend to *complete,* or round out, the character of the new discipline.

To sum up, the differences in intended function observed above with respect to deciding and knowing are reinforced by the observations that Group I approaches generally, if not always, evaluate the performance of their subjects' differently from Group II approaches. Moreover, it is clear that the analysis of the internal characteristics of choice behavior is the predominant aim of Group I approaches, while the analysis of inductive inference regarding the environment is the predominant aim of Group II approaches. Thus, Group I and II approaches appear to complement one another. Awareness of complementarity of these approaches, together with the knowledge of the supplemental contributions of IIT, should increase the likelihood that the new discipline will become a cumulative one.

Differential Function of the Single-System Case As pointed out in the earlier section (*Scope*), the single-system case is the research situation that typifies research on judgment and decision making. It is this case alone that interests DT, and occupies the greatest interest of BDT, PDT, and IIT. But this situation is different for SJT; this approach is not interested in the single-system case as the basic situation for studying and producing knowledge regarding judgment (despite all the emphasis on the single-system case that has been attributed to SJT by non-SJT researchers; for an example, see Slovic, Fischhoff, & Lichtenstein, 1977). Work within the single-system case by SJT researchers is derived, or extrapolated, from work in the double-system case involving MCPL, and the triple-system case involving interpersonal learning and interpersonal conflict (cases which the other approaches tend to ignore because of their absorbing interest in the single-system case). That is, having learned what they believe they have learned from studies in these cases, SJT researchers are prepared to extrapolate from their research in these cases to the single-system case as a descriptive (not explanatory) effort, in the interests of providng a useful remedy for the suboptimal cognitive activity they believe they have observed in studies of MCPL, etc. But SJT (or probabilistic functionalism) has not intended work in the single-system case to produce general explanations of judgment and decision making behavior.

A good example of the extrapolation of findings *from* cases other than the single-system *to* the single-system case (and others) can be found in the remedy, or cognitive aid, offered by SJT for the suboptimal performance of subjects in cognitive tasks. The remedy is offered in the form of what is called "cognitive feedback." That is, if subjects fail to perform optimally or adequately in MCPL tasks, and if it is found (as it often is) that the failure is due to inappropriate use of cue weights or function forms relative to those in the task, then SJT advocates that the subject should be provided with pictorial, easy-to-grasp information about them to aid improvement in achieving the empirically correct answer. This approach has been extrapolated to the single-system case as follows: A person's judgment policy is determined (i.e., described in terms of weights, function forms and consistency of application); the policy is displayed to the judge (cognitive feedback) so that she or he may revise his/her policy under perfect control by use of a computer console; and (ideally) the policy (as perhaps revised) is executed with perfect consistency by computers. Note again that this judgment aid is an application of the results of double-system case research to the single-system case—just the reverse of the application processes of other approaches. (More will be said about cognitive feedback below in connection with the link between cognitive models and environmental models below; see "Uses.")

IIT is deeply committed to offering descriptions (whether elevated to the level of explanations or not) of cognitive activity in the single-system case, and it is the derivatives from *this* case that are to be applied to others (say, group decision making), precisely the opposite manner of approach taken by SJT. In any case, IIT is wholly disinterested in remedies; neither suboptimality, subachievement, nor remedies for these are of interest to IIT researchers; finding the correct model to fit the integrative process is the primary problem of interest to these researchers.

We are uncertain about the AT approach. For although AT researchers do not appear to be interested in the single-system case at all, this conclusion may very well be incorrect, since proponents may provide counseling to clients that is based on results from certain experiments. Since the precise form of the counseling, if it occurs, is unknown to us, we shall assume that it is irrelevant to our present purposes. We will only point out that if such counseling does occur, the direction of extrapolation of results would, in general, be similar to that taken by SJT, namely from the more complex cases to the single-system case.

There is one indication of change in AT that may well bear on its interest in the single-system case. A recent article by Jones and McGillis indicates that AT may have taken an entirely new turn that will link it more closely to Group I approaches. These authors (in Harvey, Ickes, & Kidd, 1976, p. 404) offer a version of AT which they label "correspondent inference theory," and describe it as follows:

> Correspondent inference theory is essentially a rational baseline model. It does not summarize phenomenal experience; it presents a logical calculus in terms of which accurate inferences could be drawn by an alert perceiver weighing knowledge, ability, noncommon effects, and prior probability. But the role of the theory has been as much to identify attribution bias as to predict precisely the course of the social inference process. In a similar vein, Edwards (1968) has stated regarding decision

theories that "they specify what an ideal decision-maker would do and thus invite comparison between performances of ideal and real decision-makers [p. 34]." The theory cannot be invalidated by experimental results any more than game theory can be invalidated by the choices of players in a prisoner's dilemma game. (p. 406)

Note the references to Edwards; this statement indicates more than a recognition of common interests. Jones and McGillis go much further and suggest that they are producing a normative or prescriptive theory similar to decision theory or game theory. They also say that "Kelley's (1967) theory has a different goal than that of correspondent inference theory" (p. 406). (See also Reeder & Brewer, 1979.)

To summarize: the single-system case may be the research situation in which all approaches (except AT?) share a keen interest, but it is clear that this situation is studied very differently by different approaches because their aims are different. Equally important, the remedies that different approaches offer are different because they are directed toward different (putative) cognitive deficiencies.

Does this situation imply that complementarity exists and that a broadening of scope is possible? Or does it imply antinomies that must be resolved theoretically and/or empirically? We are not sure. Consider again Slovic's (1976) comments regarding PDT:

Subjective judgments of probability and value are essential inputs to decision analyses. We still do not know the best ways to elicit these judgments. Now that we understand many of the biases to which judgments are susceptible, we need to develop debiasing techniques to minimize their destructive effects. (p. 238)

The complexity of that task is also indicated, however, thus:

Simply warning a judge about a bias may prove ineffective. Like perceptual illusions, many biases do not disappear upon being identified. (p. 238)

Would it not be reasonable for proponents of Group II approaches to ask: If we still do not know the best ways to evoke subjective probabilities, and if they are subject to so many biases when they are evoked, and if attempts at debiasing are likely to be difficult to achieve at best and ineffective at worst, then why should not the efforts to aid the decision maker that are based on ascertaining subjective probabilities be abandoned in favor of other approaches? Perhaps subjective probabilities (and utilities) are *not* essential inputs to the decision making process. Perhaps the study of knowing *is* propaedeutic to the study of choice. Perhaps if one gains an understanding of knowing, in the manner of Group II approaches, the remedy for inadequate cognitive efforts will become, and indeed perhaps already has become, apparent.

Chapter 6

Principal Concepts

One of the primary reasons for attempting to integrate various approaches to human judgment and decision behavior is that many different concepts seem to be employed by different researchers to refer to the same phenomena. Moreover, the wide range in terminology gives rise to the uncomfortable suspicion that many authors may be using different words to refer to the same concept. Equally uncomfortable is the suspicion that the same word may be carrying different conceptual and operational meanings for different researchers. Does the Bayesian researcher's "datum" have the same meaning as the IIT researcher's "stimulus"? And does "stimulus" have the same meaning as the SJT's researcher's "cue"? Most important, does the concept of "uncertainty" convey the same meaning to all researchers in the field of "judgment and decision under conditions of uncertainty"? As we have seen earlier there is doubt as to whether judgment and decision should be used interchangeably. What about "uncertainty"?

In this section we will not try to settle such questions by references to operational definitions; these are discussed in the Procedure section. Rather, we shall consider at a conceptual level the principal concepts used by the six approaches.

6.1 DECISION THEORY

The major concepts in DT are, of course, *decision, choice, preference,* and *probability, utility,* and *aggregation.* Both probability and utility are treated as judgments that are produced in response to special circumstances (e.g., lotteries) presented to the decision maker by the decision analyst. Such circumstances are intended to permit the measurement of each in ordinal (if not interval or cardinal) form. Ideally, if a decision maker's preference is larger for one alternative than another, it will be as a result of the mathematical, analytical aggregation by the decision *analyst* of the separate probability and utility judgments made by the decision *maker.*

Consider first the probability judgment. Note that it is a dependent variable that is ascertained *directly* in response to specific circumstances. It is essential to note that the role of probability (and thus uncertainty) is that of a *dependent variable.* As such it is of primary importance in DT for two reasons: (a) it has been carried into the work of BDT and PDT in this form, and (b) it has not appeared in this form (except adventitiously) in Group II approaches. As a result, the role of probability as a psychological concept is different in these two general approaches.

Much the same can be said for the concept of utility. It is also a metatheoretical proposition within DT that the utility of an alternative exists in the mind of the decision maker and it is assumed that it is essential to measure it somehow. In contrast to the concept of probability, DT and all other approaches employ the concept of utility in much the same way, although other approaches may not employ it in every situation.

The aggregation of probabilities and utilities is the cognitive activity of the decision maker that combines, integrates or organizes the probabilities and utilities associated with various alternatives. DT is prepared to use either additive or multiplicative methods of combination, depending upon certain conditions.

DT researchers have indicated considerable interest in *scaling* and *transitivity,* and indeed, these matters have also attracted the attention of Edwards and other psychologists (e.g., Coombs; also Anderson). In addition, the mathematical consequences of nonindependence interest DT researchers. (Keeney & Raiffa, 1976, devote some space to these problems [17 pages references in the index, plus several other references to "conditionality].) Nonindependence, rather than scaling, is apt to catch the attention of psychologists interested in the question of how people cope with "causal texture" (cf. SJT and AT).

The importance of the concept of independence-dependence can also be seen by consulting the Index to Keeney and Raiffa (1976) and noting the entries under "Assumptions": These are

additive independence, 230, 295
conditional independence, 333

Perhaps the most important development in DT is with regard to decisions involving multiple, rather than single, *objectives*. Objectives, in turn, are defined in terms of their attributes. Thus, "the Postal Service *objective* 'minimize total transit time for a given category of mail' . . . was measured in terms of the *attribute* 'days' " (Keeney & Raiffa, 1976, p. 34). As a result multiple attributes must be considered, and, therefore, nonindependence; in addition, *trade-offs* must be expected. All of these concepts are also found in BDT.

6.2 BEHAVIORAL DECISION THEORY

DT and BDT share essentially the same mathematical logic and the same concepts (*decision, choice, preference, subjective probability* and *utility*) as dependent variables, and, of course, both include *aggregation* as a concept that refers to the cognitive process of combining the latter two. And as in DT, BDT takes it as a metatheoretical proposition that uncertainty exists in the mind of the decision maker and, therefore, it is essential to measure it. This is often done by requesting Ss to express their uncertainty in terms of a probability scale, odds, a likelihood ratio, etc. Explanations for, as descriptions of, the *source(s)* of uncertainty in the mind of the decision maker are not an integral part of the BDT approach and, therefore, no detail is provided by BDT on this matter (although there is some indication that if such explanations were offered they would be similar to those offered by SJT; see Edwards' introduction to Slovic & Lichtenstein, 1971). BDT also accepts DT's metatheoretical proposition regarding the need for the concept of utility and attempts to measure it; as Edwards put it: "what's at stake and what are the odds"?

All, or most all, of the concepts mentioned above in connection with DT have been investigated empirically by BDT. Note that these concepts are inherited from economic theory and Bayesian probability theory, not psychology, and, therefore, empirical work should carry implications for the *use* of the theory by decision analysts—or so behavioral decision theorists think. Thus, in empirical Bayesian research, we find such concepts as *conservatism,* the *diagnostic impact* (of a datum or event), *conditional dependence, unconditional hypothesis, independence of data, (mis)perception, (mis)-aggregation,* and *diagnosticity,* etc. All these terms were developed in the course of the research on departures from Bayesian optimality; e.g., why the conservative bias? In order to see the descriptive function of these terms we briefly consider the typical Bayesian research paradigm.

The subject is required to observe a *datum* or *event* (drawn from a population of data or events), make an estimate of the *probability* that it was produced by a given source; observe a second datum, at which point the subject revises whatever prior *probabilities* (or odds) he held prior to observing the datum, the extent of that revision providing a measure of the *impact* of the datum on his *posterior probabilities* (and thus the subject's evaluation of the *diagnosticity* of the data, as well as the *base* rate of occurrence) in addition to which the subject may *aggregate* all the information he has acquired up to this point and instead of revising his posterior probabilities may be requested to evaluate the *likelihood ratio* regarding the population which produced the event. Semipsychological concepts have been introduced into these Bayesian experiments where learning is involved (e.g., *pay-offs* and *feedback*) both of which were introduced in the effort to discover whether subjects could reduce their "conservatism" and thus behave (i.e., revise their estimates) more nearly in accord with the "behavior" of the (optimal) Bayesian model. None of these concepts are in jeopardy today in the sense of being considered wrong or useless, as for example "fractional anticipatory goal response" might be considered. But their value as descriptors of significant *psychological* processes is being questioned more and more sharply by PDT and IIT.

6.3 PSYCHOLOGICAL DECISION THEORY

This approach also includes the concepts *decision, choice,* and *preference,* as well as *subjective probabilities* and *utilities* because the point of departure for this approach is also SEU theory. In addition, we find the term "heuristics," used to describe various rules of thumb used by subjects to decide the correct answer to a problem involving a statistical inference. And it may well be that it is these heuristics that interfere with the rational use of information, and for which DT seeks to provide a remedy.

Uncertainty continues to be conceived of as a pervasive state in the mind of the decision maker, and PDT also assumes that this state of mind is to be ascertained directly in the form of a probability estimate (or choice) in relation to a set of task conditions, although, as we shall see, these conditions are far different from those employed by DT or BDT. Similarly, no detailed theoretical analysis is offered as to why such uncertainty should exist. Judgment tasks are described in statistical terms, although no special group of statistical concepts is emphasized in contrast with BDT's predilection for Bayesian concepts; rather, PDT theorists rely on the entire repertoire of statistical theory; in addition they employ a variety of methods to evaluate the optimality or correctness of any given heuristic putatively used by a decision maker.

The major significance of PDT (and the reason why we have assigned it the name we have) is that in this approach we meet for the first time the persistent use of *psychological* (in contrast to statistical) concepts to *explain* (not merely *describe*) the departure of the probability estimates of human decision makers from optimality. Such explanatory concepts are *availability*, *representativeness*, and *anchoring*. Some of these terms (anchoring) have been used before in traditional psychophysics, some (availability) in cognitive psychology (cf. Bruner, Goodnow & Austin, 1956), and one (representativeness) is new.

One of the more recently introduced explanatory concepts is that of *causal schemas*, thus, "the impact of evidence (cf. 'impact of a datum' in Bayesian research; au) on intuitive judgments of probabilities depends critically on whether it is perceived as causal, diagnostic or incidental" (Tversky & Kahneman, 1979). The use of statistical referents (see Chapter 4 SCOPE on evaluation) is illustrated by the subsequent statement: "*base-rate information* (italics ours) which is given a causal interpretation affects judgments, while base-rate information which cannot be interpreted in this manner is given little or no *weight*" (italics ours). Thus the above statement not only signifies PDT's employment of statistical logic (i.e., base rate) to evaluate a subject's use of information, it also indicates the universal (among these six approaches) resort to the psychological concept of *weight;* apparently no approach can do without it, although AT makes uncertain use of it. (Equally significant, no approach has given attention to its theoretical status, except possibly Kahneman & Tversky in *Prospect Theory,* 1979.) The employment of the concept of weight by PDT thus provides a link between PDT and all other approaches. For although the independent variables (or factors) that are believed to affect judgments of probability are different from those considered by DT and BDT, the critical question in PDT is nevertheless directed toward the differential "impact of evidence on intuitive judgment of probabilities." In other words, how much weight for a given "input" of what type? (This point is developed further in the Integration section.)

As noted above, the independent variables that PDT considers to be determinants of the "differential impact" of evidence or determinants of the "weight" that is assigned to different varieties of evidence, constitute a different class of variables than have been used by DT or BDT. The major difference is that the data presented to the decision maker is described by PDT not only in *formal* (i.e., statistical) terms, but *psychological* ones. For example, "the ordering of events by their subjective probabilities coincides with their ordering by representativeness" (p. 431, Kahneman & Tversky, 1972). Representativeness (a psychological concept) therefore *explains* the magnitude of subjective probability judgments. But what is "representativeness"? This term is defined in terms of the degree to which an "uncertain event or a sample ... is i) *similar* in essential properties to its parent population; and ii) reflects the *salient* features of the process by which it is generated" (p. 431, Kahneman & Tversky, 1972; italics ours). "Similarity" is given detailed treatment by Tversky (1977) in a paper devoted only to that topic but that material need not be discussed here. Clearly, however, "similar" and "salient" are subject-oriented terms.

Because terms such as "similar" or "salient" are subject-defined, they are members of a class of organism-centered defintions. These terms are used to represent *some* of the variables that affect judgments of probabilities. And it is these variables that give *a priori* meaning to the concept of weight, and thus explain why this piece of evidence is ignored and that piece of evidence is not. In addition, different organism-centered terms introduced by PDT seem to belong to different classes. For example, representativeness appears to be an *organism-centered* definition of an *object-attribute,* whereas availability appears to refer only to an organismic *process* (as does anchoring) without reference to object attributes. (The reasons for our uncertainty, reflected in the use of "appears," is developed in more detail in the Integration section.)

6.4 TRANSITION

The shift in orientation between Group I approaches and Group II approaches may be seen in the changes in the names of principal concepts we shall observe as we move across the conceptual watershed. No longer will such terms as probabilities and utilities be employed as primary theoretical concepts, and no longer will it be taken for granted that these concepts should be translated directly into measurable quantities. Nor is it found necessary to attack the validity of the DT approach (or SEU approach) by showing that persons do not cope with subjective uncertainty as they should. In only one of the three approaches (SJT) is uncertainty treated as a major concept and it is given far different treatment here than in Group I approaches.

New terms will be encountered among Group II approaches; for example, *cue, stimulus, percept,* and *information* are used to describe inputs to the organism, and concepts such as *organizing principle, integration, inference* and *attribution* are used to describe the cognitive activity of a "subject" or "organism" or "knower" rather than a "decision maker."

The idea of a conceptual *watershed,* rather than a gap or barrier, separating Group I and Group II approaches is particularly useful with regard to the principal concepts used by different approaches, because the change from Group I to Group II is not abrupt. Some terms (cue or stimulus, for example) are apt to have a broad range across nearly all approaches whereas others are highly restricted (e.g., SJT's use of "ecological validity"). The transition from Group I to Group II implies a continuous, if uneven, change rather than a sharp change in approach; the change is there, however, and its contours are recognizable.

6.5 SOCIAL JUDGMENT THEORY

SJT is the first approach to be encountered in moving across the conceptual watershed between Group I and II approaches because of the great emphasis on the concept of uncertainty that it shares with Group I approaches. However, as noted above, there is a clear difference in the function of this concept in Group I approaches and in SJT. For SJT postulates the emergence of uncertain (probabilistic) behavior as a function of an uncertain and, therefore, generally *ambiguous* environment. And although SJT might find it advantageous in some circumstances to request subjects to make judgments about probabilities (paralleling the work of Group I approaches) such judgments simply constitute one instance of the general class of judgments. (The same is true for IIT; see, for example Shanteau, 1975; Lopes, 1976, and would be true for AT if it requested probability judgments from its subjects.)

The concept of utility (as this term is used in Group I approaches) has no special role in SJT. As in the case of probability judgments, value and utility judgments are simply one member of a class of judgments. Far more emphasis is placed on *achievement,* that is, the correct attainment of the distal variable, and that emphasis points to the fact that the fundamental, primary conceptual paradigm for SJT is *not* the single system case (as it is for DT, PDT, and IIT).

Uncertainty in the organism is inferred from the organism's semierratic *behavior* as it attempts to cope with a semierratic task (see the large series of studies carried out by Brehmer and his colleagues on MCPL). It is not ascertained by requiring the person to make a judgment of probability values, or choices between lotteries as in Group I approaches. If probability judgments are requested at all by SJT (or IIT, or AT) such judgments are treated merely as another instance of a general class of inferences about a not-directly-observable state; thus, uncertainty is inferred by the analyst from the judge's inferential behavior in this case as well as others. In short, when Group I investigators study uncertainty, they use techniques to evoke persons' expressions of their subjective *feelings* about their uncertainty, whereas Group II investigators study uncertainty by observing its occurrence as inconsistency in the *behavior* of their subjects. So far as we know, the significance of this distinction in the role of probability and uncertainty in judgment has never been explored.

The following material taken from the most recent statement of the general principles of SJT should indicate the principal concepts employed by this approach.

BASIC CONCEPTS

Relationships: The Fundamental Units of Cognition

The fundamental concept ordinarily employed to describe an environmental "input" to the organism is the stimulus. That concept is rejected here. Although both Tolman and Brunswik used this term, they did not make a complete conceptual commitment to it; both argued that the objects and events apprehended by an organism do more—and less—than "impinge" upon it. Not only does the organism cognitively act on the "input," but the perceived object carried implications for *other objects*. That is why Tolman's position was labeled an S-S theory (that is, a "sign-significate" theory) and contrasted to an S-R (stimulus-response) theory by competing theoreticians of his time. And that is why Brunswik used the word "cue" to refer to various dimensions of the perceived world. Both these terms, "sign-significate" (or as Tolman also put it, "sign-Gestalt") and "cue," have in common the notion that the raw materials of perception point outward from the organism toward various aspects of the person's ecological surroundings. And whereas "sign-significate" and "cue" point *outward* from the organism to the environment, the concept of stimulus points *inward*. It is for this reason that S-R theories in general do not include concepts relating to the environment and that S-R judgment theories, in particular, do not include concepts referring to the properties of judgment tasks (see, for example, Anderson, 1971).

Because "cues" and "sign-significates" point outward, they involve a relation between two variables—proximal and distal, the given and the inferred. Choice of that relation as the fundamental unit of cognition has profound consequences, of course, and it was this choice that eventually led Tolman to introduce the concept of the "cognitive map" in 1948; he argued that cognition involves a subjective representation of the inter-relations of goal paths in the organism's environment. Brunswik went further; he demanded a more detailed analysis of the *environment* and a less detailed analysis of the *organism*. Thus, for example, he remarked:

> Both the organism and environment will have to be seen as systems, each with properties of its own ... Each has surface and depth, or overt and covert regions. ... It follows that, much as psychology must be concerned with the texture of the organism or of its nervous properties and investigate them in depth, it must also be concerned with the texture of the environment. [1957, p. 5]

Brunswik's admonition to psychologists to "be concerned with the texture of the environment" gives clear direction to the student of human judgment; his first step must be to learn about and to understand the texture (and by that we mean the causal ambiguity) of the relationships among variables in the tasks which require human judgment. (The methodological corollary is that such ambiguity among relations must be represented in the judgment tasks used to study human judgment.)

Principle of Parallel Concepts

As can be seen in the above quotation, Brunswik indicated that organismic and environmental systems should be described in symmetrical terms. That symmetry is represented in what Brunswik called the "lens model" of behavior indicated in Figure 1. (Space does not permit more than a cursory reference to the conceptual implications of the lens model; the best of several original sources is Brunswik's "The Conceptual Framework of Psychology," 1952; a secondary source which presents parts of what is contained in several original articles is Hammond's *The Psychology of Egon Brunswik,* 1966.)

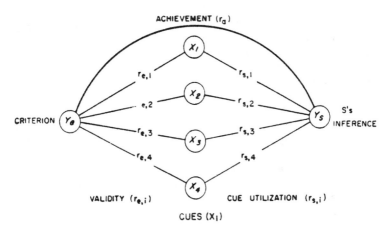

Brunswik's lens model.

As Brunswik describes the lens model, it becomes clear that he employs a principle of parallel concepts, for each concept on one side is paralleled by a similar concept of the other. Thus, cues on the task, or ecological, side vary in *ecological validity,* and on the organismic side there is variation in *cue utilization* by the subject. And just as the relations between cues and distal variables on the ecological side may assume various (linear, curvilinear) *forms,* according to the principle of parallel concepts, the relations between cues and judgments may also assume various function forms on the organismic side. The investigator has similar interests with regard to both sets of variables: to what extent ecological validities are matched by cue utilization and to what extent ecological function forms are matched by subjective function forms. Social judgment theorists are also concerned with the extent to which the principles of organization that control the task system are reflected in the principles of organization that control the cognitive system of the subject.

It is the principle of parallel concepts, therefore, that produces the symmetrical relation between the descriptive terms applied to the organismic system and to the environmental system, and it is this principle that is responsible for the fact that Social Judgment Theory (SJT) includes a set of concepts which apply to task systems as well as person systems.

Distinction between Surface and Depth

This distinction is essential to SJT. It derives from the proximal-distal separation in perception theory and thus refers to the separation between what is given and what is inferred. *Surface* data are (given) cues to (inferred) *depth* conditions in the judgment task. By virtue of the principle of parallel concepts, this distinction also applies to organismic judgment systems (see Figure 1). Separation of surface and depth is critical to any theory of judgment (or inference), for it raises the question of the properties of the region that intervenes between them. Because of the importance of this region, we have named it the *zone of ambiguity*.

The Zone of Ambiguity

The region between depth and surface variables in a given judgment task involves the relations between cause (depth) and effect (surface). Because a single effect may be produced by several causes, as well as because multiple effects may be produced by a single cause, there is ambiguity from cause to effect and effect to cause. Because causes may be related, and because effects are interrelated the network of task relations can be said to be entangled. Moreover, causal ambiguity is produced because (1) surface data are less than perfectly related to depth variables, (2) functional relations between surface and depth variables may assume a variety of forms (linear, curvilinear), and (3) the relations between surface and depth may be organized (or combined) according to a variety of principles (for example, additivity or pattern). These circumstances give more specific meaning to the term "causal texture," or causal ambiguity.

In short, causal ambiguity within the zone of ambiguity is the source of the human judgment problem, as well as a source of the misunderstandings and disputes that occur when judgments differ. (Hammond, Stewart, Brehmer, & Steinmann, 1975, pp. 272-275)

6.6 INFORMATION INTEGRATION THEORY

This approach takes us further in the direction of a traditional psychological approach. Measurement of probabilities, utilities and measurement of the analytical aggregation carried out by the decision analyst are activities far removed from the principal business of IIT, that of discovering lawful relations between stimulus and response in circumstances involving cognitive activity. The character of IIT can be seen in the names of its principal psychological concepts. These are *stimulus, response, information, integration, valuation,* and *weight.* The concept of *discounting* takes on a special significance because it relates to (conflicting) cue interdependency. Thus (as in the case of SJT), Information Integration Theory omits subjective probabilities or utilities from its fundamental descriptive terms, and makes no argument for any specific aggregational rule, organizational principle, or integrative mechanism to be applied to the weighted, subjective scale values of stimuli. *Information integration* mechanisms are given a prominent place in this approach and the generic term *cognitive algebra* (e.g., adding, averaging of differentially weighted and scaled values of stimuli), is used in contrast to some single analytical mechanism such as the Bayesian rule in DT, or the pervasive additive principle in MAUT. Additionally, IIT refers to *responses* of the organism or subject (not a decision maker) which must be subject to the same scaling analysis as are *stimuli.*

IIT may be further discriminated from SJT by IIT's omission of uncertainty (and its derivative, probability) from its list of fundamental concepts. Thus IIT moves further from General Approach I than SJT in that (a) uncertainty is not a fundamental part of its conceptual system, (b) it does not emphasize inductive inference as an epistemological function, nor (c) include detailed consideration of the environment as a source of cognitive uncertainty. When IITs use the term *judgment* it is often in its psychophysical sense (as in judging the weights of hefted objects), although judgment is apparently also intended (as in SJT) to carry the same meaning as *"inference,"* as in the inference of a distal, impalpable state of affairs. Additionally, the term "impression" is often used to refer to the more general (distal) cognitive activity of inference (thus, the term "impression formation" is used in studies of how impressions of personalities are "formed"). But IIT apparently sees no compelling reason for distinguishing among the terms judgment, impression, inference or attribution; and the terms choice, or preference are simply considered to be instances of inference.

6.7 ATTRIBUTION THEORY

The key concept, of course, is *attribution.* As indicated above, this term is directly translatable into a special case of the term *inference* or *judgment* (see

Harvey, Ickes, & Kidd, 1976, p. 4, for Heider's definition of attribution). It is important to note that choices of action, or preference for friends, say, *follow* from different attributions; AT is, however, primarily concerned with *causal* attributions (or, inferences about causality).

The concept of probability does not play a large role in this approach. Indeed, although the originators of AT (Heider) and SJT (Brunswik) shared a mutual intellectual respect (and friendship), frequently cited one another's work, and were particularly interested in "causal texture," in Heider's theory probability is simply subjective uncertainty arising from ambiguity; it does not receive theoretical treatment as it does in Brunswik's work. For example, "probability," is not indexed in Heider's book, nor is "uncertainty," or "weight," although "mediation, ambiguous" is. Heider emphasizes the *organization* of the person's environment, not its *statistical* structure, not *relative frequencies* of the co-variation or co-occurrence of events when discussing ambiguity and the problem of inference (see pp. 35-44 in Heider, 1958). And the same is true for contemporary AT. Although one might say that one finds in Heider a "grudging" acknowledgement of the "grain of truth" in Brunswik's argument about the probabilistic nature of man (and other organisms) that acknowledgement is overwhelmed by Heider's return to an emphasis on the organism's search for the *in*variances in the environment (see especially p. 44 of Heider, 1958); that is, the search for (psychologically defined) cues that are "structurally safe" (our term) and which, therefore afford stable reference points for the organism. And despite numerous opportunities for contemporary attribution theorists to link their aruguments to judgment and decision research, such links almost never occur, mainly, we believe, because of the large role assigned to the concept of uncertainty in judgment and decision research (a conclusion also reached by Fischhoff, 1976). (For a particularly clear example of a missed opportunity, see Wortman in Harvey, Ickes, & Kidd, 1976; for examples of links, see Jones & Davis, 1965; Jones & McGillis, 1976; Fishbein & Ajzen, 1975.) *Utility* is a different matter, it is given considerable importance by AT, but it is discussed in terms of valence or value.

Despite his aversion to a probabilistic approach, Heider is keenly aware of the role of interdependency among cues in creating ambiguity. In a section entitled "Economy of interpretation—redundancy," he says:

> *Economy of interpretation—redundancy.* We have seen that a stimulus which is ambiguous as long as it is given singly, may become unequivocal with the addition of further data. It is important to stress that this specificity is established through the meaningfulness of the integrated perceptual field. But of two equally meaningful integrations, the one that is less complex, the one that requires fewer assumptions, fewer data in general, seems in general to be preferred. This is sometimes referred to as the principle of parsimony, a principle well known in the philosophy of science, and which may have its analogue in perception.

It is sometimes said that the objective of science is to describe nature economically. We have reason to believe, however, that some such process of parsimonious description has its beginnings on a fairly naive perceptual level ... It appears likely that a major function of the perceptual machinery is to strip away some of the redundancy of stimulation, to describe or encode incoming information in a form more economical than that in which it impinges on the receptors. (Attneave, 1954, p. 189)*

Now to illustrate economy in perception. Let us assume that stimulus x is ambiguous, that it could be interpreted as mediating either a or b, two

different features belong to the distal sphere, i.e., the environmental world. In the same way stimulus y could be seen as b or c. If x and y are given together, they can be "explained" by the hypothesis "b is there," or by the hypothesis "a and c are there." The first hypothesis is "cheaper"; it refers the stimuli to only one underlying entity, whereas the second hypothesis assumes two entities.

The same principle can be applied if two of several meanings underlying ambiguous data imply each other. For instance, suppose that

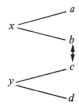

x means a or b, y means c or d, and that b and c imply each other mutually. Then, if x is interpreted as b, it also transmits the information that c is there, since b implies c. Or, it is a simpler hypothesis to interpret xy as bc than as ad, since a and d are two independent facts and bc makes an integrated group and contributes only one fact according to the restrictions of the system. It will be seen that the first example above in which two meanings are identical is really just a special case of this one. (Heider, 1958, pp. 51-52)[†]

(Note how Heider's discussion of one hypothesis being "cheaper" than another and thus more likely to be used is related to Tversky and Kahneman's "Causal Schemas." Also, recall the extensive reference to "independence" in Kenney & Raiffa's assumptions mentioned above.)

Curiously, the concept of cognitive *organization* (or *aggregation* or *integration*) is not indexed by Heider, nor does it seem to be singled out for analysis by AT, although one somehow gains the impression that the process of cognitive organization has a large role in AT, possibly because of the emphasis on "structure."

In the second phase of the development of AT we find that Kelley gives considerable attention to interdependency (as we noted was the case with Heider) as well as to the integrative process (not addressed as a major topic by Heider; but cf. Anderson's assistance provided for AT in Berkowitz, 1974).

Definite recognition of the entangled nature of task dimensions can be found in Kelley's (1973) statement on attribution theory. For example, "our attributor ... sometimes treats ... cases ... as being interdependent ... " (p. 122) as do scientists, although the latter "know that causes do not occur independently and in all combinations. We conduct experiments precisely for the purpose of creating such circumstances ... At the same time, we know that such separation and independence are not characteristic of real-life. ... It seems reasonable to assume that the lay attributor shares this awareness of the possible interdependence among causal factors ... " (p. 123). Moreover, "if and when the layman makes such assumptions, the inferences he will draw ... *may shift in a drastic manner*" (p. 123, italics ours).

In Kelley's version of the theory, persons cope with the difficulties of entangled task dimensions by applying the principles of the orthogonal components design (called the "ANOVA cube" by Jones & McGillis, 1976). Thus, Kelley asserts that the orthogonal components design is the basis of ordinary human inference, or "common sense." That is, (unaided) human inference follows, or attempts to follow, the logic of modern experimental design (in effect, Mill's Canons) in coping with the inference problems of everyday life.

There is some recognition by Kelley (1973, p. 123) of the asymmetry between the nature of the inference task and the cognitive processes he believes are brought to bear on it. We are left, however, only with the warning that the asymmetry "poses a problem for a complete theory of the attribution processes" and its associated methodology.

Since Jones has been a leading contributor of AT, it should be mentioned that he and McGillis present a chapter in Harvey, Ickes, and Kidd (1976) entitled "Correspondent Inferences and the Attribution Cube." They indicate that "correspondent inference theory" is "essentially a rational baseline model" (p. 104 in Harvey, Ickes, & Kidd) and thus bring it near to Group I approaches. Fig. 6-1 indicates that Jones and McGillis are prepared to

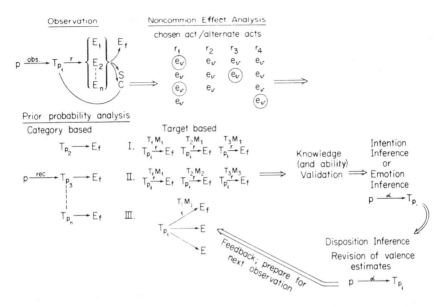

Figure 6-1 Diagram showing the inclusion of probabilistic concepts (action sequence in an integrated attributional framework) in a recent presentation of Attribution Theory. Key: p, perceiver; Tp, target person; e, effect; ⓔ, noncommon effect; obs, observe; rec, recall; α, attribution; T, time; M, modality; E, entity; Ef, figural entity; S, setting; c, circumstance; v, valence. From Jones & McGillis, 1976, p. 415. Copyright © 1976 by Lawrence Erlbaum Associates. Reprinted by permission.

see the attribution process in probabilistic terms closely associated with the Bayesian view. If "correspondent inference theory" as depicted in Fig. 6-1 were to become an integral part of AT the latter would be changed significantly, for the concept of probability would be systematically introduced into a much more general theoretical structure (see also Jones, 1979).

6.8 INTEGRATION

6.8.1 Integration within Group I Approaches

Integration within these approaches will require some direct efforts by those working within the framework of decision analysis to come to grips with what appear to be significant antinomies. On the one hand, Keeney and Raiffa's 1976 book was awarded a major prize by the Operations Research Society of America (ORSA), and thus endorsed as a highly valued representation of decision theory by their peers. On the other hand, the validity of the principal concepts in this book has been sharply challenged and the value of the approach seriously called into question by Kahneman and Tversky, other

PDT researchers (see Slovic, Fischhoff, & Lichtenstein, 1977) and other operations researchers (Cochrane & Zeleny, 1973).

The following paragraphs provide some indication of how probability and utility were seen at the beginning of the merger between economics and psychology and how they are seen now:

1 Subjective probability
  a Edwards (1961):

> In 1954 it was already clear that expected utility maximization models were unsatisfactory and that the crucial necessary change was to replace objective with subjective probability in such models. But it was by no means clear what a subjective probability is. In 1960 it is clear what a subjective probability measure is, but it seems unlikely in the face of the data that subjective probabilities conceived as measures are any more adequate than objective probabilities. Less restrictive definitions of subjective probability, which do not require them to be measures in the sense of measure theory but which still preserve a form of the SEU model, are in much the same state of ambiguity and ill-definedness as in 1954. (p. 478)*

  b Slovic (1976):

> Subjective judgments of probability and value are essential inputs to decision analyses. We still do not know the best ways to elicit these judgments. Now that we understand many of the biases to which these judgments are susceptible, we need to develop debiasing techniques to minimize their destructive effects. (p. 238)

2 Utility
  a Edwards (1961):

> In 1954 there was general agreement on what utility is and that it can be measured, but no real agreement on how to measure it. In 1960 there is at least a conceptually adequate method of measurement (assuming a SEU model)—but some doubt about whether a SEU model, and therefore any measurement methods based on it, can stand up to the facts. (p. 475)*

> There is no indication by Raiffa in 1968 that the concept of utility as he employs it (as a choice between lotteries) "can stand up to these facts" that imply that the concept of utility still defies measurement.

Nor is there any concern about this indicated by Keeney and Raiffa roughly 10 years later. Should there be?

b   In 1975, at least some decision theorists thought decision theorists ought to pay attention to the empirical "facts" produced by psychological research. Thus, Cochrane and Zeleny in their introduction to the proceedings of the 1972 conference wrote:

> The results of psychologists and other social scientists—that individuals and groups do have multiple goals, none of which can be pursued to the complete detriment or sacrifice of the others—have been ignored. Even further, these goals often change not only in the course of time but also in the course of their pursuit. Finally, these goals are certainly not independent of the means used to pursue them. The traditional utility approach, suggesting that the alternative with the highest utility will be chosen, is not of much help under such conditions. About the only property this simple idea has is transitivity. Transitivity, however, is not the behavior people manifest when facing situations characterized by multi-attribute consequences. (p. xiii)*

The references to "the results of psychologists and other social scientists" and the reference to "the behavior people manifest" suggest that these authors believe that there is an interface between DT and the empirical research carried out by behavioral scientists. But it does not appear that the issues that divide these approaches can be settled by resort to empirical behavioral test. Keeney and Raiffa are no doubt aware of the challenges to DT from PDT (and BDT as well), but DT is not an empirically-oriented approach, and therefore, the issues are not likely to be met head on by empirical research. Rather, they are more likely to be left in the realm of argumentation until the issues involving intended function, limits of competence and the relation between logic, behavioral and psychological knowledge, and practical application are examined in detail. Of course, we intend the present effort to constitute a first step in that direction.

6.8.2   Integration within Group II Approaches

The principal concepts employed by Group II approaches imply different metatheories concerning the knowledge process. For example SJT metatheory describes an organism, *any* organism, in its cognitive efforts to achieve stability (and thus survival) within an environment that is "semi-erratic." Therefore, in its largest sense it lays the groundwork for a theory of cognitive evolution. It does this by providing concepts that permit the description of cognitive tasks that test the organism's ability to achieve stability. These

*Copyright © by University of South Carolina Press.

task-descriptive concepts are not only of grand theoretical interest, however; they turn out to be of considerable practical interest because they show the *ecological* task conditions under which human beings' (and other animals') achievement will be high or low. Thus, *ecological analysis* indicates that man functions well "as an intuitive statistician" when *perceiving* (in the correct use of the word), and much less well when making quasi-rational judgments that involve *thinking* as well. (The corruption of the word perception by judgment and decision researchers, particularly those who discuss "risk perception," has not helped their scientific work.)

The same problem was addressed by Heider. He also theorized about cognitive achievement in the real world and tried to incorporate and do justice to the structural complexity of the ecology of that world in his theoretical work. As a result of (a) a common interest in the ecology and (b) a rough agreement on the ecological circumstances that create the ambiguity that is an obstacle to such achievement, a general set of concepts has been created by SJT and AT that makes constructive integration a reasonable and worthwhile aim.

Much of what has been done since the publication of Brunswik's major work in 1956 and Heider's in 1958 has been directed toward the investigation of the empirical worth of their approaches. The work following from Brunswik (as represented by SJT) has on the whole been far more quantitative in character, and less psychological by far, than the work that has followed from Heider. Reconciliation of those different emphases would go far toward a "third phase" that could contribute to creating a cumulative discipline of judgment and decision making.

Curiously, that "third phase" of integration might be said to have already begun with Anderson's 1974 paper. Anderson's quantitative formulation of some of Heider's hypotheses and work within the general spirit of AT was set forth in that paper. Yet, as noted earlier, this effort has been ignored (at least in the most recent compendium) by attribution theorists. Since the reduction of verbal formulations to quantitative ones is ordinarily rejected by AT's on metatheoretical grounds, one might suppose that Anderson's efforts toward integration have already been set aside by attribution theorists. In our view, that would be unfortunate inasmuch as previous efforts in this regard appeared to be fruitful. For example, in 1971 and 1972 attribution theorists Jones, Kanouse, Kelley, Nisbett, Valins and Weiner produced a volume which contained numerous references to IIT; moreover, they actually used IIT's functional measurement in their research and employed many of IIT's principal concepts. But Anderson does not reference that work in his effort toward integration in 1974. Perhaps this sort of unevenness and distressing lack of cumulative work is to be expected until metatheoretical similarities and differences are ironed out between these approaches. It is difficult to see, for example, how AT's original emphasis (from Heider) on environmental structure (e.g., cue intercorrelation, equifinality) and the ambiguity it produces, are to be reconciled with IIT's indifference to this matter. But on the positive side, if the phenomenological aspects of AT can be successfully represented within the concepts of subjectively weighted and subjectively scaled stimuli, and the cognitive algebra that integrates them, then a cumulative integration may develop, with AT providing the psychological flesh for the quantitative bones of IIT.

Integration of SJT and IIT may prove to be easier precisely because SJT is more quantitative in character than AT and thus similarities and differences between SJT and IIT will be easier to detect; moreover, quantification will make empirical tests of crucial differences, if any are found, easier. Metatheoretical differences may preclude such tests, however, for their *different metatheories give rise to different concepts, methods and procedures.*

The metatheory of psychophysics (IIT) places man in a Newtonian world in which there are (largely) *independent,* orthogonal physical dimensions of space, time and mass to which man reacts. Since physical dimensions are critical, psychological measurements should be made in parallel with them; hence the work on subjective scaling of physical, or more broadly, independently-defined dimensions. The metatheory of Brunswik and Heider, on the other hand, places man in a biological Darwinian world in which *interdependence* is the critical characteristic, to which man *adapts,* rather than *reacts.* Study of the single-system case (IIT's base) is sufficient for the study of reaction; study of adaptation requires the double-system case (SJT's base). The quantitative (mathematical) psychologist is mainly interested in the single-system case in which orthogonal dimensions are emphasized, therefore, subjective scaling (i.e., of psychophysical relations) assumes considerable importance. But the biologically-oriented psychologist finds that the physicists' world (described in terms of the c.g.s. system) is not the appropriate world for the study of psychology.

The distinction was made by Brunswik in 1956 in a manner calculated to move psychologists away from traditional psychophysics, thus:

> Many of the environmental stimulus variables mentioned by psychologists, such as "physical size" or "physical color," seem at first glance simply to be taken over from physics or chemistry. Others, such as "food," "sit-upon-ableness" (William James), "likability of a person," etc., are obviously conceived with an eye to potential effects upon organisms. . . . Upon closer inspection, however, even the former often reveal psychological entanglement when they appear in the context of a psychological experiment. For example, the "sizes" of physical objects (more precisely, of physicist's objects) . . . are in fact to be specified as "sizes of objects of attention, i.e., of potential manipulation or locomotion, of a certain human being" . . . It is the type of organism-centered specifying redefinition mentioned above which may be summarized by

saying that *stimulus variables are "ecological"* rather than purely "physical" or "geographic" in character.

In other words, "many of the . . . variables mentioned by psychologists" only appear to be physical; they are in fact "ecological." Emphasis on the ecological, rather than the physical nature of the world insofar as the behaving organism is concerned leads to an emphasis on interdependence and thus intersubstitutability of information and the ability to use such information. This emphasis may be seen in the following paragraph from Hammond's 1955 paper quoted favorably by Heider (1958, p. 29) to indicate the congruence between Brunswik (SJT) and Heider:

> Observers of the state of anger may agree that such a state exists (i.e., high reliability may be achieved), *but* they may not be able to communicate the basis for their decision . . . (Hammond, 1955, p. 257.) [Consider] the clinician [who] is attempting to discover the patient's motive. The patient substitutes one form of behavior for another as he attempts to achieve his goal (equifinality). The clinician perceives these behaviors, as they substitute for one another, as cues which also substitute for one another (equipotentiality). Because of vicarious functioning, then, the clinician is hard-pressed to point at, to communicate, the basis for a decision . . . *Vicarious functioning . . . lies at the heart of the private, quasi-rational nature of the clinical decision.* (Hammond, 1955, p. 258)

It is these metatheoretical principles that move SJT (and its parent, probabilistic functionalism) away from the single-system case to the double-system case so that environmental characteristics will be included in the research. SJT follows probabilistic functionalism by emphasizing adaptation and those cognitive strategies undertaken to achieve rapport with the distal layers of the environment. Thus, for example, the Lens Model Equation (see Hammond, Stewart, Brehmer & Steinmann, 1975) in its most general form reads as follows:

$$r_a = GR_eR_s$$

where r_a is the correlation between the person's judgment and the empirical "answer" or response or distal variable of the environment; G is the correlation between the person's judgment and the distal variable of the environment corrected for the inconsistency (or uncertainty) in either system; R_e is a measure of the uncertainty in the environment and reflects the fact that for Brunswik and Heider (and SJT) the environment is a semi-erratic medium; R_s is a measure of cognitive control (i.e., consistency of information utilization in judgment).

The important point to be observed is that this equation shows that SJT is interested in a *relation* (r_a) between two systems, not merely the response of one system, as in the case with Group I theories (including PDT) and IIT. And this can also be shown to be the case for AT.

6.8.3 Integration of Group I and Group II Approaches

There is one point of departure that may well serve to integrate the six approaches and provide a means for a cumulative effort, and that is Brunswik's lens model (see above, Fig. 4-1). It is so much a part of Heider's work that it might have deserved the term "Brunswik-Heider lens model." And a similar "model" has been used by Anderson (1970) and Shanteau and Phelps (1977); see Fig. 6-2. At the risk of appearing "imperialistic" we shall try to make use of the lens model as an integration device.

A casual glance through Heider's 1958 book shows his constant use of lens modeling diagrams to show both vicarious mediation of information on the part of the environment and vicarious functioning (intersubstitutable use of information) on the part of the subject. In his book "An Introduction to Attribution Processes" (1975) Shaver offers the diagram on the third page of the first chapter after the introduction.

Although Shaver's replica of the lens model is not precisely accurate, it serves well the purpose of indicating a basic platform of agreement. Shanteau's "lens model" indicates similarities, but differences as well; the reader will

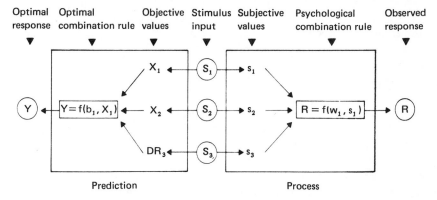

Figure 6-2 Diagram showing the similarity of IIT to SJT. General judgment diagram illustrating Prediction analyses (on the left) and Process analyses (on the right). Circled stimulus inputs (S_i) are common to both Prediction and Process. Capital letters on the Prediction side represent objective values; small letters on the Process side represent psychological values. Numeric subscripts (e.g., X_1) refer to individual dimensions, whereas alphabetic subscripts (e.g., X_i) refer to dimensions in general. From Shanteau & Phelps, 1977, p. 258. Copyright Academic Press, 1977.

observe that the *environmental* segment of the lens model is absent, and that it is replaced by an optimal model of the *psychological* process. These diagrams can be taken seriously; they indicate the differential emphasis in the double- and single-system case, and they illustrate the common emphasis on ambiguity arising from multi-dimensionality and thus multiple mediation of environmental information, a matter of concern to all Group II approaches.

In short, the integrative value of the lens model lies in its clear depiction of (a) the organism's effort to organize or integrate or combine or aggregate (b) various inputs or stimuli or cues or pieces of information or evidence or data, that (c) are more or less inter-related or interdependent into (d) a judgment or choice or preference or decision or impression or attribution about (e) something not immediately given.

Aside from the clarity of the depiction (easily seen to be related to the decision tree of Group I approaches) the lens model points to two concepts, (a) a cue or stimulus (etc.) and (b) the weight attached to it; these two concepts offer integrative potential. As an example of that potential we shall try to integrate the approach taken by PDT with other approaches by using the concepts of *cue* and *weight* as the point of departure. Our aim is to classify the principal concepts that PDT introduces to explain what a probability estimate will be and PDT uses to predict which heuristic will affect the judgment and make it what it is. (Our description will omit constant references to "appears to be" and "apparently" in order to save space; the reader should understand, however, that our treatment is tentative.)

According to PDT, a person's judgment of a probability is influenced (moved up and down a probability scale) by the differential *weight* of various pieces of information. The general psychological principle(s) that control the manner in which these weighted pieces of information are *combined* is (are) not specified, however; therefore, we write

$$J = f(w_i)$$

simply to indicate that this aspect of other judgment theories (e.g., $J = \Sigma w_i x_i$) is absent. (See also Shanteau & Phelps', 1977, comment on the absence of conceptual treatment by PDT of organizing principles.)

PDT indicates that the meaning of (subjective) weight can be found in the variables that affect its magnitude (and sign). These variables are of three kinds: (a) objectively defined statistical varibles, (b) subjectively defined attributes of an object, and (c) types of cognitive processes. Each is discussed in turn.

Objectively Defined Statistical Variables (Such as Base-Rates or (Comparative) Relative Frequencies of the Occurrence of Objects or Events) Results of experiments that indicate the impact of these variables (e.g., "base rates are given little weight when . . . ") lead PDT researchers to evaluate the accuracy of the cognitive activity that leads to probability judgments. PDT generally employs problems or cognitive tasks for subjects in which hard statistical data provide "cues" for the subject who is required to infer the correct state of affairs. It is important to note that such cues have one important characteristic: they are generally (ecologically) valid cues. In other words, they are "univocal" cues that are "equivocal" psychological cues.

Such objective, or "axiomatically safe" cues (e.g., base rates) can be set in analogy to perceptual cues that are *"geometrically* safe" cues to size or distance (e.g., those used in the study of optics). Complete reliance on univocal cues (cues that are perfectly ecologically "safe" or valid) produces perfect achievement in either case. Under ordinary circumstances, however, persons do not have access to geometrically safe perceptual cues, unless they are provided by technological aids such as range finders, etc. (That is why perception is as interesting a problem as judgment.) And, to continue the analogy, we can ask to what extent persons have access to "axiomatically safe" cues such as base-rates under ordinary circumstances. Undoubtedly there are some problems that require probability judgments in which such "axiomatically safe" cues are available, but their frequency and importance is uncertain.

Subjectively Defined Attributes of an Object (Such as "Representativeness") In addition to representativeness, a further set of imputed object-attributes has recently been introduced by PDT; thus, "the impact of the evidence depends critically on whether it is perceived as *causal, diagnostic* or *incidental"* (Tversky & Kahneman, 1979). "Specifically, we hypothesize i) that causal data has a greater impact than diagnostic data of equal informativeness, and ii) that incidental data are given little or no weight, in the presence of causal or diagnostic data" (p. 2). Results of the empirical analysis of the operation of these psychological variables thus provide the basis not only for (a) *describing* and thus (b) *comparing* actual probability judgments with optimal judgments, but also (c) *explaining* why the departures from optimality occur, and (d) *predicting* when they will occur.

The reader will, of course, want to raise the methodological question of the *a priori* status of these organism-centered definitions, for these are always defined in terms of plausibility arguments rather than in terms of empirical operations. That is, PDT researchers rely on the reader's willingness to agree that it is plausible to assume that a given set of circumstances is more representative than another, or that a given set of conditions implies causality whereas another set implies diagnosticity rather than carrying out experiments which provide independent evidence of subjective representativeness, etc. Few would dispute the plausibility of the assumptions made in the experiments, but it must be noted that (a) plausibility arguments do not have the status of empirical evidence, (b) the (somewhat indistinct) road of advances in psychology is littered with the wreckage of plausibility arguments, and (c) that it may well be difficult to ascertain organism-centered definitions of these variables in the more ambiguous circumstances of real world (test) questions. (Cf. the rise and fall of the concept of "cognitive dissonance".)

Be that as it may, as indicated above, few would (and indeed, no one has) dispute(d) the plausibility of the operational definitions of these organism-centered variables in any specific case, nor have the psychological definitions received any criticism, a matter to which we turn in a moment.

Before turning to the third class of variables, we should note that the research method used by PDT is similar to that used by Group II approaches, namely, to "confront" various types of cues with one another in order to discover their relative weights under various conditions. PDT frequently pits objective cues such as base rates against subjective cues such as representativeness. That is, the task is presented in such a way that it offers the subjects a choice between "axiomatically safe" information (e.g., base rates) and "psychologically safe" information (such as personality data). (See especially Kahneman and Tversky, 1973). [Note: the terms "axiomatically safe" and "psychologically safe" are introduced by the authors, not PDT researchers]. The general results of these "confrontation" studies that are emphasized by PDT indicate that "axiomatically safe" information is ignored in favor of "psychologically safe" information. Recent efforts ("causal schemata"), however, are more specific and indicate under which conditions each type of information will carry how much weight. Confrontation studies of this sort have a long history in psychology, particularly in perception, where various types of cues are pitted against one another; see Brunswik's (1955) use of the term "diacritical confrontation" with regard to this method.

Types of Cognitive Processes (Such as "Availability" or "Anchoring") Data from the empirical analysis of the operation of these psychological processes also provide the four functions of (a) describing, (b) comparing, (c) explaining, and (d) predicting indicated above in relation to "subjectively defined attributes."

Distinctive Differences among the Three Classes of Variables Are these three classes of variables separate and distinct? We are uncertain. For although objective denotation of statistical variables is simple enough, and therefore this class of variable is easy to separate from the two subjectively defined classes of variables, separation of the latter is not so simple. Yet separation is required. In particular, separating the denotation of *attributes* from *process variables* is not as easy as one might hope, although the attempt at separation was made by PDT at the outset. Thus, availability was described at the time of its introduction by Tversky & Kahneman, (1973) as "associative distance," to be contrasted with representativeness, which was described as "connotative distance" (p. 208): "one estimates probability by assessing similarity or connotative distance. Alternatively, one may estimate probability by assessing availability or associative distance." That distinction indicates that we have two types of "distance," and the distance appears to apply to objects, that could perhaps be scaled in these terms. Thus, we are dealing with attributes of objects. But we could not find this distinction appearing again. There are, however, numerous references to *representativeness* as a quality or attribute assigned by the person to independently real objects or processes: Example: "Which is more likely? This series (HTTHTH) or this series (HHHTTT)?" Persons say the former because, PDT argues, it subjectively "best represents both the population proportion (1/2) and the randomness of the process" (p. 208). That is, representativeness is a subjectively defined *attribute* of a "process" (or object or event) and can be used as a cue by subjects when they infer the likelihood of the occurrence of processes (or objects or events).

Availability, on the other hand, is described as "the ease with which the relevant mental operation of retrieval, construction or association can be carried out" (1973, p. 208). Availability therefore refers to the process of recall: some objects or events are more available than others because of their special characteristics, notably their "associative bonds." Thus, "the availability heuristic exploits the inverse form of this law, that is, it uses the strength of association as a basis for the judgment of frequency. In this theory, availability is a mediating variable, rather than a dependent variable [see above] as is typically the case in the study of memory" (pp. 208-209). Here we encounter difficulty; availability refers to the ease with which a "mental operation . . . can be carried out" in memory (p. 208) as a result of the association between objects (or processes). But the associative distance between objects can also be thought of as an attribute of an object or objects, and thus can be considered to be a (subjectively defined) cue. Indeed, Tversky and Kahneman refer to it in just those terms: "Availability is an *ecologically valid* clue for the judgment of frequency because, in general, frequent events are easier to recall or imagine than infrequent ones" (italics ours, p. 209). Possibly because this is a clear misuse of the term "ecologically valid," this definition was later changed to read: "availability is a useful clue . . . because instances of large classes are usually recalled better" (Tversky & Kahneman, 1974, p. 1127). The point remains, however; availability is used to refer to an attribute of independently real objects, as well as to the process of recall itself.

Steps toward integration might be taken, then by means of careful examination of the concepts of *cue* and *weights* attached to them. Other concepts that might provide a means for integration include a central concept of SJT, namely "cognitive control"; it refers to the control persons can exercise in the execution of the knowledge they may possess (a concept that has turned out to be of particular value in Gillis's application of SJT to the judgment processes of schizophrenics and the differential effects of various psychoactive drugs; see Hammond & Joyce, 1975). Although SJT explains variations in cognitive control as due largely to environmental circumstances (mainly uncertainty), as well as to biochemical interventions, Tversky's treatment of choice as "elimination by aspects" (1972a) also suggests an internal source of decreased cognitive control.

> The EBA model accounts for choice in terms of a covert elimination process based on sequential selection of aspects. Any such sequence of aspects can be regarded as a particular state of mind which leads to a unique choice. In light of this interpretation, the choice mechanism at any given moment in time is entirely deterministic; the probabilities merely reflect the fact that at different moments in time different states of mind (leading to different choices) may prevail. According to the present theory, choice probability is an increasing function of the values of the relevant aspects. Indeed, the elimination-by-aspects model is compensatory in nature despite the fact that at any given instant in time, the choice is assumed to follow a conjunctive (or a lexicographic) strategy. Thus, the present model is compensatory "globally" with respect to choice probability but not "locally" with regard to any particular state of mind. (p. 296)

This quotation suggests that over a series of judgments ("globally") choice may be seen as changing, "at any given moment" the "choice mechanism . . . is entirely deterministic;" however, "at different moments . . . different states of mind . . . may prevail." SJT's use of "cognitive control" refers to the same phenomena, its interest lies in the extent to which persons can exert sufficient control "at any given moment" to make the same choice of judgment as they made at a previous "moment."

Whether the use of the lens model as an integrative device will be found to be acceptable within Group II approaches remains to be seen, and whether the lens model analogy can be usefully pushed further into the domain of Group I approaches than PDT also remains to be seen. We shall point to that possibility in our discussion of the *loci* of the concepts employed by various approaches.

Chapter 7

Loci of Concepts

In this section, the concepts employed by judgment and decision making theorists are described in terms of their location within a reduced form of Brunswik's "lens model" diagram. Our use of the lens model diagram does not, of course, imply that the reader must become immersed in, or committed to, the Brunswikian framework. We use the diagram simply because it is broad enough to accommodate the concepts employed by all six approaches, and thus serves as a useful device for locating redundancies as well as gaps in our theoretical efforts. Thus, for example, Fig. 7-1 indicates seven areas of the judgment and/or decision process to which theoretical concepts can be applied.

In what follows we shall attempt to indicate the extent to which the six approaches have developed concepts (or have assigned theoretical importance to) each of the following seven areas:

1 Refers to general problem of selecting the cues that enter into a judgment;

2 Refers to problems where intuitive judgments provide basic data; problems of turning "soft" data into "harder" data;

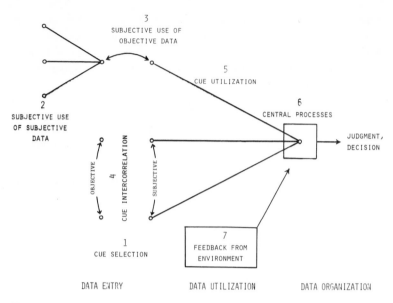

Figure 7-1 Diagram used to locate various concepts used by the six approaches. See text for details.

3 Refers to problems of subjective use of objective, "hard" data; scaling;
4 Refers to problems involving ecological and subjective intercorrelations among cues;
5 Refers to problems involving subjective weights; function forms;
6 Refers to problems involving principles of organization, e.g., additive or configural principles, cognitive control;
7 Refers to problems involving feedback from the environment, including other persons.

7.1 DECISION THEORY

This approach locates its concepts *centrally;* there are no theoretical concepts that refer to what is now called the "processing" of information prior to the person's expression of a subjective probability. Judgments of probability are the result of prior knowledge, that is, knowledge gained from experience, education, theory, etc., prior to the elicitation of the probability judgment. For example, when the decision maker offers a subjective probability (p) that an event (e) will occur, she or he is offering a complex judgment based on information that is somehow organized into judgment. Decision theorists, are, of course, prepared to decompose, indeed, to *urge* the decomposition of "larger" subjective probabilities (and utilities) into "smaller" ones by means of decision trees, that is, to "divide and conquer." But there is no theoretical attention given to the psychological process by which past or present information, or data, is transformed into subjective probabilities, nor to the process by which such division is made. In short, processes (items 1 through 5) are not given theoretical attention. Careful *procedural* attention is given, however, to the matter of obtaining and measuring, i.e., calibrating, the decision maker's probabilities and utilities based on the acceptance of a metatheory regarding psychological measurement shared with BDT, PDT and IIT (but not SJT or AT; see below).

Such procedures (e.g., the use of lotteries) are justified on either (a) pragmatic grounds ("this technique works better than that one, at least in my experience") or (b) theoretical-logical assumptions about measurement. There is no explicit theoretical concern for the objective world of event-frequencies and utilities and the psychological process by which these give rise to subjective probabilities.

Finally, the decision theorist "knows" that the central cognitive process of *aggregation* of probabilities and utilities is nearly always suboptimal by any prescriptive criterion. Without considering the wide variety of possible forms that psychologists have imagined cognitive activity might take, the decision theorist prescribes the logically defensible form and substitutes it for whatever actual form (or forms) it (or they) might be, and thus "aggregates" the probabilities and utilities *for* the decision maker. In short, all the major concepts employed by the decision theorist are located *centrally*. The activities of the decision theorists are directed toward developing measures of these central concepts, with little or no regard for psychological research that might bear on proximal-central relations or procedures used to measure them.

Research, therefore, is logical-theoretical rather than theoretical-empirical; it is devoted to the development of the mathematics of the prescriptions for various types of problems. Empirical work is given over to applications that consist of case histories indicating the usefulness of certain steps (e.g., divide and conquer) toward rational decision making. Although the extent of that work is impressive (see Keeney & Raiffa, 1976), it is not evenly distributed over the major concepts of DT. As Keeney and Raiffa note in their Preface (p. viii) decision theorists have given far more attention to the "uncertainty phase" (that is, the ascertaining of probabilities and the development of axioms of probability theory) than to the "value or preference side of the picture." Both concepts have received considerable theoretical attention elsewhere, however—probability mainly from mathematical statisticians, utility mainly from economists. We do not include these theoretical efforts as part of the present discussion, however, because the theoretical differentiations in that literature have little relevance to the present work of DT.

7.2 BEHAVIORAL DECISION THEORY

The work carried out within this approach is best understood if research and application are separated.

7.2.1 Research

Many of the concepts employed by researchers in this approach flow from the Bayesian model of organizing data concerning events into a probability judgment about the truth or falsity of hypotheses. As a result, the research includes concepts that refer to "hard" events (e.g., a "datum"), on the periphery of the organism (item 3 in Fig. 7-1) and concepts that refer to the utilization of data, that is, translation of external data into a judgment of a probability regarding the likelihood of the truth of a hypothesis (item 5), and, of course, central concepts of judgments of subjective probability (item 6) and their revision (with or without feedback, item 7).

Bayesian researchers construct decision tasks, manipulate the parameters of such tasks (in contrast to DT researchers), and, therefore, they employ a set of concepts to describe the task circumstances. These include probabilities, events, situations (e.g., "stationarity"), and relations between events (e.g., dependence, item 4) as noted above. In particular, Bayesian research includes the concept of "optimality" with regard to the subject's behavior. "Optimality" is evaluated in terms of the extent to which the subject's (posterior) probability judgments about the truth of a hypothesis approach those produced by the Bayesian model. Because (a) the parameters of a task are specified and manipulated, and (b) a criterion regarding the achievement (Bayesian optimality) of a subject is provided, Bayesian research may be said to be conducted within the framework of the "double-system" case (the task constituting one system, the subject constituting the other). Therefore, insofar as Bayesian research is concerned, the above single-system lens model (that characterizes DT) must be extended to include the "second system" that represents the task (as in the original lens model diagram). Thus Bayesian research includes learning. (See relation to SJT with regard to *cognitive* feedback.)

There are (a) distal (causal) categories $(H_1, H_2 \ldots H_n)$, (b) objective descriptions of cues (e.g., colors of poker chips, and thus proximal stimuli), and (c) there can be conditional dependence, etc. between cues, and (d) cue utilization can be observed in the "impact of a datum" per event, as well as (e) organizational principles imputed (as a hypothesis) to the subject, such principles being expressed in the form of a "likelihood ratio" or Bayes' theorem. And it is the comparison between the Bayesian likelihood ratio (or some other aspect of Bayes' theorem) and the subject's likelihood ratio (or other aspect of the subject's central data processing mechanism) that provides a measure of the subject's achievement as an "intuitive statistician" (a term introduced by Brunswik) or adaptive cognizer, under conditions of uncertainty.

Thus, it appears that the research paradigm employed by **BDT** regarding the "extraction of information" (generally) is one which explicitly employs theoretical concepts that apply to all seven areas of the diagram (including items 1 and 2). It should be noted, however, that all of the concepts converge on a *single* end term (or response) namely the expression of a *probability* judgment.

7.2.2 Application

The distribution of theoretical concepts in the *application* (MAUT) of Bayesian theory is not as clear as in the *research* situation. First, we observe that MAUT has been applied to two sets of task circumstances (a) the n-system case in which the multiple systems are several decision makers without a known task system (in contrast to the situation described above in which the two systems include one decision maker and one task) and (b) the single-system case in which there exists only a decision maker, the task parameters being unknown. We discuss the n-system case first.

Here we follow Gardiner and Edwards (1975) in their description of the application of MAUT to social decision making in which it is assumed that interpersonal and intergroup conflict will occur. Leaving no doubt about the importance of this application the authors say (p. 35) that "We consider the idea of resolving value conflicts at the level of decision rules rather than at the level of individual decisions to have the potential of revolutionary impact on land-use management—and many other public-decision contexts as well."

The outline of the process of application of MAUT indicates four main phases.

Phase 1. Definition of the nature of the problem and its dimensions. This step is primarily substantive. It refers primarily to the specification of the attributes (cues in Fig. 7-1) that the decision makers want to consider; item 1 in Fig. 7-1.

Phase 2. Probability evaluation. This step involves extracting a probability judgment. Gardiner and Edwards say (1975, p. 10) that "other names used for the same process in other contexts are diagnosis, intelligence evaluation, data gathering and interpretation, and so on." But the "output is a set of posterior probabilities of states." They also indicate, however, that "less formal judgments of probability . . . and such formal ones as the acceptance or rejection of statistical hypotheses, also fit here and might be substituted for the Bayesian version of the process."

Probability evaluation can thus also be a cognitive process that intervenes between (a) the subject's observation of the several attributes of various objects and (b) the subject's response that indicates the probability of occurrence of various "states." In this case, if Step 1 refers to dimensions (cues, attributes; item 1 of Fig. 7-1), Step 2 refers to the judgment (item 6 of Fig. 7-1) of the probabilities of occurrence of the states so described.

Phase 3. Outcome evaluation (SMART). This step refers to "the attachment of values ... to outcomes." Part of what makes this process difficult is the fact that outcomes include a "multiplicity of value dimensions" which "presents a multiplicity of problems" (p. 13). Thus, the process of outcome evaluation *parallels* the process of probability evaluation. (See also SJT). Gardiner and Edwards make it clear that without the assistance of a MAUT decision analyst, ordinary decision makers confuse these two processes; a decision analyst will separate these processes, however, and combine them analytically and thus produce a rational choice for the decision maker. (Note the similarity here with DT.)

As in probability evaluation, a set of attributes (dimensions) characterizes each of a number of outcomes. And as in the case of probability evaluation, direct estimates (of amounts of *probability* in the case of probability evaluation, of amounts of *importance* in the case of outcome evaluation) are obtained simply by asking the decision maker for them (in contrast to decision theorist's more complex method of requiring the decision maker to choose between lotteries, or SJT's or IIT's "wholistic" method of extracting them post hoc).

Interdependence between cues. (Item 4, Fig. 7-1). Interdependence of cues or data is of considerable theoretical importance to MAUT. Two types of interdependence are acknowledged within the SMART approach (interdependence is given detailed analysis in Bayesian research by Edwards and his colleagues). One type of interdependence is that of *value* interdependence, the other is called *environmental* interdependence. (Note: Gardiner and Edwards, 1975, have labeled these "value independence" and "environmental interdependence"; p. 20.) Since values are entirely subjective and environmental facts are objective (i.e., measured independently of the decision maker) this distinction is represented in Fig. 7-1 as the distinction between objective and subjective intercorrelations. As Gardiner and Edwards observe (p. 20) these may not match.

Therefore, MAUT approaches the problem of ascertaining (or externalizing) utilities or values precisely as it does probabilities. That is, from a theoretical point of view, in both cases it specifies cues, their interdependencies, their differential utilization and their organization.

7.3 PSYCHOLOGICAL DECISION THEORY

Because the PDT approach takes the SEU theory as its point of departure, its fundamental concepts are probability, utility, and (although seldom mentioned) aggregation. But the PDT approach has argued that the empirical evidence indicates that the departures from optimality begin with *systematic* errors in estimating probabilities, and that these systematic errors are explained by psychological concepts such as *availability, representativeness* and *anchoring* (see Principal Concepts for definitions).

As noted above, all of these concepts are explanatory, rather than descriptive. That is, they explain why some cues are over- or under-utilized, and thus explain why judgments are often found to be in error. These concepts are directed toward the formal aspects of the judgment task as well as substantive aspects of the task. That is, Kahneman and Tversky have pointed to situations where the *statistical properties* of the judgment task themselves give rise to errors of judgment because of their *(un)representative* character, as well as situations where the *substantive materials* of the task give rise to errors of judgment because of their *(un)representative* character.

Because of their explanatory nature, these concepts cover three major aspects of the judgment process: (a) cue-utilization, (b) weight, and (c) central processes. That is, use of the availability heuristic, the central activity, explains why certain cues are weighted more or less heavily in any specific situation. (Approaches that are largely descriptive do not make such links.)

Areas of the lens model diagram (Fig. 7-1) affected by these explanatory concepts are (a) cue selection, (b) subjective use of subjective data, (c) subjective use of objective data, (d) cue-utilization (weight) and (e) central processes. It should be mentioned that, although the explanatory concepts clearly refer to central processes, they do not address the matter of *organizing principles*—the form of aggregating or integrating data into a judgment. No examination of learning has been undertaken by PDT and it has therefore not addressed the problem of feedback.

7.4 TRANSITION

Theoretical concepts within the first three approaches to which the probability-utility-aggregation premise is basic can be found at all critical points of the lens model representation of the judgment process. There are large differences among the three approaches, however. DT emphasizes the central region, PDT has focused its efforts intensively on the input region, but neither has engaged in the more extensive analysis engaged in by BDT.

7.5 SOCIAL JUDGMENT THEORY

This approach includes theoretical concepts that apply to all seven areas of the lens model diagram (as in the case of BDT). In addition to applying theoretical concepts to the seven areas of the single-system case, SJT includes several overall concepts that apply to the double-system case (e.g., zone of ambiguity, causal texture, etc.) and gives special emphasis to the concept of feedback with regard to learning to improve judgments (as does BDT) and with regard to the difficulty if not impossibility of improving achievement in the absence of such feedback.

SJT also has developed theoretical concepts that apply to the processes of interpersonal learning (both from and about others) as well as to interpersonal conflict.

7.6 INFORMATION INTEGRATION THEORY

This approach has by and large restricted its work to the single-system case although there have been demonstrations of its ready applicability to learning and to group judgment making.

Specific and detailed treatment is given to peripheral, mediating, and central phenomena. IIT employs a variety of concepts concerning peripheral (i.e., stimulus) data, some from psychophysics (e.g., contrast), and some from social psychology (e.g., change of meaning). Treatment of mediating processes ("cue" utilization) is given less theoretical attention; the concept of weight is a major one, but no special attention is given to it. Central processes are described wholly in terms of organizing or integrating functions that can be described algebraically (e.g., data are added, averaged, or multiplied). Primary emphasis has been given to the concepts of (a) valuation (item 2), (b) weight (item 5) and (c) integration (organizing principle) (item 6); among these major concepts, the organizing principle, or integration process, has received greatest emphasis. All other aspects of the lens model diagram but one have been dealt with in some form (e.g., item 4, subjective intercorrelation among cues, has been treated in terms of "discounting"). The major omission is that of feedback; no theoretical analysis of the concept has appeared as yet, presumably because IIT's major emphasis lies in the study of the single-system case.

7.7 ATTRIBUTION THEORY

Heider's approach includes concepts that apply to all seven areas of the single-system case. In addition, this approach also includes, and gives detailed treatment to, one aspect of the judgment and decision problem none of the other approaches do; that is the effect of the subjects' *actions* on their attributions, inferences, judgments and decisions, as well as the reverse. But little or nothing is said about weight, an omission that very likely follows from the lack of quantitative emphasis. Note that when Anderson's functional measurement is applied to AT (see above) the concept of weight is readily employed. This suggests that when AT becomes a more formalized theory of inference more attention will be given to that concept.

7.8 INTEGRATION

If a lens model diagram were to be constructed showing the loci of all the theroetical concepts employed by the six approaches considered here, it would indicate that each of the seven areas in the diagram would be covered by concepts from at least two approaches. And, as Mumpower (1976) has shown, there is considerable overlap between AT and SJT in the case of interpersonal learning. Therefore, if one assumes that the lens model diagram (Fig. 7-1) does in fact adequately depict the major aspects of the judgment and/or decision making process, then it may be said that all aspects of this process have received, at the least, some description, and on occasion, some explanation. Redundancies rather than omissions characterize the situation.

The next question, of course, is: Can these heterogeneous concepts be "integrated," or somehow merged into a single, semantically unified set of concepts, or are there antinomies among them that must be settled either by further analysis of their meaning or empirical test.

Consider this example of integration: BDT researchers recognize and give due importance to the concept of "interdependence among attributes"; SJT researchers also emphasize the importance of what they call the "ecological intercorrelation" among cues. Therefore, one could decide that the Bayesians' term "conditional dependence" should be applied to the interdependence among categorical or nominal attributes, while the SJT term "ecological intercorrelations" should be applied to the interdependence among continuous attributes. Recognizing that both terms refer to different types of contingencies or covariation between objective variables would be a simple matter; such terminological agreements would certainly be advantageous for all concerned.

Antinomies are another matter, however. For example, when Kahneman and Tversky (1972) assert that "man is apparently not a conservative Bayesian: he is not Bayesian at all" (p. 450), we have an antinomy between BDT and PDT that should be resolved analytically or empirically, unless one assumes that the antinomy results from the present use of a coarse theoretical framework. Future analyses that use a finer method of description and comparison may find that such apparently intractable antinomies disappear. At present, however, we conclude that (pride of authorship aside) it would not be difficult to move toward a cumulative discipline by developing a semantically-unified theoretical framework.

Chapter 8

Intended Uses
of Research Results

It may appear strange to include this topic in a discussion of theory. But all of the Group I approaches and at least one of the Group II approaches (SJT; possibly IIT also, see Shanteau & Phelps, 1977) have made it clear that they intend their work to be used not only by other scientists but by *policy makers*, and, indeed, by anyone who has to make a decision of more than trivial consequence. Therefore, we need to discover to what extent the theoretical framework of these approaches encompasses judgment and decision making in the real world, as well as in the controlled conditions of the laboratory. For example, it is generally acknowledged that in the real world, task variables (as they are ordinarily described by the judgment maker or decision maker) are interdependent. But including such interdependencies in empirical research creates severe problems of interpretation and it is seldom done. One question that can be asked, therefore, is: to what extent is such interdependency included within the *theoretical* framework of those approaches that intend to apply their work to the real world? What theoretical guidance is provided for dealing with interdependencies among task variables? More generally, how does theory guide method in application, if, indeed, it guides it at all? In addition, all but two approaches (IIT, AT) have indicated their interest in developing *aids* for the policy maker and/or decision maker. To what extent and in what way do the concepts included in these theories direct the construction of such "aids"? And to what extent are judgment aids different from decision aids? These questions cannot be answered properly in this report but they deserve an answer; we need to know whether theory and the results of basic research control application, whether application proceeds independently, or whether, in fact, the distinction between basic research and application can be made at all in the study of judgment and decision making.

8.1 DECISION THEORY

The mathematical research that elaborates and extends the logical entailments of SEU theory is intended to be used to aid decision makers to achieve a better procedure for reaching decisions. "Better," of course, is defined in terms of the approximation of the procedure to the axioms of DT. It follows that if the decision procedure can be justified in terms of the mathematical logic of DT, and if it is followed, the decisions themselves will be better. In short, the use of DT is entirely justified by the logical consistency of the mathematics that supports the prescriptions it offers to decision makers.

Although it is obvious that DT is thus prepared to defend the objectives it seeks, it is uncertain whether DT would argue that it does not matter much *how* logical consistency is achieved. Is there, for example, a proper amount of persuasion and an improper amount? If so, how much persuasion is improper? But almost certainly decision theorists would not concur with the argument that the application of DT should be postponed until the research is done that will tell us whether indeed it does matter *how* logical consistency is achieved. Decision Theory's primary procedural consideration seems to be directed toward reducing the likelihood that the probabilities and utilities are those of the decision analyst rather than the decision maker. And that seems to be entirely a matter of personal technique.

Operational questions aside, however, it is clear that the theory that supports the *aims* (not the specific techniques) of decision analysis does have a strong directive influence; it certainly tells the decision analyst what information he or she might get under specific circumstances and, very often, what approximations are satisfactory under specific circumstances.

8.2 BEHAVIORAL DECISION THEORY

BDT theorists see two uses for the results of their research: (a) descriptions and explanations of decision making behavior that will find a place in the basic science section of psychology, and (b) the development of procedures (decision aids) that will enable decision makers to make better (i.e., logically defensible) decisions. It is only with regard to (a) that the efforts of the behavioral decision theorists differ significantly from the efforts of the decision theorists.

8.2.1 Basic Research Uses

BDT efforts are generally directed toward questions of whether "do people do this or do that." Do people aggregate probabilities and utilities by adding or multiplying them? To what extent do people organize information and act on it cognitively (intuitively) as if they were Bayesian statisticians? In general, departure from the Bayesian model are of central interest.

8.2.2 Application

The results of Bayesian research have been applied in a variety of decision making situations (see, for example, Edwards, 1972; Fryback, 1974; and Edwards, 1978). Present uses of BDT involve SMART (see Gardiner & Edwards in Kaplan & Schwartz, 1975). Bayesian research is hardly mentioned in that application, although MAUT is described in detail. The same is generally true with regard to the use of SMART in evaluation research; the results of Bayesian research do not bear directly on the use of SMART. In Gardiner and Edwards (1975), for example, there is little reference to research regarding the number of dimensions employed, how weights are to be ascertained, methods of coping with interdependencies, etc. (points which are discussed in detail in the Procedures section). Nor is there any reference to any research dealing with interpersonal conflict or interpersonal learning.

    In short, although BDT differs from DT in that it carries out empirical behavioral research, the results of that research are not often brought directly to bear on efforts to aid the decision maker.

8.3 PSYCHOLOGICAL DECISION THEORY

Until Kahneman and Tversky's article in *Management Science* (in press), it could be fairly said that although PDT had pointed to the fallibilities rooted in human judgment and decision making, PDT had not indicated what remedies were to be applied. Remedies are indicated in the *Mangement Science* article, however, and it is clear that these are developed directly in response to the "biases" that these authors and others have found in their research. In short, having found certain biases, they offer "debiasing" procedures. Lichtenstein, Slovic, Fischhoff, Layman, and Combs (1978) have also pursued this matter.

    These debiasing procedures are entirely statistical; for example, "to correct for nonregressiveness, the intuitive estimate should be adjusted toward the average of the reference class" (Kahneman & Tversky, in press, p. 12). Thus, PDT offers logical mechanics to guard against the use of psychological mechanisms. As noted earlier, however, PDT has yet to develop a theory regarding central, organizing principles and does not address the problem of interdependencies among "inputs." Since no mechanisms for dealing with these are offered, it seems fair to say that theory and assistance proceed independently.

There is no empirical proof of the utility of the remedies offered by Kahneman and Tversky in their *Management Science* article, but in one sense none is needed; the statistical logic offered has a better claim to truth than the "psychological logic." In another sense, however, proof is needed as it is in the case of other decision aids. Can this specific debiasing procedure be used? Will it be used? With what effect?

Lichtenstein, Slovic, Fischhoff, Layman, and Combs (1978) attempted to debias their subjects without success. In this case, the debiasing method was used; it simply didn't work. But since this was an initial attempt, one can only conclude that debiasing that is not simply application of statistical techniques may require hard work. Be that as it may, it is clear that efforts to debias decision makers follow directly from the results of basic research as well as from the logic of DT.

8.4 TRANSITION

The conceptual distinction between judgment (knowing) and decision (getting) that was made above (see Intended Functions of the Theories) can be seen in its operational form in the differences in the construction of "decision aids" within Group I and "cognitive or judgment aids" constructed within Group II. That is, Group I aids always center on assisting the decision maker to assign the correct probabilities (to various outcomes or alternatives, etc.) whereas Group II judgment aids may include probability judgments only as *one* instance of a variety of judgments.

8.5 SOCIAL JUDGMENT THEORY

As anticipated, Group I provides decision makers with information about their subjective probabilities and utilities (a) in the "divide and conquer" approach to a decision tree (DT), (b) in SMART or MAUT (BDT), and (c) in debiasing (PDT). Group II judgment analysts (represented only by SJT), on the other hand, provide policy makers with information about relations between their judgments and cues, as well as information about other persons' judgments in relation to task properties. SJT insists upon such cognitive feedback because such relations are argued to be the basic unit of knowing; indeed, SJT insists that such cognitive feedback is the primary means of inductive learning, inside and outside the laboratory. Thus it might be concluded that decision aids that deal with probabilities and utilities address themselves to the *results* of inductive knowing, that is, to the cognitive state of an individual subsequent to the acquisition of knowledge, whereas judgment *aids* address themselves to the *sources* of those probabilities and utilities, thus illustrating the distinction between deciding and knowing. (See, for example, Hammond & Adelman, 1976).

As noted earlier SJT derives its arguments for its form of an aid for judgment from the results of theory and research regarding the double- and n-system cases. The clearest examples of the insistence of the SJT theorist upon environmental representation in judgment research can be seen in the recent development of judgment aids that links environmental models with models of judgment systems (see, for example, Hammond, Mumpower, & Smith, 1977; Hammond, Klitz, & Cook, 1978; Mumpower, Veirs, & Hammond, 1979.) These three studies present worked-out examples which are intended to show that neither modelers of environmental systems nor modelers of cognitive systems can work effectively in isolation, and that the policy maker must have access to both models and their interactions if she or he is to be successful. This argument, of course, follows directly from Brunswik's admonition:

> Both organism and environment will have to be seen as systems, each with properties of its own . . . Each has surface and depth, or overt and covert regions. . . . It follows that, much as psychology must be concerned with the texture of the organism . . . it also must be concerned with the texture of the environment. (1957, p. 5)

Until the advent of the computer model of the environment this admonition was honored more in its breach than in its execution, mainly because of the technical difficulties of bringing the full complexity of the environment into contact with the organism in a controlled way. Computer models can effectively solve that problem, however, and can bring the interaction between policy makers and the complexities of their environment under analysis. It is in this way that SJT follows the above metatheory regarding the organism and the environment in its effort to aid the policy maker.

8.6 INFORMATION INTEGRATION THEORY

This approach has generally stood aside from the matter of application. The only example is that provided by Phelps and Shanteau (1978) regarding the judging of animals. Even in this case, however, the investigators seemed more interested in testing the descriptive accuracy of various models than in providing a judgment or decision aid.

8.7 ATTRIBUTION THEORY

Although AT clearly intends that its research results are used to develop general laws of inductive knowing or inferences about the locus of causality, and although there are neither direct efforts to apply the results of AT research to specific real-world problems nor attempts to develop "attribution aids," still, there is at least an implicit suggestion that the results of AT research can be directly applicable to behavior in the real world. Indeed, because of its social, rather than physical, character, the empirical work in AT implies that the results grow out of or are based on simulations of the real world and are thus directly generalizable to it. The realization of these aims seems to be far in the future, however. (But see Frieze, Bar-Tal, & Carroll, 1979.)

8.8 INTEGRATION

The intended uses of the research results produced by decision analysis (Group I) and judgment analysis (Group II), although different, are not highly divergent. Group I intends its theory to be useful to decision makers in general and policy makers in particular; DT, BDT, PDT and SJT clearly ask their theory to be useful, to guide them toward producing results that not only contribute to knowledge about the psychology of information processing, but also to contribute toward the development of aids for policy makers. All four approaches want to be able to point to theory-based, research-based, applications. But there are major differences between and within these four approaches that follow from their theoretical (and metatheoretical) orientations. To what extent can these differences be resolved and/or set aside in this development of aids to the policy maker?

We offer only one suggestion: if judgments and decision processes can be usefully separated with regard to their intended *theoretical* function (as described above) then they may be usefully separated with regard to their *pragmatic* function. That is, Group I approaches may aid the policy maker to explicate his probabilities and utilities and to organize these in a logical manner, thus avoiding the biases and fallibilities of unaided cognitive efforts, whereas Group II approaches may aid the policy maker to see sources of these probabilities and utilities, and to see the relations between various judgment policies and their implementation in a world simulated by models that vary in their "hardness," or analytical strength. The combination of these two approaches to providing aids for the policy maker (or decider) demands exploration, theoretically and methodologically as well as empirically.

Before leaving this section we should point to the similarity in the claims that are made by the proponents of various approaches with regard to their value as aids to decision makers.

8.9 CLAIMS FOR THE VALUE OF VARIOUS APPROACHES

In the course of our study of the different approaches, we frequently encountered claims of benefits that were made on behalf of those approaches. This was particularly true for those approaches that have been used outside the laboratory. We have collected and categorized some of those claims in the belief that such claims can serve as useful criteria for evaluating and comparing the different methods and procedures, although we have not yet undertaken that task. At the very least, these claims indicate important psychological issues which need further exploration in the context of judgment and decision making. Almost all proponents, for example, claim that their respective methods are useful for teaching novices how to arrive at better judgments, or how to resolve group conflict about a decision. The most striking feature of the list of claims is that seldom have these claims been verified experimentally; rather they rely on references to case histories.

The categories in the list below are not always mutually exclusive (that may be impossible and undesirable anyway) and the list is undoubtedly incomplete. We have only included those claims seen in print; often a direct quotation making the claim is presented. Because the claims of the approaches (at least for DT, BDT, and SJT) are so similar and because we would be surprised if any approach would deny that its method *could* produce such benefits, we do not indicate the sources of the quotations.

Claim 1: Aids Clear Thinking

Almost all claims fall into this category, although they are usually indirect. Examples: "a framework for straightening out one's mind," "creating cognitive aids for human judgment," "extending the limits of human judgment."

Claim 2: Educates the Decision Maker

Whether or not these methods help decision makers think better, almost everyone claims that such methods make decision makers wiser about their particular problem; for example; "There is educational value in asking more specific questions, getting specific utility functions, and so on. It sensitizes the decision maker." Below is a list of more specific educational claims.

a. Makes hidden assumptions and implicit tradeoffs explicit: "we should not underestimate the important intellectual and emotional impact that arises when we are forced to express vexing tradeoffs in unambiguous terms"; "it helps management articulate some of its basic assumptions."

b. Forces full consideration of all consequences of a given action: Why conduct an experiment or do an opinion survey if there is virtually no expectation that action will be altered by the information obtained? "Explicit definition of the possible outcomes tends to prevent this common trap."

c. Identifies what is important for making decision and where more information is needed: "Examination of value of information in a decision context helps suggest the gathering, compilation, and organization of data from new sources;" the decision maker "can come to grips with the critical determinants of his decision;" causes the decision maker to "grapple with fundamental issues."

d. Identifies what is *not* important for making the decision: This claim is obviously a by-product of (2c). The decision maker can avoid wasting time on either facts or values that really have no impact on the decision. Usually this is accomplished via sensitivity analysis.

e. Forces explicit recognition of uncertainty: Decision makers often either do not understand or try to duck issues of uncertainty. Analysis forces the decision maker to deal with uncertainty.

f. Understanding of the complete problem: "the detailed quantitative work in doing the full-scale study probably helped the [decision maker] to better understand the *qualitative* implications of the problem, and it was this qualitative understanding that helped him influence the governmental officials;" force the decision maker "to scrutinize his problem as an organic whole."

Claim 3: Communication

Better communication is often claimed: "executives most satisfied with the approach valued it as a vehicle for communicating reasoning amongst decision makers." A number of good outcomes are presumed to follow from this improved communication.

a. Advocacy, defense of decision: "helps the decision maker defend and communicate his decision . . . makes the point that decision was not frivolous and that all factors were considered;" "provides an effective basis for the justification of a particular recommendation."

b. Conflict resolution, reconciliation: This claim is made for virtually every approach that aims at application. However, justifications for this claim often are rather murky—conflict resolution seems to happen as a by-product of the improved communication. "useful as a mediating device . . . can quickly focus on those issues on which they have fundamental disagreements; . . . will sharpen the specificity and sophistication of the arguments;" "can spell out explicitly what the values of each participant are, show how much they differ, and in the process can frequently reduce the extent of such differences;" "isolate and quantify differences of opinion among experts."

c. Teaching: "The documentation of an analysis can serve as a briefing report for a new decision maker;" judgment and decision analyses are frequently alluded to as valuable teaching devices for such diverse disciplines as medicine, airline piloting, and livestock grading.

d. Explanation and intellectual discussion (problem-solving): Even if there is no conflict, analysis aids an intellectual, nonemotional discussion of critical issues facing society; "can be meaningfully discussed by experts and laymen;" "it is easier to discuss the issues with our colleagues."

Claim 4: Policy Focus (Variable) rather than Specific-Action (Object) Focus

All approaches, in one way or another, claim that their methods and procedures promote a policy focus and thus "shift the decision maker's attention from specific actions to the values these actions serve." The advantages of so doing include the following.

a. Saves time, money, and unhappiness: "eliminate the need for costly time-consuming case-by-case adversary or negotiating proceedings."

b. Easy to adapt to new information or changing values: "provides a framework for contingency planning and for the continuing evaluation of new facts that is necessary as the dynamics of a problem unfold;" "such policies can easily be changed in response to new circumstances or changing value systems;" "provides the opportunity for cumulative knowledge."

c. Easy to pass on to next administrator: (same claim as Teaching [3c] and Adapt to new circumstances [4b]).

d. Inform those affected by policy: "Such policies can be easily, efficiently, and explicitly disseminated;" "by publicizing a set of values, a decision making organization can in effect inform those affected by its decisions about its ground rules."

Claim 5: Fact-Value (Probability-Utility) Separation

This separation "distinguishes the decision maker's preferences for consequences, including his attitudes towards risky situations, from his judgments about uncertainties;" "separating judgments of probabilities from those of values permits rational analysis." Some of the advantages claimed to follow from this separation include:

a. To each his own: "The separation phase permits elected representatives to function exclusively as policy-makers, and scientists to function exclusively as scientists."

b. Easy to integrate information from experts: "each expert can give testimony in an unambiguous quantitative manner that can be incorporated in the overall analysis," "formal framework makes it easier to incorporate the opinion of another expert."

Claim 6: Synergistic Effect, Creates New Solutions

This benefit leads to "aid in generating creative alternatives;" "there is always the possibility that these analyses will uncover new insights that result in a different alternative—one that is perceived as better than any of the original alternatives."

Taken out of context (and they have often been taken out of context by those who are scornful of the scientific study of human behavior) these claims may appear to be strident, or boasting, if not absurd. And it may indeed be that we are witnessing the overconfident claims of a new discipline much in the same stage of development as, say, clinical psychology or psychiatry was in the early 1900s. It must be acknowledged that these claims are not entirely, or even largely, based on research resembling, say, clinical trials of new drugs. Rather, they tend to be based on reasonable extrapolations from laboratory research, or reasonable observations of behavior in real world decision making, the most dangerous sort of material on which to base a claim of any sort.

It will be well to remember, however, that all these claims are made in reference to circumstances in which these decision aids are absent; thus, claims about the efficacy of decision aids for improving communication are made in relation to the communication via written or spoken language. Does the reader need to be reminded how often this form of communication fails in situations where judgments and decisions are involved? Or how often conflict is increased rather than reduced by the usual efforts at conflict reduction?

If the reader believes that the conventional methods of judgment and decision making of commensuration, conflict reduction, and the like need no improvement, then he or she will consider the above claims to be exaggerations. If, on the other hand, the reader believes these activities are of a poor quality, then she or he will find the above claims to be credible. We leave this judgment to the reader.

Method

Chapter 9

Introduction to Method

This section analyzes the six approaches to judgment and decision making with respect to their methodologies. The distinction between methodology and procedure (the latter being the topic of the next section) is sometimes nebulous. We have tried to include in methodology those issues which pertain to strategic choices for testing or implementing a judgment and decision theory and to reserve tactical choices for the procedures section. For example, the decision to analyze group or individual data is a strategic choice and is discussed in this section, while operational definitions of the key concepts identified in the previous section on theory are included in the procedures section rather than here. Of course, there is inevitably some overlap; therefore there are a few redundancies in our quest for systematic coverage of the important dimensions on which the six approaches can or do vary.

The organization of this section is much the same as that of the preceding section: each approach is described in terms of theoretically neutral dimensions and an attempt at integration follows the descriptions for each dimension. We arrived at the list of dimensions used in this methods section by simply asking what strategic choices had to be made in order to design a complete judgment and decision making study or application. Basically, the investigator designing a study must decide what stimuli in what tasks to present to which judges or decision makers, when and how to decompose the stimuli and judgments for analysis, and whether to group the data from different subjects before or after analysis of model fit. Each of these choices is a dimension upon which we describe and compare the six approaches; consideration of each dimension forms one chapter. Chapter 10, "Idiographic vs. Nomothetic Analysis" describes the choices made by the various approaches as to when during the analysis to aggregate data from different judges and decision makers. This chapter also contains an extensive discussion of the implications following from a particular choice upon this dimension. Chapter 11, "Diversity in Subjects, Objects, and Tasks" describes differences among the six approaches with respect to the number and diversity of subjects, objects, and tasks included in judgment and decision making studies. We examine diversity and its effects on generalizability both within and across studies of each approach.

Chapter 12, "Stimulus-Object Decomposition," considers the issue of whether the stimuli presented to subjects are decomposed into theoretical components before or after the subject responds to them. If before, then the judge or decision maker is explicitly aware of the aspects upon which the stimuli vary; whereas, if after, the investigator usually takes great pains to ensure that the judge does not guess the theoretical decomposition. Once the characteristics of the stimuli are decomposed into meaningful components, then the investigator must decide what methods to use to decompose the judgments into similar components. Strategic analytical choices, such as testing axiomatic versus statistical predictions, are discussed in Chapter 13, "Judgment Decomposition." In order to illustrate some of the important differences in the methods used for judgment decomposition, we present a hypothetical data set and examine how several of the approaches would perform the required analysis. Finally, Chapter 14, "Methods of Partitioning the Judgment/ Decision Problem," describes how the three approaches which have attempted policy applications partition the judgment/decision problem into manageable components.

In essence, this section describes the methodological choices made by each approach with respect to aggregation and decomposition in the study of judgment and decision making. While the dimensions upon which we describe the methods of the six approaches are logically distinct, it is important to note that a methodological choice on one dimension often constrains the available choices on another dimension. Throughout we try to note not only the constraints implied by choices on other dimensions but also the constraints imposed by both theory and practicality. In the "Integration" subsection of each chapter we note similarities and differences among the approaches and note any antinomies requiring empirical, logical, or conceptual reconciliation.

Chapter 10

Idiographic
versus Nomothetic Analysis

In this chapter we examine an important strategic choice each approach must take with respect to analyzing the data from a judgment or decision making experiment or task. Before describing that choice, it is first necessary to describe the analysis problem in the abstract and to introduce a bit of notation. Fig. 10-1 shows a data matrix obtained from a typical judgment and decision making study. In such studies the data consist of responses (judgments, decisions, etc.) to each of m stimuli (profiles, decision situations, gambles, etc.) by each of n judges. The rows of the data matrix in Fig. 10-1 correspond to the judges and the columns to the stimuli. An entry in the matrix is represented by r_{ij} and corresponds to the response to the j-th stimulus by the i-th judge. The goal of analysis is to reduce this data matrix so that theoretical predictions might be tested and/or so that functional relationships might be established between the responses and characteristics of the stimuli and the judges.

There are basically two processes involved in reducing a judgment and decision making data matrix. One of these processes is *aggregation across responses* (across columns of the data matrix) and the other is *aggregation*

STIMULI

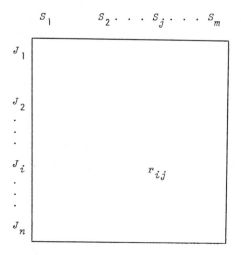

Figure 10-1 Prototypical data matrix from a judgment and decision making study. The J_j correspond to different judges, the S_j to different stimuli, and r_{ij} is the response of the *i*th judge to the *j*th stimuli.

across judges (across rows of the data matrix). Aggregation across judges is usually the simpler process and involves the calculation of descriptive and summary statistics (measures of central tendency and variability, frequency distributions, etc.). Aggregation across responses is more complex because there are many different techniques for accomplishing such aggregation. The same descriptive statistics as for aggregation across judges are sometimes appropriate. In addition, aggregation across responses may involve parameter estimation and model fitting as well as statistical tests of theoretical predictions.

Using only one of the two aggregation processes does not generally provide a sufficient reduction of the data matrix for hypothesis testing or presentation in a scientific publication. Thus, although there are important exceptions, almost all analyses of judgment and decision making matrices include aspects of both aggregation processes. We can now describe the important strategic methodological choice which each of the approaches to judgment and decision making must make in order to analyze data. That choice is simply which aggregation process to do first—to aggregate across judges first and then across responses, or to aggregate across responses first and then across judges? We refer to the first choice as the "nomothetic" method and the second as the "idiographic" method. Each is described in turn.

10.1 NOMOTHETIC METHOD

The key assumption of the nomothetic method is that with respect to the given judgment or decision task all judges are essentially replicates of one another—that except for random error all the responses within any column of the data matrix of Fig. 10-1 would be identical. With such an assumption the obvious first step in data reduction is to aggregate across judges in order to increase the reliability of the responses and consequently to increase the power of the statistical tests. After (or sometimes simultaneous with) the aggregation across judges, model parameters are estimated, hypotheses tested, etc. in order to accomplish the aggregation across responses. If only the aggregation across judges is used, then the data matrix of Fig. 10-1 is reduced to a single row containing average responses for each stimulus. More often nomothetic data analysis reduces the matrix to a functional relationship of the following form:

$$r_{ij} = f(s_j, a, b)$$

where a and b are estimated parameters of the model (two parameters are used here for illustration; there may be any number of parameters including none). It is important to note that there are no subscripts corresponding to the judges (J_i) on the right side of this equation; that is because of the nomothetic assumption that individuals are replicates so that it should be possible to describe responses only in terms of characteristics of the stimuli (the s_j in the function) and model parameters (a and b in this case). The functional relationship might be either complex as in an explicit mathematical equation or it might be as simple as a statement such as "increases in variable X result in increases in the proportion of response type Y."

Because judges are considered to be replicates of one another, large numbers of judges are generally used to increase statistical power. The use of the nomothetic method has no implications for m—the number of stimuli; m may range from 1 (a data matrix with a single column) to many times the number of judges.

10.2 IDIOGRAPHIC METHOD

In contrast to the nomothetic assumption that individual judges are replicates of one another with respect to the judgment and decision task, the key presumption of the idiographic method is that there exist important and reliable individual differences between judges with respect to the given task—that differences among responses within a column of the data matrix are not simply due to random error. This implies that no single model with a single set of parameters is likely to be able to describe the functional relationship between the responses and the stimuli; in the extreme case there may be a separate functional relationship and a separate set of parameters for each judge. With such individual differences, it is imperative to analyze within judges first (i.e., to aggregate across the responses of the data matrix) and then do any aggregation across subjects that is possible. The result of the first aggregation produces functional relationships of the following form:

$$r_{ij} = f_i \ (s_j, a_i, b_i)$$

which differs from that for the nomothetic model because of the subscripts corresponding to judges (J_i) on the right side of the equation. That is, both the parameters (a_i and b_i) as well as the nature of the functional relation (f_i) may be dependent upon the judge. Again, the functional relationship represented by f_i may be either complex as in an explicit mathematical equation or simple as in a statement such as "the responses of judge X do not satisfy the predictions of model Y." After the aggregation across responses, it is then possible to aggregate across judges. Such aggregation usually results in statements of the form, "model X is appropriate for $Y\%$ of the judges and model Z is appropriate for the remainder" or if the same functional relation applies to all judges, "the average parameter values are $\bar{a}$ and $\bar{b}$."

In the idiographic method, because of the need to make separate inferences or model fits for each judge, it is generally advantageous to observe many responses from the same judge so that m—the number of stimuli—tend to be rather large. In contrast, the burden of separate initial analyses for each judge serves to limit the number of judges included in any one study. So compared to a typical nomothetic study, the idiographic method usually has smaller values of n and larger values of m.

10.3 NOMOTHETIC VS. IDIOGRAPHIC

The obvious question is which is the better method for the study of judgment and decision making—nomothetic or idiographic? There is no answer because each method has its advantages and disadvantages. If differences across judges are either small or not important, then the nomothetic method offers the advantages of greater statistical power and reliability as well as simpler analytical procedures. On the other hand, if differences across judges are either large or important, then the idiographic method offers the advantage of individual analysis with the disadvantage of greater procedural complexity. The choice between nomothetic and idiographic is analogous (but not identical) to the choice of between and within subject designs in the analysis of variance, so many of the considerations that apply to that choice apply here as well. A more complete discussion of the reasons for selecting each method is presented later. The important point is that the choice of either nomothetic or idiographic methods is a real choice, for there is no reason to expect that a nomothetic and an idiographic analysis will yield the same conclusions. For example, only under very special and restrictive conditions is it true that the parameter estimates given by the nomothetic method using grouped data (say, a and b) will be the same as the average of the parameter estimates from the idiographic method ($\bar{a}$ and $\bar{b}$).

We now turn to a consideration of the methodological choices with respect to aggregation across and within judges made by each of the six approaches.

10.4 DECISION THEORY

The primary methods of DT are clearly of the idiographic type. In most applications there is only one judge or decision maker so that there is never even an opportunity for nomothetic analysis. This methodological choice obviously derives from theory. Because probabilities and utilities (the important parameters of DT models) are presumed to be personal and subjective there is no expectation that differences between people are due only to random error as is required by the nomothetic approach. Rather the expectation is that people will have different parameters and thus their judgments will require individual analysis. Nomothetic analysis simply makes no sense in the context of the theory.

In those instances in which there are multiple decision makers—as in group decision making problems or social choice situations—DT still opts for the idiographic method of aggregating within judges before aggregating across judges. Keeney and Kirkwood (1975) and Keeney and Raiffa (1976, see Chapter 10) provide an interesting application of the idiographic method in the context of group decision making. They use a "supra Decision Maker" model for aggregating individual utilities into a joint decision. Individual utility functions are first determined and then combined into a single utility function using the supra Decision Maker's weights for each individual.

10.5 BEHAVIORAL DECISION THEORY

A variety of methodological approaches has appeared in the work of BDT. The earliest studies within this tradition relied mostly on the idiographic method (e.g., Mosteller & Nogee, 1951; Edwards, 1953, 1954; Davidson, Suppes, & Siegel, 1957). In these studies there is often no or very little aggregation across judges as there are generally separate results, figures, analyses, etc. reported for each subject (or at least for a selected sample of subjects).

The "conservatism" studies of probabilistic information processing often abandoned the pure idiographic approach for the nomothetic. For example, in the three experiments of Phillips and Edwards (1966) the probability estimates from several (5 to 12) subjects are averaged and *then* those average estimates are compared to the probabilities predicted by Bayes' Rule. Parameter estimates follow the aggregation across judges (e.g., in the equation $\Omega_1 = L^c \Omega_0$ the parameter c is estimated only for the group data).

Finally, the most recent work on multiattribute utility theory (the SMART method described in Gardiner & Edwards, 1975) has returned to the use of the idiographic approach (see their Fig. 5) although some nomothetic results are also reported (see their Fig. 6).

10.6 PSYCHOLOGICAL DECISION THEORY

The work within PDT also exhibits a variety of methodological approaches; it is not unusual for both idiographic and nomothetic methods to be used in the same study. To complicate matters further it is often difficult to categorize some PDT methods as being either idiographic or nomothetic.

Recent experiments on "prospect theory" (Kahneman & Tversky, 1979) provide good examples of PDT's use of nomothetic methods. The following is a typical result from that paper in which subject behavior is compared with predictions from the axioms of subjectively expected utility (SEU):

Percent selecting gamble A over gamble B: 67%
Percent selecting gamble A' over gamble B': 22%

The gambles are constructed so that in order to be consistent with SEU axioms, a choice of gamble A implies choice of gamble A' and a choice of gamble B implies choice of gamble B' (as well as both converses). Subject behavior is apparently not in agreement with such implications because a majority choose A in the first pair and B' in the second pair. This is the nomothetic approach because there is never a count of exactly how many individuals switch from A to B' or B to A' (in the present example the proportion of *individuals* violating the SEU predictions could range from a low of 45% to a high of 89%).

On the other hand, Tversky and Kahneman (1979) in their paper on "causal schemas" use an idiographic method with the same two-choice paradigm as employed in the prospect theory studies. Instead of reporting choice percentages for each pair, they report "A large majority of our subjects (56 or 68) stated that $P(A/B) > P(A/\bar{B})$ and that $P(B/A) < P(B/\bar{A})$, contrary to the laws of probability" (p. 10). This is idiographic analysis, for it is clear that most individuals do indeed make simultaneous, contradictory choices. These two examples illustrate that the choice of idiographic or nomothetic analysis can be independent of other aspects of the experimental procedure.

The methods of the heuristic studies (e.g., Kahneman & Tversky 1972, and Tversky & Kahneman, 1973) are not so easily classifiable. Classification is difficult because although the typical study involves large subject samples with only one judgment or choice per subject—the usual large n, small m pattern characteristic of nomothetic methods—the data are often (but not always) analyzed using an idiographic method. That is, on the basis of a few responses (and often only a single response) each individual is categorized as either exhibiting or not exhibiting the given error or bias and then the numbers in each category are counted. For example, in Tversky and Kahneman (1973) 105 of 152 subjects evidence an availability bias by incorrectly believing that more words had a given letter in the first than in the third position for a *majority* of five letters (K, L, N, R, V). It should be noted that in the idiographic method used in heuristics experiments, statistical tests are applied *only* to the process of aggregating across judges although in principle there is nothing to preclude statistical analyses for each individual when aggregating across responses. For example, in the above letter frequency problem, the null hypothesis (that a subject is equally likely to choose first or third position as more frequent for any given letter) can be rejected (at $p < .05$, one-tailed) for only those *individuals* who choose the first position for all five letters. Still other heuristics studies use nomothetic methods. For example, Kahneman and Tversky use only between-group comparisons to demonstrate that sample size is often ignored in estimating subjective-sampling distributions.

Finally, there are many PDT studies which use pure idiographic methods in which there is no aggregation across judges; in contrast to the nomothetic experiments which demonstrated systematic violations of SEU axioms and the consequent need for prospect theory, Kahneman and Tversky (1979) estimate the parameters for their theory (uncertainty weights and value functions) separately for each individual. Tversky (1967, 1969, 1972a) also employs the pure idiographic methodology (e.g., see Figure 10 in Tversky, 1967).

10.7 SOCIAL JUDGMENT THEORY

Proponents of SJT specifically advocate the use of the idiographic method. Because different individuals may use cues in different ways (i.e., different weights and function forms) it makes no sense to average judgments across individuals or to fit one set of parameters to data from a group of individuals. Thus in the typical study separate weights and function forms are estimated for each individual and a separate measure of fit (R^2) is computed for each person.

Many, but not all, SJT studies then go on to aggregate across judges. Summary measures (R^2, G) for each individual are averaged within groups in order to assess the effects of such between-group manipulations as cognitive vs. outcome feedback (Adelman, 1977), linear vs. curvilinear function forms in multiple cue probability learning tasks (Brehmer, 1974; Hammond, 1971) and correlated vs. orthogonal cues in interpersonal learning (Mumpower & Hammond, 1974).

The recent use of cluster analysis (Rohrbaugh, 1977) to group individuals with similar judgment policies is also an example of aggregating across judges after first aggregating across responses within judges.

10.8 INFORMATION INTEGRATION THEORY

It is difficult to classify the work within IIT as being either idiographic or nomothetic. Anderson (1974) explicitly advocates within-subject designs, but in such designs judgments from different individuals are still averaged when the model is tested and parameters are estimated. Thus, in most IIT studies only group (i.e., nomothetic) analyses are reported. However, reports of those studies usually also include a disclaimer to the effect that individual (idiographic) analyses confirm the nomothetic results. For example, Shanteau (1975) states:

> All the results reported up to this point have been based on group data. However, it is well known that group analyses can mask model discrepancies for individual subjects (see, for example, Shanteau & Anderson, 1969). Accordingly, each of these studies was also analyzed at the single-subject level. For the most part, these anlyses have substantiated the group results in support of the multiplying model. Where discrepancies have occurred, they tend to be small with no consistent trends. (p. 118)

When group analyses might mask important individual differences then IIT investigators do use idiographic analyses and report separate parameter estimates for each subject or a representative sample of subjects (e.g., see Shanteau & Nagy, 1976). It seems reasonable to conclude therefore that IIT prefers nomothetic methodologies but is quite willing to use idiographic methods when the data indicate that group analyses are inappropriate. The preference for nomothetic methods stems from convenience (group analyses are much easier to report) and from statistical considerations (grouped data have larger degrees of freedom and much greater statistical power for detecting model deviations).

10.9 ATTRIBUTION THEORY

Almost all attribution studies use nomothetic methods. The study by Jones, Davis, and Gergen (1961) provides a typical example. In their experiment, Jones et al. presented a single stimulus (actually an experimental condition) to each subject and different subjects received different stimuli. With only one response from each subject and that one response not coming from the same stimulus, idiographic analysis is virtually impossible. (As noted earlier, Tversky & Kahneman, 1979, were able to perform an idiographic analysis with only one response per judge but in that case all responses were made to the same stimulus.) For those AT studies in which subjects do make multiple judgments (e.g., Weiner & Kukla, 1970; Frieze & Weiner, 1971; and many other studies reviewed in Frieze, 1976), nomothetic methods are still used exclusively.

A few attribution studies do use idiographic methods of analysis. For example, Jones and Goethals (1971, p. 36) report the percentages of their subjects using various distinct strategies in an impression formation task. However, even in studies of "individual differences" in attributions (e.g., see Frieze, 1976) nomothetic analysis is the overwhelmingly predominant choice of AT.

10.10 INTEGRATION

Unlike many of the other theoretical and methodological dimensions considered in this report, the distinction between Group I and Group II approaches is not reflected in the choices of idiographic or nomothetic methods. Instead both types of methodologies are found in each group. In terms of this issue, we can match each Group I approach with a corresponding Group II approach. DT and SJT generally depend on idiographic analysis; BDT and IIT are the most likely of these six approaches to use a combination of nomothetic and idiographic methods; PDT often uses and AT almost always uses nomothetic methods. So the use of both idiographic and nomothetic methods can already be found on either side of the conceptual watershed.

Is further integration necessary? We think so, for often the choice of an idiographic or nomothetic method is based on convenience or tradition rather than on any conceptual or logical analysis of which method is more appropriate for studying or measuring judgments, preferences, and decisions. Only SJT and IIT have thought the issue important enough to advocate which method type should be used in what situations. One might also argue that the issue is moot for DT.

A complete conceptual analysis of the strengths and weaknesses of each method type is not appropriate here, but we can suggest a few of the important issues.

10.10.1 Group Analyses Which Result from Aggregating across Judges First Can Yield Very Misleading Indicators of Individual Behavior

As noted earlier, idiographic and nomothetic methods do not necessarily give the same results. Grouped data may fit a given model even though the judgments of every individual do not, and grouped data may not fit a model even though the data from all individuals do fit that model. As Tversky (1972a) has noted:

> most studies [of preference, choice, and judgment] report and analyze only group data. Unfortunately, group data usually do not permit adequate testing of theories of individual choice behavior because, in general, the compatibility of such data with theory is neither a necessary nor a sufficient condition for its validity. (p. 291)

Shanteau and Anderson (1969) have empirically demonstrated such problems. and hypothetical examples are easy to construct (e.g., see Luce, 1959, p. 8). This consideration obviously favors the use of idiographic methods.

Group analyses are likely to be misleading to the extent that there are individual differences among the subjects. In a pure judgment task for which it is reasonable to assume that everyone has the same point of view, group and individual analyses are likely to yield the same results. However, for a decision task for which the value structures differ across individuals, idiographic and nomothetic analyses will very probably lead to different interpretations of the data. For example, group aggregation before analysis will cause little difficulty if we ask subjects to rate a series of paint chips according to their "degree of yellowness" because everyone will have a common definition of "yellow." On the other hand, group analysis of preference data, say asking subjects to rate the paint chips according to their ideal for an automobile color, will likely be hopelessly confusing due to the lack of a common ideal. Furthermore, it is still possible for group analyses to hide important individual differences even in judgment tasks which do not involve different value structures (e.g., if there were a few color blind subjects in the "degree of yellowness" study). Thus, any approach using nomothetic analysis should be aware that the "group" model derived from such analysis may apply to none of the individuals in the group when considered separately; ideally any nomothetic analysis would include specific methodological checks against that possibility.

The idea that nomothetic methods might be suitable for those judgment and decision tasks which do not involve different value structures across subjects and that idiographic methods might be appropriate for those that do suggests an explanation of the varying use of those methods in BDT and IIT. That is, nomothetic methods are used in the BDT subjective probability revision studies in which values are not involved and idiographic techniques are employed in the multiattribute studies for which value structures are obviously relevant. Similarly, those IIT studies which have reported results from idiographic analysis have involved preferential choice (of sandwiches, of dating partners, etc.) rather than knowledge or perceptual judgments.

There are many applied group decision making or judgment problems which require aggregation across judges in order to obtain a single decision or judgment for the group as a whole. The goal is often to obtain a "compromise" decision or judgment. It is an open question as to whether idiographic or nomothetic analysis is more likely to produce a good compromise in the group situation. Despite the importance of the problem of group decision making, the six approaches considered here have devoted little attention to the methodological problems inherent in aggregating across judges to produce a single result for the group. The one exception is DT which has provided (Keeney & Kirkwood, 1975; Keeney & Raiffa, 1976) within the context of an idiographic method a theoretical rationale and a procedure for aggregation across individual decision makers to reach a group decision function. This is certainly a problem that deserves further theoretical and methodological consideration from the other approaches to judgment and decision making.

10.10.2 The Strength of Any Conclusion is Affected by Whether Nomothetic or Idiographic Methods are Used

Unfortunately there is at least one consideration which favors the nomothetic and one that favors the idiographic. With an idiographic method, analysis is concentrated on a few individuals and one is never sure how representative the resulting parameter estimates and model fits are of the general population; thus population generality may be stronger with nomothetic methods. On the other hand, with a nomothetic analysis we are never sure that the results apply to any *one* individual; that is, situational generality may be stronger with idiographic methods. For example, in the nomothetic data from Kahneman and Tversky (1979) discussed above, while the majority of subjects selected A from the first pair and a majority of subjects chose B' from the second pair, it does not follow that a majority of the subjects selected *both A* and B' and thereby violated the SEU axioms. In this instance, as few as 45% of the subjects may have made this joint choice, or as many as 89%. If the actual percentage were closer to the higher value, then an idiographic analysis would have produced a much stronger conclusion relatively immune to methodological second-guessing.

The example illustrates another point as well. If one's goal is to falsify the predictions of a particular model as opposed to showing that a particular model adequately describes judgments, then the weaker conclusions from a nomothetic analysis may be strong enough. In this case, even if the lower value (45%) for the number of subjects violating the SEU axioms is correct, that value is certainly large enough to be very disquieting for anyone proposing SEU theory as a descriptive model of human judgment. Thus, there may be circumstances for which a nomothetic result is "strong enough" to reject a model, and the greater analytical complexity of the idiographic method becomes unnecessary. However, idiographic methods are more likely to be required if the goal is to show that a model is "correct," for failure to find violations with a weaker nomothetic analysis would not be conclusive that such violations did not exist. This distinction between falsifying models and fitting parameters of models seems to explain the alternation between nomothetic and idiographic methods in PDT and possibly in BDT. That is, when the goal is to reject, say, probability axioms or SEU axioms as principles of judgment, then PDT and BDT are likely to use nomothetic methods; but when the goal is to fit a specific model, say, to describe value functions in prospect theory, or to describe attribute weights in SMART, then PDT and BDT are likely to use idiographic methods.

10.10.3 Presenting Multiple Judgment of Decision Tasks to Each Subject May Create Demand Characteristics Which Alter the Judgment Process Being Studied

This issue clearly favors nomothetic designs in which the judge sees only a few stimuli. Such demand characteristics are a problem particularly for certain AT experiments which use elaborate, realistic scenarios and vary only a small part of the scenario from condition to condition. For example, most subjects would have been able to infer the manipulation in the Jones, Davis, and Gergen (1961) study had they been able to listen to more than one of the recorded interviews. While some investigators using multiple judgments dismiss the demand problem—for example, Anderson (1974) claims that many of his experiments control for demand characteristics, and that those that do not produced the same pattern of results—remarkably little formal research attention has been devoted to this issue. The dilemma facing any investigator is aptly stated by Ostrom, Werner, and Saks (1979).

> One of the difficulties in drawing conclusions in the present experiment is that parameter estimates were obtained on a group-wide basis rather than for individuals. This resulted from the decision to counterbalance stimuli across set sizes on a group basis rather than on an individual basis. If parameter estimates are desired on an individual basis, it would require having each subject see all stimuli in all set sizes. Each stimulus item, then, would be seen more than once by each subject. Whether this design alteration would change the processes involved in juridic judgments is unknown at present. (p. 448)

10.10.4 Even after a Choice Has Been Made to Use Either an Idiographic or Nomothetic Method, the Investigator Still Must Decide on the Relative Emphasis to Be Placed on the Two Aggregation Processes

The strength and type of the aggregation within judges may be very weak and nonstatistical (e.g., classification of individuals on the basis of one response in some PDT experiments), strong and nonstatistical (e.g., examination of all an individual's many choices for consistency with each other and with DT axioms), or strong and statistical (e.g., statistical analysis of an individual's many judgments using regression or ANOVA techniques by SJT and IIT). The subsequent nomothetic statistical test may then involve relatively weak, nonparametric techniques or more powerful ANOVA methods. Such choices for both aggregation stages raise immediate questions—questions which we do not try to answer here. Should formal statistical tests be employed for both stages? If so, what is the effect of "double" statistical tests on the experiment-wide significance level? Should the aggregation across responses test be very liberal (say, $p < .30$) and the aggregation across judges test be more conservative (the usual $p < .05$), or vice-versa, or should the respective significance levels be equal? And how would a Bayesian statistician analyze idiographic data?

The issues discussed above are just a sampling of the considerations involved in making a choice between idiographic and nomothetic methods. A more complete integration of the six approaches will require further analysis of these and other related issues. Agreement on the idiographic vs. nomothetic choice may well be the most critical methodological issue for the integration of these approaches. While awaiting a resolution that may or may not exist, it is important that investigators in the field of judgment and decision making be aware of the consequences of the choices they are making when they select an idiographic or nomothetic methodology.

Chapter 11

Diversity in Subjects, Objects, and Tasks

No judgment or decision study presents one subject or stimulus to one subject, judge, or decision maker. For any one study, however, the number of subjects can vary from one to many, as can the number of object stimuli presented. The six approaches differ in the characteristic sample sizes for both subjects and objects, and in the relative importance of diversity of subjects and objects.

Within a single judgment or decision-making study, but more usually across studies, the task or context can vary in two ways. *Substantive* variations are those in global context or problem area: does the task concern land-management policies, medical diagnoses, evaluations of people, or lifting weights? *Formal* variations pertain to changes in presentation mode or response type independent of substantive task content: hypothetical or real gambles, open or closed response formats, intercorrelated or orthogonal cue sets, etc. The distinction between substantive and formal task characteristics was first suggested by Hammond (1966).

Typical sampling patterns for subjects and objects, and degree of diversity in substantive and formal task characteristics are discussed below for each approach. It should be noted that we use the term "sample" in a very loose sense; in particular we do not restrict use of that term to truly random samples from well-defined populations. Rather we refer to a sample as any selection, arbitrary or not, of subjects or judges, and of objects or stimuli. Our concern is not so much the mechanics of the selection process but rather the size of the samples from each domain.

11.1 DECISION THEORY

The methods of DT are usually applied to a single decision maker in any one study. There are exceptions (e.g., Roche, 1971) but the norm is certainly for subject samples of one. The emphasis in DT is on collecting as much information from that single decision maker as is necessary to understand and structure the problem, to conduct an analysis of the various options, to construct the required probability distributions and utility functions, and to gain insights and help for the individual who must make the final decision. For a complete analysis this method may require hundreds of judgments and decisions from a single decision maker (see Keeney, 1977, for an example of an extensive interview with a single person). Across studies, DT methods have been applied to diverse substantive tasks (see Chapters 7 and 8 of Keeney & Raiffa, 1976). Finally, there is some variation of formal task properties in terms of the type of response required. For example, to test the validity of the axioms, the decision analyst may present pair comparison choices, request indifference judgments, or explain the axiom to the decision maker and ask the decision maker to evaluate its validity directly. However, selection of formal task characteristics seems to depend on the situation and convenience and there are no studies evaluating the effect of such formal task variations.

11.2 BEHAVIORAL DECISION THEORY

Studies within the context of BDT generally use more than one subject, but sample sizes are typically not large. On the other hand, samples of stimulus objects tend to be quite large. For example, in Phillips and Edwards (1966) there are from 5 to 12 subjects per experimental group and in Experiment I each subject made 480 judgments. This same pattern of small subject samples and large object samples is repeated in many other BDT studies (e.g., Fryback, 1974; Fischer, 1977).

Across experiments, BDT studies have investigated a wide variety of substantive tasks including such diverse topics as military intelligence and medical diagnosis although many early experiments concentrated exclusively on gambling and bookbag-and-poker-chip tasks (e.g., Peterson, DuCharme, & Edwards, 1968). Formal task characteristics are also of particular interest in the BDT approach. Examples of formal task variations include different probability response modes (Phillips & Edwards, 1966), scoring rules (Jensen & Peterson, 1973) and wholistic vs. decomposed SMART judgments (Gardiner & Edwards, 1974). Work in progress comparing different formal methods for assessing the same multiattribute utility structures can also be considered as focussing on formal task characteristics.

11.3 PSYCHOLOGICAL DECISION THEORY

The recent studies withing PDT (heuristics and prospect theory) reverse the pattern of BDT with respect to subject and object sampling. That is, typical PDT experiments use rather large subject samples with only a few judgments collected from each subject. For example, in Kahneman and Tversky (1979) each subject made at most 12 choices and each choice problem was judged by from 66 to 115 subjects. Tversky's (1978) rationale for this sampling strategy, which is characteristic of the heuristics studies, illustrates the practical and theoretical tradeoffs which influence choices with respect to sampling domains.

> Our choice of research strategy was guided by the fear that the responses to many repetitive questions do not add significant new knowledge, and by the hope that the answers to a few, simple, carefully worded questions will provide useful information about values and beliefs. (p. 8)

A few nonheuristic studies switch the relative emphasis on subject and object replication. For example, Tversky (1967) used only 11 subjects with 225 responses per subject.

The demonstration of heuristic biases—representativeness, availability, anchoring with adjustment, etc.—in a wide variety of substantive tasks (e.g., judging occupation types, guessing letter frequencies, estimating binomial sequence relative likelihoods, and answering almanac questions) has received great emphasis. In contrast, PDT studies have usually not varied formal task characteristics. However, those few studies which have done so provide dramatic evidence of the considerable impact that formal task variations may have on empirical results. Because those studies figure prominently in our integrative comments to follow, we consider several of these studies in some detail.

Kahneman and Tversky (1979) presented subjects with pairs of paired choices between gambles, such as the following problem illustrating the "isolation" effect.

1 In addition to whatever you own, you have been given $1000. You are now asked to choose between:
   A. (Win $1000 with probability .5) or
   B. (Win $500 for sure).

2 In addition to whatever you own, you have been given $2000. You are now asked to choose between:

A′. (Lose $1000 with probability .5) or
B′. (Lose $500 for sure).

According to the SEU axioms, these two choices are equivalent because in either case the effective choice when viewed in terms of final consequences is between:

A′. (Win $2000 with probability .5; otherwise win $1000) and
B′. (Win $1500 for sure).

This formal variation—the appearance but not the substance of the gambles changes from A to $A′$ and B to $B′$—reverses the preference of the majority; the majority prefer B to A and $A′$ to $B′$ (but see the caution in interpreting this result in the discussion above of idiographic vs. nomothetic methods).

Lichtenstein and Slovic (1971) used a bidding procedure to obtain their subjects' maximum buying price (MBP) for a number of gambles. These same subjects were also given the opportunity to choose that gamble (from the same set) which they would most like to "own" or to play. Contrary to axiomatic predictions, for many subjects the gamble with the highest MBP was not the most preferred gamble in the choice task! That is, the formal task variation—changing the response mode from bidding to choosing—resulted in a different preference. A detailed attempt by Grether and Plott (1979) to explain this result as an artifact only succeeded in confirming the original Lichtenstein and Slovic result.

Finally, Tversky (1967) found that utility assessed in riskless situations systematically differed from utility measured in risky situations. Risky utilities exceeded the corresponding riskless utilities (again contrary to SEU axioms) at all points for all but one subject. Again, a formal change which theoretically should not have changed behavior did in fact do so.

11.4 SOCIAL JUDGMENT THEORY

The clear preference of SJT is for small sample sizes (1 to 10) and moderate object samples (20 to 50). In recent policy applications of SJT "subject samples" have consisted of all members of small, identifiable groups (e.g., city council members, labor-management negotiators in a specific dispute, state cabinet officers). A few survey applications of SJT (e.g., Rohrbaugh, 1977) have involved several hundred subjects but these studies are the exception. SJT has also been applied to a variety of substantive topics including clinical judgment, perception, probability learning, and public policy. The diversity of topics within the public policy domain is very similar to the variety of substantive applications of DT and BDT.

More than any other of the six approaches, SJT emphasizes formal task characteristics. In fact in many of the multiple cue probability learning and interpersonal conflict studies (e.g., Mumpower & Hammond, 1974) the emphasis is so much on formal properties (linear vs. curvilinear function forms, intercorrelated vs. orthogonal cue sets, etc.) that the specific judgment task includes a substantive topic mainly for the purpose of holding the interest of the subject.

11.5 INFORMATION INTEGRATION THEORY

In most IIT studies there are moderate-sized samples of both objects and subjects. Typical sample sizes are 10 to 15 subjects and 9 to 25 judgments per subject. As with PDT, there is emphasis on use of a diversity of substantive tasks. In an attempt to show the wide applicability of cognitive algebra IIT has, it seems, applied its methods to the widest variety of substantive tasks of any of the six approaches. Examples include perceptual illusions (Massaro & Anderson, 1971), impression formation (Anderson, 1965), jury decision making (Kaplan & Schersching, 1978), and livestock judging (Shanteau & Phelps, 1977). In fact, IIT has even been applied to characteristic substantive tasks of several of the other approaches: Shanteau's (1970, 1972) experiments on the probabilistic information processing tasks of BDT and Anderson's (1974) attribution studies. Formal task properties have received less but still important attention within IIT. Formal task variations include studies of order effects (primacy-recency), redundancy, inconsistency, etc.

11.6 ATTRIBUTION THEORY

Most studies within the tradition of AT have used rather large subject samples (e.g., 258 in Weiner & Kukla, 1970), and very small object samples (e.g., 118 subjects judged a single object-person in Nisbett & Wilson, 1977). Not only does each subject often receive only one judgment object or stimulus condition, but even between groups there is usually only a limited number of different stimuli presented. There are exceptions; some of the Weiner experiments have used object samples comparable to those used by SJT or IIT (e.g., Frieze & Weiner, 1971, presented 54 combinations of information to each subject for judgment).

AT has investigated a wide variety of substantive tasks. For example, work on self-attribution has been conducted within the contexts of obesity (Nisbett, 1968), insomnia (Storms & Nisbett, 1970), and psychotherapy (Valins & Nisbett, 1971).

With respect to formal task variations, Kelley's covariation principle leads directly to an interest in the effects of information consistency (a formal property) across occasions, objects, and actors. Thus, McArthur (1972) may be viewed as a study of the effects of formal task variations. Order effects in sequential presentation of information are one formal property that has been an important empirical topic within AT (e.g., Jones & Goethals, 1972; Frieze, 1976).

11.7 INTEGRATION

Table 11-1 summarizes the variations across approaches in sample sizes for subjects and objects and in diversity of substantive and formal task characteristics. Of particular note is that every approach has used a wide diversity of substantive tasks. As a body, the six approaches have investigated an impressive variety of substantive topics in the context of judgment and decision problems. The diversity is so great—from economics to psychotherapy—that it seems as if virtually every important topic in the social sciences can be or has been interpreted as a judgment or decision problem by one of the six approaches.

The differences between approaches that do exist in Table 11-1 are (a) the relative sizes of the subject and object samples and (b) the diversity of formal task variations. We comment on each of these issues in turn.

We emphasize that all approaches use both multiple subjects (with the possible exception of DT) as well as multiple judgments or choices per subject. From Table 11-1 it is clear that DT, BDT, SJT, and IIT place more importance on object sampling whereas PDT and AT devote more attention to subject sampling. We note that these differences in relative emphasis are mostly independent of whether an approach uses idiographic or nomothetic methods. The only dependence is that very small samples of either subjects or objects inhibit, respectively, nomothetic or idiographic analysis; yet many studies in all approaches use sufficient sample sizes for either analysis type. Within the four approaches emphasizing object sampling we find the use of both nomothetic and idiographic methods. Evidence exists that a change in the relative emphasis on subject and object sampling can affect a study's

Table 11-1 Sample Sizes and Task Diversities of the Six Approaches

| Approach | Sample size | | Diversity of task or context | |
	Subjects	Objects	Substantive	Formal
DT	1	Large	Wide	Some
BDT	Small	Large	Wide	Yes
PDT	Large	Small	Wide	Few, but significant
SJT	Small	Moderate	Wide	Yes, special emphasis
IIT	Moderate	Moderate	Wide	Yes
AT	Large	Small	Wide	Some

results. For example, Cliff (1959), using large samples (about 200) of subjects and small samples of adverbs and adjectives (about 40 combinations in each experiment), found that a multiplicative model described judgments of the evaluative meaning of adverb-adjective combinations. McClelland (1974) studied the same judgment task using a contrasting sampling strategy—small sample of subjects (21) and a large sample of judgment objects (over 200 adverb-objective combinations) and found serious violations of the multiplicative mode; an "unfolding" model (Coombs, 1964) provided a much better fit to the data. Further, presenting large numbers of repetitive judgments to a single judge might change that person's process for making such judgments. The issue of the relative emphasis of subject vs. object sampling thus certainly deserves additional theoretical work from the six approaches.

Systematic variations of formal task properties have received differential emphases across the six approaches, as is shown in Table 11-1. Further, while the same substantive topics appear in studies across approaches (e.g., gambling tasks in DT, BDT, PDT, and IIT; impression formation tasks in SJT, IIT, and AT), experimentation on any specific formal task variation is generally limited to only one approach. Such specificity is partly due to the theoretical bases of each approach, for often the language necessary to describe any given formal variation is unique to one approach. For example, the formal equivalence of gambles in terms of final consequences as studied by Kahneman and Tversky (discussed above) has meaning only within the Group I approaches which have their origins in axiomatic utility theories (DT, BDT, & PDT) and, for example, variations of intercorrelation patterns among informational cues as studied by SJT are really only describable within the theoretical frameworks of SJT and possibly AT.

Is it important for each approach to investigate the impact of formal task variations? We think so if for no other reason than most studies which have studied formal task properties have found them to have significant and often dramatic impacts (e.g., Mumpower & Hammond, 1974). Of course, it is possible that many investigations of such formal manipulations which did not find effects were not reported. Reactions by researchers to the existence of such potent formal manipulations have been extremely varied. For example, Coombs and Bowen (1971) dismiss effects due to different formal presentations of equivalent gambles as rather uninteresting "display effects" not central to basic theory. Conversely, Kahneman and Tversky (1979) and Tversky (1972a, 1972b) use such effects as a basis for discarding old theories and building new ones—prospect theory and elimination-by-aspects, respectively.

One formal task property that varies across approaches—the use of judgment ratings vs. pair comparison choices or rank order—deserves special attention. The Group I approaches (DT, BDT, and PDT) with their decision theory origins tend to use choice methods for collecting data· that is, the subject or decision maker is confronted with various alternatives (often only two at a time) and must indicate either a preference or indifference among these alternatives. On the other hand, the Group II approaches (SJT, IIT, and AT) usually have the subject make ratings on numerical scales (often presumed to have interval scale properties). There are of course exceptions to that general rule, such as probability estimates in BDT Bayesian studies, choice problems in IIT studies (e.g., Anderson & Alexander, 1971), and "direct preference measures" in DT, but let us proceed with the basic argument. Given such a split in basic methodology, the results of Lichtenstein and Slovic (1971) and Grether and Plott (1979) which show that maximum buying prices (akin to worth ratings) and choice preferences do not give the same results are extremely disturbing, and represent an important barrier to the integration of judgment and decision approaches. Tversky (1969) also suggests that considering alternatives singly as in the case for ratings versus alternatives in pairs as for choices may activate different evaluation processes (e.g., additive vs. additive difference models), thereby producing different results.

The Lichtenstein and Slovic and Tversky results are extremely troublesome for any attempted integration of the Group I and II approaches for they mean that the methods as well as results of one of the two groups may not be transferable to the other. For example, must we ask whether SJT rating methods when applied to choice and decision problems (as in Hammond & Adelman, 1976) actually select the most "desirable" outcome with "desirable" being defined in terms of a choice methodology? We need to answer that and similar questions for the other approaches before a true integration is possible. We should note, however, that Shanteau (1972) obtained the same results using preferential choice ratings (i.e., subject rates his preference for one alternative over another) as with subjective-worth judgments of single alternatives. Similarly, McClelland and Rohrbaugh (1978) found the same violations of the Pareto axiom regardless of whether subjects rated or ranked potential arbitration decisions.

The potency of formal task variations, particularly as compared to the seemingly minimal effects of substantive task variations, suggests that formal task properties require greater attention from all approaches. Conversely, the generalizability of both methods and results over such a diverse range of substantive topics indicates that variety in substantive contexts need no longer be a goal in itself. Further studies of the effects of formal variations would certainly aid the work toward integration.

The prevalence of effects due to formal task variations also bears on an important theoretical issue. It argues that the models of the various approaches are more models of the formal tasks (or at best of the task-judge system) rather than models of people's judgment processes. Brunswik (1952), Brehmer (1969), Edwards (1971) and Dawes (1975) among others have discussed the possibility that our models primarily model the task rather than the person. If such is the case, then differences in the formal properties of the judgment and decision tasks used by different approaches are much more than just methodological idiosyncrasies. Rather, these formal task differences may be the key barriers to effective integration; a resolution of such differences (e.g., a comprehensive theory for both choice and judgment) is fundamental for any attempt to find common ground across judgment and decision approaches.

Chapter 12

Stimulus-Object Decomposition

Each approach must make a methodological as well as a procedural choice about the form of the stimuli or objects to be presented to the subjects or judges. We identify the following three distinct methodological choices for stimulus-object decomposition.

12.1 WHOLE, NON-DECOMPOSED OBJECTS

In this case, the subject sees complete real objects as opposed to the hypothetical, abstract stimuli described below. These objects may be relatively simple (e.g., a photograph) or extremely complex (e.g., a description of the procedures and results of a psychological experiment as in Nisbett & Borgida, 1975, or a complete scenario recorded on tape as in Jones, Davis, & Gergen, 1961). For there to be any interpretable results, the objects must be decomposed prior to the data analysis into relevant variables, attributes, cues, etc. Even with the very complex, complete stimuli, this decomposition process may not be difficult. Often only small portions of the stimuli will vary, so that the appropriate decomposition is obvious to any observer who sees all the stimuli. However, these prior conceptual decompositions of the stimuli are not apparent to the subject, who usually sees one or only a few of the stimuli when whole, nondecomposed objects are used.

12.2 SCHEMATIC STIMULI

The obvious alternative to presenting complete objects is to display a conceptual decomposition of these objects to the judge in schematic form. That is, the stimuli are described in terms of the key variables, cues, etc. that are of interest in the study. So instead of a real object, the subject judges (or selects between two, etc.) only a "profile" that may correspond to a real object or may be hypothetical.

12.3 VARIABLES AS STIMULI

The ultimate decomposition is to ask the judge to respond directly to the variables of interest without ever presenting any real or hypothetical objects. For example, a judge might indicate the weight that he or she would like to place on each variable in a multiattribute decision problem.

A brief example may help make these three distinctions clear. To study the judgments or decisions of a high school student evaluating undergraduate colleges, we can construct three different basic kinds of tasks corresponding to the three methodological choices described above. For the whole object approach, we would ask the student to rate, rank order, or whatever various colleges and universities after visits to a number of campuses or after viewing films about each institution. In the schematic approach, we would ask for responses to colleges described on a number of variables such as student/teacher ratio, number of students, size of library, and quality of football team. Except for profile values on the variables presented the colleges would be unidentified; the profiles may or may not be based on real colleges. Finally, we might ask the student to indicate directly which variables are important for the decision and which are not, or to rank order the variables without presenting descriptions of any real or hypothetical college on those variables.

While we think the three types of decomposition are mutually exclusive, we make no claim that they are exhaustive. They do seem to cover the methodological variety among the six approaches and we now turn to a description of each approach's methodological choices with respect to stimulus decomposition.

12.4 DECISION THEORY

Decision analysts almost always pose their questions to the decision maker in terms of schematic objects, especially in multiattribute applications. There are two distinct types of schematic decompositions employed within DT. The first is decomposition of an alternative into probabilities and outcomes. For example, in a medical context, a decision maker might be asked to consider a given surgical option described in the following schematic form:

Outcome	Probability
Complete recovery	.50
Recovery with disability	.30
Death	.20

The second is decomposition of alternatives into multiple attributes. For example, different sewage disposal alternatives might be described in terms of costs, water pollution, land pollution, and air pollution.

It should be noted that the schematic multiattribute decompositions used in the assessment of utility functions are almost always hypothetical in that they have no real referent and are often very implausible (e.g., a profile with maximum values on all attributes but one with a minimum value on that one). The use of implausible schematic stimuli was until very recently a procedural necessity dictated by practical constraints. It is desirable to assess the relevant model parameters during the interview with the decision maker so that the decision analyst may give the decision maker feedback and also decide which questions are best to ask next. To do so requires that the decision analyst solve relevant DT equations during the interview. Judgments and decisions based on extreme, and hence implausible, alternatives—each attribute in the profile is either at its maximum or minimum value—generate the simplest equations in the context of DT. However, the recent development of interactive computer support systems for decision analysis (Keeney & Sicherman, 1976) suggests that the dependence of DT methods upon the use of extreme, implausible stimuli will decrease.

12.5 BEHAVIORAL DECISION THEORY

Various experiments within BDT have used all methodological choices for decomposition; the following examples demonstrate this methodological variety. In Fryback (1974), undecomposed stimuli consisting of intravenous pyelogram films were presented to radiologists. Gardiner and Edwards (1975) used schematic stimulus profiles (hypothetical coastal developments described in terms of number and density of dwelling units, feet from high tide line, etc.) as well as eliciting importance ratings and rankings of directly presented variables.

12.6 PSYCHOLOGICAL DECISION THEORY

In the heuristics experiments, the subject usually receives a rather complex, undecomposed stimulus—for example, the "personality" descriptions in the base rate studies (Kahneman & Tversky, 1973). Certainly, the important variables which differentiate stimuli are not apparent to the judge. (But see Lichtenstein, Slovic, Fischhoff, Layman & Combs, 1978, for an explicit attempt to make subjects aware of the representativeness and availability variables on which their stimuli varied.) In other studies, however, Tversky (1967, 1969, 1972a) has used schematic, decomposed stimuli in which the differences between objects (or profiles) were purposely made quite clear to the subject.

12.7 SOCIAL JUDGMENT THEORY

Early SJT studies often used real objects of considerable complexity. For example, Hammond and Kern (1959) had medical students judge various characteristics of 36 patients from sound motion pictures of patients being interviewed. In order to analyze the results of such studies, the complex stimuli were sometimes decomposed by having other subjects (sometimes experts) rate the real objects on a number of dimensions (see McClelland & Auslander, 1978, for a recent example of this technique).

In contrast, recent SJT studies (see Hammond, Rohrbaugh, Mumpower, & Adelman, 1977, for many examples) have used schematic stimuli almost exclusively. The subject in a typical experiment judges a series of "profiles" which are descriptions (usually numeric) of an object on a number of variables or cues. These profiles may be descriptions of either real or hypothetical objects. In selecting or constructing these profiles, SJT emphasizes that the set of schematic stimuli should be representative (in terms of formal properties such as means, ranges, and intercorrelations) of the real objects the subject is likely to encounter in the environment. Finally, there are a few SJT studies which ask subjects to respond directly to variables, as is the case when judges indicate the relative importance of cues in their judgment policies by distributing 100 points across those cues (Cook & Stewart, 1975).

12.8 INFORMATION INTEGRATION THEORY

The typical methods of IIT are difficult to place into one of our three categories. Many IIT studies have certainly used complex, real stimuli such as photographs (Lampel & Anderson, 1968; Shanteau & Nagy, 1976) and paragraph descriptions of events during the terms of each U.S. President (Anderson, 1973).

Such stimuli are often combined with each other in factorial designs and then presented as units to the subjects. For example, in a study of the choice of dating partners, Shanteau and Nagy (1976) presented subjects with photographs of prospective partners and probability phrases indicating how likely it would be that the person in the photograph would accept a date from the subject (e.g., "somewhat unlikely"). Each stimulus presentation consisted of both a photograph and a probability phrase; in the analysis, these stimulus pairs are decomposed into their constituent parts—a photo variable and a probability variable—but the complex elements of the photograph are not decomposed further. Thus, despite the use of whole, nondecomposed objects as parts of the stimulus, the method of IIT is more appropriately viewed as an instance of the use of schematic profiles. In this example, the profile consists of two attributes—a photo and a probability label—with the specific photos and labels defining the levels of those attributes. These profiles differ from those used in the other approaches in that only nominal levels of the attributes are specified in IIT studies while other approaches generally use numerical values to designate levels. One of the advantages of IIT's functional measurement methodology (Anderson, 1970) is its ability to measure the subjective values of such nominal attribute levels without the necessity of prior assignment of numerical values to the levels in the schematic profiles. Therefore, it seems that the methods of IIT are best described as being between the whole object and schematic profile approaches as we have defined those.

12.9 ATTRIBUTION THEORY

Of all the six approaches, AT uses the most complex, undecomposed objects. The subjects often respond to elaborate scenarios (recorded on tape or acted live) in which the important variables are purposely not apparent. While the complex stimuli used in many AT experiments have the practical disadvantage of being difficult to construct, they have the advantage of being more complete and more realistic than the schematic stimuli commonly used by the other approaches. Again, we note that the overt complexity of the stimuli does not imply that the conceptual decomposition of the stimuli and the data analysis must also be complex. Indeed, usually only small portions of the stimuli are varied from condition to condition in AT studies so that the decomposition and analysis are generally simpler than in the other approaches.

When schematic stimuli are used they are often like those used by IIT; that is, levels of relevant variables are defined verbally rather than numerically for both subjects and later analyses. For example, Weiner and Kukla (1970) defined student profiles in terms such as "has ability, did not expand effort, has a borderline test result," and generally there are only two levels for each variable (e.g., has ability vs. does not have ability).

12.10 INTEGRATION

All six approaches have sometimes used schematic, decomposed objects as stimuli. Such similarity across approaches should not be surprising, for as many have noted, including Shanteau and Phelps (1977), "decomposition may well be the common foundation of judgment analysis" (p. 259). But "common" is still not "identical" and an important methodological difference does exist among these approaches. That is, IIT and AT use what we might label "minimal decompositions" while the other approaches favor "maximal decompositions," at least when they use schematic decomposition. The IIT and AT decompositions are minimal in the sense that the stimulus presented to the subject still contains more or less real objects (photos, paragraphs) and specification of the levels of variables is via verbal labels. Such labels are minimal because it is still the subject's task to decide which level is more than another as well as how much more. For example in an IIT impression formation experiment the subject must decide, say, whether "methodical" or "organized" is the more likable trait and how much more likable.

In contrast, the maximal decompositions used in DT and in some BDT, PDT, and SJT studies involves the presentation of relatively abstract stimuli which contain few if any components that could be considered as real objects. Instead, the schematic stimuli or profiles of these approaches describe objects mainly in terms of numerical values on specified variables, attributes, or cues. For example, in the Mexico City Airport study (Keeney, 1973a, and deNeufville & Keeney, 1972) alternative airport siting plans are described strictly in terms of numerical quantities such as cost, access time in minutes, number of aircraft operations per hour, number of people displaced by development, etc. There is clearly no ambiguity about whether one level of an attribute is "more than" another level though, of course, the decision maker still decides which level is better.

We are not prepared to argue here whether minimal or maximal decomposition of the schematic stimuli is more appropriate for work in judgment and decision making. Most likely both are necessary in the complete approach and the choice depends on situational constraints as well as purposes for research or application. For example, minimal decomposition is obviously the preferred mode if the purpose of a basic research study is to discover empirically how people interpret information from real objects. On the other hand, if the purpose in an application were to prevent decision makers from using irrelevant or improper variables to evaluate alternatives (e.g., "Is this potential airport site near to the property I own?"), then maximal decomposition which makes explicit or eliminates such variables would be chosen. We suggest therefore that any integrated methodology for judgment and decision making must be able to employ both types of schematic decomposition.

While there seems to be agreement on the usefulness of some type of schematic decomposition, there is less agreement on the presentation of whole, nondecomposed objects or on the use of variables as stimuli. The choice to use decomposed vs. whole stimulus-objects is closely related to the choice of idiographic or nomothetic methods. Approaches such as AT which use real, complex stimuli tend to favor nomothetic methods because of difficulties in constructing many stimuli, while idiographic methods based on many judgments of different objects more often require the use of easily constructable and repeatable stimuli.

Only BDT within the context of the SMART methodology (see Gardiner & Edwards, 1975, or Edwards, 1978) advocates the direct rating of variables in judgment and decision tasks. The claim is that the methods and procedures involved with presentation and analysis of whole objects or schematic stimuli are more complex than simply having the decision maker rank order and rate the importance of the key variables or attributes. Gardiner and Edwards argue that greater methodological complexity is not warranted because most of the models of judgment and decision making are insensitive to error in the estimation of parameters; however, see McClelland (1978) for a cautionary note about this supposed insensitivity.

Chapter 13

Judgment Decomposition

Whatever methodological choices are made with respect to stimulus-object decomposition, each approach must also decide how to decompose the judgments, choices, or preferences during analysis. The general similarities across approaches with respect to judgment decomposition are remarkable: all six approaches analyze judgments in terms of *weights* and *function forms* representing the relationship between object levels of a variable and the person's judgments. Of course, the terms "weight" and "function form" are not used by all approaches, but all use concepts with essentially the same meaning; see the Theory section. However, the similarity ends there, for each approach uses quite distinct methods and procedures in order to decompose responses into weights and function forms. We briefly examine the methods of judgment decomposition employed by each approach.

13.1 DECISION THEORY

In either its unidimensional or multiattribute forms DT is based on a set of axioms which specify a set of conditions which must be satisfied *before* it makes sense to decompose a set of judgments into weights and function forms. Thus many of the DT data collection and analysis methods and procedures are devoted to testing those axioms. What to do when the axioms are violated is not entirely clear. Sometimes the decision analyst finds other attributes or combination rules which remove the violations. In other cases, the analyst explains to the decision maker the meaning and implications of a particular axiom and shows how the decision maker's judgments violate that axiom. The decision maker may then wish to change some judgments in order to be consistent with the axiom. For example, when informed of the intransitivity of their judgments, many decision makers wish to change their judgments so that transitivity is satisfied. The important methodological point is that the decomposition does not proceed until it has been verified that the axioms are reasonably appropriate for the given context. Once the axioms are checked, choice and indifference procedures (described later in the Procedure section) are used to determine the actual weights and function forms.

13.2 BEHAVIORAL DECISION THEORY

Gardiner and Edwards (1975) recognize that their **SMART** methods and procedures depend on several assumptions or axioms. For example, they discuss the "value independence" assumption, but unlike DT do not consider its formal test in the data to be important. Indeed, in the data which they do collect—direct importance ratings of attributes—such tests would be impossible. They dismiss the need for such tests by appealing to the robustness of linear models and by noting the inconvenience of the methods and procedures of the other approaches. Because of this orientation BDT takes the most direct approach to assessing the weights and function forms. First, the judge directly estimates the weights on a ratio scale. The judge may then either specify the function form directly by, say, drawing a picture or provide maximum and minimum feasible values and a direction for each attribute, which are used to construct linear function forms.

13.3 PSYCHOLOGICAL DECISION THEORY

As yet prospect theory of the PDT approach has not been formally tested; it has only been proposed as an explanation for the systematic violations of SEU axioms which have been observed. Thus, although Kahneman and Tversky (1979) present an example of a decomposition (see their figure 4), it is not clear what methods should be used to decompose choices into the uncertainty weights and value functions which are the key components of prospect theory. Tversky (1967) used conjoint measurement to check the suitability as well as to produce the decompositions of his subjects' judgments of risky and riskless alternatives. Other studies in the PDT tradition (e.g., Lichtenstein,

Earle & Slovic, 1975) have used decomposition methods very similar to those of SJT, which are described below.

13.4 SOCIAL JUDGMENT THEORY

Multiple regression is the decomposition method of SJT. Statistically determined beta weights estimate the judgment weights and function forms are derived by adding power terms (e.g., X^2) to the regression analysis. Unlike DT there are no axioms which must be satisfied in order to justify decomposition. Instead the adequacy of the decomposition is assessed post facto by examining the multiple R^2 obtained from the regression. The advantage of this method over DT is that data analysis does not require that the judge satisfy any particular axioms. The disadvantage is that the interpretation of a low R^2 is ambiguous. A low value may be due either to inconsistency by the judge or to the inappropriateness of the particular decomposition (e.g., use of wrong variables or combination rules). This ambiguity is recognized by SJT and methods for its resolution are indicated in Hammond, Stewart, Brehmer, and Steinmann (1975).

13.5 INFORMATION INTEGRATION THEORY

The methods of IIT have in common with SJT the use of a statistical procedure for the decomposition of judgments into weights and scale values. The decomposition into scale values is slightly less restrictive than decomposition into function forms in that conceptual decomposition of the stimuli into attributes is not required prior to analysis; see the discussion of minimal and maximal schematic decomposition in Chapter 12. The major difference between SJT and IIT is that IIT uses analysis of variance (ANOVA) instead of regression designs. This has the disadvantage of strongly favoring the use of orthogonal sets of stimuli because of the statistical complexity associated with nonorthogonal designs. The benefit is the ability to test statistically the "axioms" underlying various combination rules. For example, a significant "row by column" interaction invalidates an additive model and concentration of the ANOVA interaction term in the "linear by linear" or "bilinear" component suggests a multiplicative model (see Anderson, 1970). The essence of the IIT methodology of functional measurement is to check the validity of a specific algebraic model statistically and then to use that validated model to solve for the parameters necessary for the judgment decomposition.

13.6 ATTRIBUTION THEORY

AT is the only one of the six approaches which does not formally decompose judgments into weights and function forms. Because most AT experiments have only two levels for each variable, the concept of function form has no use. Although weights are not explicitly measured, the concept of relative weight is used implicitly in AT research. For example, results on situational versus dispositional attributions can be summarized by a statement such as "actors give more weight to situational variables in explaining their behavior while observers place more weight on dispositional factors for explaining the same behavior." Instead of decomposing judgments into weights and scale values, AT studies generally pit two opposing hypotheses against each other in each judgment task. Thus, at most only relative weights are determined (e.g., "subjects give more weight to this attribute than to that attribute in making causal attributions"). It should be noted, however, that explicit measurement of weights would not be incompatible with most specific attribution theories— particularly with Kelley's "ANOVA cube" model.

13.7 INTEGRATION

While the theoretical concepts of weights and function forms exist for prospect theory and attribution theory, the methods for obtaining them have either not been developed or have not been adequately enough described to allow further discussion here. We will therefore focus our comments in this section mostly on the methods of DT, BDT (specifically SMART), SJT, and IIT.

When applied to a policy problem all four approaches produce results remarkably similar in form: descriptions of judgment or preference policies in terms of weights and function forms. The very different methods for arriving at the decompositions are summarized in Table 13-1 in which the approaches are categorized according to their use of statistical analysis and formal tests of decomposition suitability.

IIT and DT include formal checks for the suitability of decomposition which is not performed unless the necessary conditions are met. The methods of SJT and SMART do not include any similar assessments of the appropriate-

Table 13-1 Classification of Judgment
Decomposition Methods Formal Tests
of Decomposition Suitability

Statistical analysis of decomposition	Decomposition suitability	
	Yes	No
No	DT	BDT (SMART)
Yes	IIT	SJT

ness of further analysis and decomposition. SJT does not perform such tests because it views the statistical procedures of multiple regression analysis as being generally appropriate for assessing the relationship between any set of interval-scale judgments and the cues or attributes upon which those judgments are based. BDT admits the importance of the underlying axioms but omits their verification on the grounds that the axioms are generally true anyway, at least if the decision analyst is careful in developing the set of attributes, and because the typical linear model is very robust even when mild violations of the assumptions exist.

The use of statistical analyses and associated error terms by IIT and SJT allows for a certain amount of inconsistency in the judgments. By contrast, DT and SMART have no formal mechanism for dealing with inconsistency. BDT simply claims that the robustness of the model obviates the problem. DT in its axiomatic form assumes no inconsistency, and the DT methods and procedures take great care to assure this: the decision analyst is almost always present to assist and check each judgment.

13.8 ILLUSTRATIVE EXAMPLE

To explicate further the methodological differences and similarities among these approaches, we now examine how each of the four (DT, BDT-SMART, SJT, and IIT) would analyze a common data set. The hypothetical data set we shall use is based on a study of family composition preferences by Coombs, Coombs, and McClelland (1975). We choose this particular problem because as originally presented the judgments are not suitable for decomposition into weights and function forms. The data are listed in Table 13-2. The example is based on actual data with a few adjustments and assumptions added to make the data amenable to analysis by all four approaches. The first two columns show values on each stimulus on two attributes; the next two show the judge's ratings and rankings of each stimulus. The final columns, "transformed attributes," are explained later. We now examine how each approach would detect and respond to the inappropriateness of judgment decomposition for these data.

13.8.1 Decision Theory

Keeney and Raiffa (1976) would begin by checking the validity of the preferential independence axiom. The essence of that axiom is that if one prefers profile (x, y) to (x', y) then one should also prefer (x, y') to (x', y') no matter what value y' has. The point is that evaluation of x and x' should not depend on whether they are combined in the schematic stimulus with y or y'; in other words, the function form for attribute X should not depend on the level of attribute Y. In this problem, Keeney and Raiffa would be likely

Table 13-2 Hypothetical Data for Comparing Decomposition Methods

Attributes		Judgment	Rank order	Transformed attributes	
X	Y	(rating)	(1 = best)	X*	Y*
0	0	0	16	3	0
0	1	6	12	2	1
0	2	18	7	1	2
0	3	17	8	0	3
1	0	9	11	4	1
1	1	27	3	3	2
1	2	28	2	2	3
1	3	10	10	1	4
2	0	23	4	5	2
2	1	31	1	4	3
2	2	19	6	3	4
2	3	2	14	2	5
3	0	20	5	6	3
3	1	15	9	5	4
3	2	5	13	4	5
3	3	1	15	3	6

to present the judge some of the pairs listed below and ask the judge to select the best or most-preferred member from each pair. Because they have a number of alternate procedures we cannot be stronger than "likely," but they do illustrate this procedure in their 1976 book. Based on the "Rank Order" column of Table 13-2 (with "1" being most preferred), our hypothetical decison maker's response is listed to the right of each pair.

Pair	Choice
A; (0, 0) vs. (1, 0)	(1, 0)
B: (0, 3) vs. (1, 3)	(0, 3)
C: (1, 1) vs. (1, 2)	(1, 2)
D: (2, 1) vs. (2, 2)	(2, 1)

From Pair A we would conclude that level 1 of attribute X is more valuable than level 0 since attribute Y is fixed. However, Pair B implies just the opposite conclusion, thereby violating preferential independence. Pairs C and D demonstrate another violation of independence, this time with X fixed within each pair. Many other pairs of pairs from the data set also violate preferential independence. DT would therefore conclude that no decomposition into weights (they would call them scale factors) and function forms is feasible. The next step (we are now guessing somewhat) would be to explain the principle of preferential independence to the decision maker and to try to determine whether the violations were "real." The analysis would not proceed until either the decision maker modified the choices to conform to preferential independence or until the analyst restructured the problem so that the alternatives could be described on a set of attributes for which preferential independence was satisfied.

13.8.2 Behavioral Decision Theory (SMART)

Gardiner and Edwards (1975) state that "value independence" is necessary for decomposition. In other words, "the extent of your preference for location $[x]$ over location $[x']$ of dimension $[X]$ is unaffected by the position of the entity being evaluated on dimensions $[Y, Z, \ldots]$" (p. 20). Value independence is the same as Decision Theory's preferential independence. However, in the SMART method there is no procedure for checking this property. In this case, they would presumably ask the decision maker to rate the relative importance of each attribute and to draw a value function for each. As we shall see later, while X and Y are reasonable attributes for describing the alternatives, they are not the appropriate attributes for decomposing the judgments. We are not sure, therefore, what would happen next. There are two possibilities: the decision maker might (a) give up in despair and complain that the task made no sense because these are not the attributes useful for making the decision, or (b) simply be compliant and try to provide the necessary parameters. In the latter case, BDT might still detect the problem by comparing wholistic judgments with SMART-produced evaluations of the 16 alternatives.

Thus, we cannot be sure that SMART would detect the inappropriateness of further analysis, nor is it clear what methods would be employed in case the impasse were discovered. Also note that monotonicity (either more of an attribute is better than less or vice-versa throughout its range) which is partly the basis for the robustness claim is clearly violated for these data.

13.8.3 Psychological Decision Theory (Conjoint Measurement)

We have not explicitly considered conjoint measurement as a judgment and decision approach elsewhere. However, it seems appropriate here to examine how conjoint methods would analyze our hypothetical data for two reasons: (a) Tversky, whom we have identified as one of the key investigators within the PDT approach, has also been one of the primary developers of the theory and method of conjoint measurement (e.g., Krantz, Luce, Suppes, & Tversky, 1971; Krantz & Tversky, 1971) and (b) conjoint measurement was the method used in the study on which our example is based.

Conjoint measurement would check the independence or monotonicity axiom (identical to preferential independence in DT and value independence in BDT) and would find it seriously violated. The response of Coombs et al. to such violations was to determine whether the rank orderings and the axiom violations they implied were replicable; the thought was that maybe only the top two or three choices were really definite. However, the replication revealed that each subject produced essentially the same rank ordering as before so further analysis with conjoint measurement was not possible. This began a search for a transformation of the attributes for which independence was satisfied.

13.8.4 Social Judgment Theory

The decomposition method of SJT would be to enter these two attributes as independent variables and the judgment ratings as dependent variables in a multiple regression analysis. POLICY 2, a special computer program which does the regression and then algebraically determines an appropriate weight-function form decomposition, yields the results in Fig. 13-1. The R^2 of .42

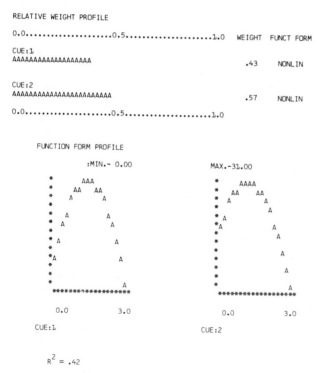

Figure 13-1 Analysis of hypothetical data by SJT (Output from POLICY 2).

would be regarded as an unacceptably low value by SJT. A likely followup would be to present replications to the judge, just as in the conjoint measurement approach, to determine the consistency of the judgments. If consistency were confirmed, then SJT might search for transformations of the attributes which would improve R^2.

13.8.5 Information Integration Theory

Because there is only one subject and there are no replications in our data set, the standard IIT functional measurement methodology using ANOVA would not be possible. Instead, IIT would most likely turn to a graphical test of the parallelism property required of any additive model. Parallelism is essentially equivalent to value and preferential independence: the shape of the function form for one attribute must not depend on the levels of the other attributes. Figure 13-2 shows that parallelism is clearly violated for these data. Each curve represents the function form for one attribute for each possible level of the other. A minimal requirement for parallelism is that the function forms should not intersect; the numerous crossings in these figures rule out constant function forms. IIT would view these figures as evidence of configurality and would not proceed further with the decomposition into weights and scale values. What other algebraic models would be tried next is not clear.

13.8.6 The Transformation

Coombs, Coombs, and McClelland (1975) discovered that an appropriate transformation of attributes for these data is $X^* = X + Y$ and $Y^* = X - Y + 3$. Once this transformation is made (see Table 13-2 again) all the problems blocking the decomposition methods of each approach are resolved. For DT preferential independence is now satisfied; for example, $(5, 2)$ is preferred to $(5, 4)$ and $(1, 2)$ is preferred to $(1, 4)$. Value independence is also satisfied for SMART, and the decision maker is now able to draw a value function for each attribute; however, it is still not monotone in the sense that more is always either better or worse. The function forms derived by SJT decomposition are displayed in Fig. 13-3; the respective relative weights are .26 and .74. R^2 is improved but still is only .78. A decomposition for these data does exist for which $R^2 = 1$; POLICY 2 fails to find it because the actual function forms are more complicated than the parabolas which the program tries to fit to the judgments. The conjoint measurement analysis now proceeds smoothly; details as well as evidence that this transformation is appropriate for describing the family composition judgments of most people can be found in Coombs et al. The parallelism test of IIT is graphed in Fig. 13-4. Because the transformation does not produce a complete factorial design only even-

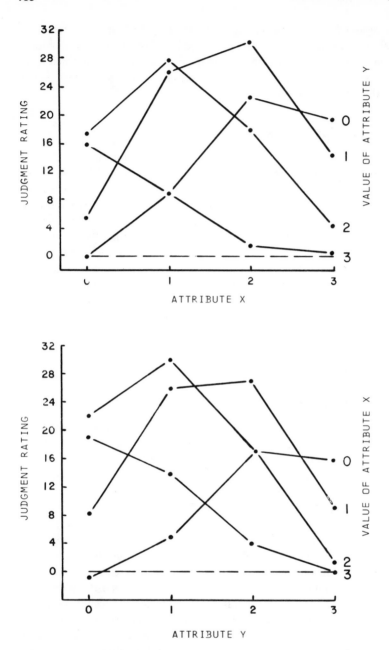

Figure 13-2   IIT's parallelism test for hypothetical data set.

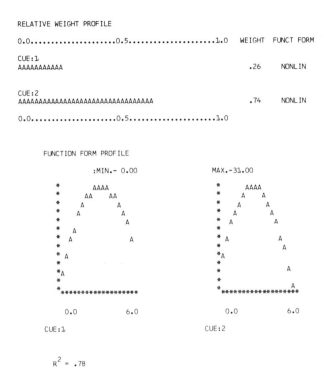

```
RELATIVE WEIGHT PROFILE

0.0....................0.5.....................1.0   WEIGHT  FUNCT FORM

CUE:1
AAAAAAAAAA                                             .26    NONLIN


CUE:2
AAAAAAAAAAAAAAAAAAAAAAAAAAAAAAAAAAAA                   .74    NONLIN

0.0....................0.5.....................1.0
```

```
    FUNCTION FORM PROFILE

             :MIN.- 0.00                MAX.-31.00

        *       AAAA                *        AAAA
        *     AA    AA              *      A    A
        *    A        A             *     A      A
        *   A          A            *    A        A
        *                A          *   A          A
        *   A                       *
        *  A               A        *  A            A
        *                           *                 A
        * A                         * A
        *                           *                A
        *A                          *
        *                           *                 A
        ********************        ********************

           0.0        6.0             0.0        6.0

        CUE:1                         CUE:2
```

$R^2 = .78$

Figure 13-3 SJT analysis of transformed data (Output from **POLICY 2**).

numbered attribute levels should be compared to other even-numbered levels and similarly for odd-numbered levels; when this is done parallelism is clearly staisfied. In summary, analysis now goes reasonably well for all approaches.

13.8.7 Lessons

What have we learned from this rather extended example? We think that there are at least three very important conclusions which we consider in turn below.

First, this example demonstrates that despite the very different methods used to check model validity (e.g., axioms vs. statistics) all approaches have sufficient warning flags to discover inappropriate decompositions—at least for the rather blatant model violations contained in the untransformed version of these data. The main difference lies in the point during analysis at which the problem is discovered. For DT and conjoint measurement discovery comes before decomposition, for IIT it is during attempted decomposition, and for BDT and SJT it is after. Of course, more subtle model deviations may not be detected by all approaches (see Anderson & Shanteau, 1977) but it is

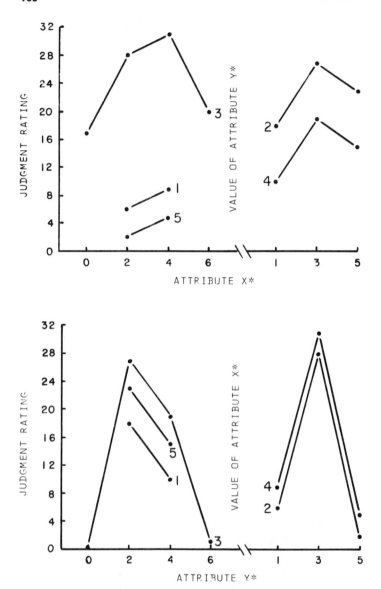

Figure 13-4   IIT's parallelism test for transformed attributes.

encouraging that the very different decomposition methods are sensitive to the suitability of those decompositions.

Second, this example shows that having the correct attributes is essential for a successful decomposition. The original attributes X and Y were quite reasonable for the preference judgment Coombs et al. asked of their subjects. The substantive topic was parents' preferences for alternative family compositions; $X =$ number of boys and $Y =$ number of girls seemed perfectly reasonable attributes for describing the alternatives. However, those attributes clearly fail for analysis, while the transformations $X* =$ family size and $Y* =$ sex balance are quite appropriate.

Third, because having the correct attributes is so critical for a successful analysis, it is striking that in contrast to the explicit, detailed decomposition methods, the different approaches provide no real methods for elicitation and refinement of the attributes. All the approaches insist upon attribute elicitation, but give little instruction about how it should be done; the elicitation process is left as an art. It is interesting to ask whether any of the various decomposition methods would have had any advantage over the others in finding the correct transformation, a 45° axis rotation, in the above example. Of course we know that investigators using conjoint measurement did find the appropriate transformation. However, there does not seem to have been anything specific in the methodology of conjoint measurement which aided Coombs et al. in their search. They simply generated a number of plausible decision rules which their subjects might have used and then tested the implications of those rules in the data. Any method which allows the testing of alternative composition rules or organizing principles (i.e., DT, SJT, or IIT but not SMART of BDT) could have done much the same. Raiffa (1968, p. 258) has considered precisely this transformation as a means of achieving judgmental independence for certain problems, so DT could claim that it is at least aware of the need to look for such transformations. But does DT have any explicit methods for the search? Unfortunately not. Raiffa (1968) states:

> We can generalize and say that it is sometimes possible to circumvent the problem of judgmental dependence by concocting meaningful, auxiliary, mathematically related quantities that are judgmentally independent. This is one of the *tricks of the trade.* (italics ours) (p. 259)*

Indeed, all approaches seem to have left the problems of eliciting, defining, and transforming attributes as "tricks of the trade." Again, this stands in sharp contrast to the extremely explicit methods advocated for using those attributes once obtained.

A final point concerning the example: this attempt to apply the various methods to a common data set has convinced us that such a procedure is an invaluable tool for highlighting methodological similarities, differences, and gaps among the approaches. Other attempts to apply the methods of the approaches to a common problem (e.g., Shanteau & Phelps, 1977) have also been extremely informative, so we can only conclude that further integration of judgment and decision approaches will require many more such efforts.

*Howard Raiffa, *Decision Analysis,* © 1968, Addison-Wesley, Reading, Massachusetts, p. 259. Reprinted with permission.

Chapter 14

Methods of Partitioning the Judgment/Decision Problem

As a result of attempts to make complex decision and judgment problems tractable both for decision makers and for research, DT, BDT, and SJT have developed explicit methods by which the decision maker can "divide and conquer" the decision or policy problem. The general methods used by the various approaches are so similar that separate descriptions of each would be redundant. Therefore, communalities and differences between Group I and Group II approaches are noted first.

14.1 METHODS FOR COMPLEX DECISIONS

Figure 14-1 depicts the prototypical decision or policy problem. The adjective "prototypical" is justifiable because more or less the same figure appears in publications from DT (see Fig. 1 in Keeney, 1976, and Fig. 7.6 in Keeney & Raiffa, 1976), BDT (Fig. 3 in Gardiner & Edwards, 1975) and SJT (Fig. 2 in Hammond, Rohrbaugh, Mumpower, & Adelman, 1977). As indicated in Fig. 14-1, there are two basic steps to solving any decision or policy problem. The first is the "knowledge" step: identification of the options and description of

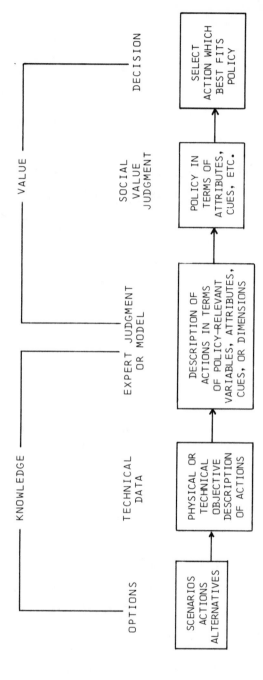

Figure 14-1 Diagram of prototypical decision problem.

them in terms of variables (dimensions, cues, attributes, etc.) upon which a meaningful policy can be based. For example, when Hammond and Adelman (1976) helped a city council select handgun ammunition for a police department, the options—bullets—were described in terms of injury, stopping effectiveness, and danger to bystanders—attributes that were meaningful for policy judgments but far removed from the physical properties of the original bullets. Second is the "value" step, involving a description of the system to be used to evaluate or judge an option described on the variables resulting from the first step. The value step culminates in selection of the option that best "fits" (usually maximizes, but other definitions are possible) the policy or the decision maker's values.

The emphases of the knowledge and value steps in Fig. 14-1 correspond to the different interests of the Group I and Group II approaches defined in the Theory section. Historically, Group II psychological theories of judgment have aimed primarily at questions of knowledge, with judgment for choice or decision treated as a special case, if at all. This statement is true not only for SJT, IIT, and AT but also for other psychological approaches to judgment. The central problem in the knowledge step is locating an entity on various judgment dimensions. For example, all research on clinical judgment fits into this paradigm. But until recently most judgment theories have had little interest in the value portion of the process. As a consequence most of the methods of psychological approaches were developed to describe, explain, or predict a judge's knowledge.

On the other hand, Group I approaches have concentrated traditionally on questions of value, giving less attention to knowledge questions. For example, in their pioneering work, von Neumann and Morgenstern (1947) simply assume the objective probabilities are known and then produce an axiomatic theory for the measurement of values. So while elaborate methods have been developed to measure values or utilities, less attention has been given to measurement of "facts." "Knowledge" traditionally entered DT usually only in the form of probabilities—either objective or subjective. Although sophisticated assessment procedures for subjective probabilities have been developed, there is usually no attempt to uncover the bases of a person's subjective probabilities; they are simply assessed and taken as is as long as they are consistent. One exception is the use of Bayesian statistics to incorporate new information, but that is an organizing principle which says nothing about the origin of the subjective probabilities.

The above stereotypes are too pat, but probably not overly unfair. However, while the stereotypes of basic judgment and decision methods apply to the historical and traditional approaches, the distinction has become increasingly blurred since about 1970, which for some reason seems to be a watershed year. Raiffa's first multiattribute utility (MAUT) paper was in 1969 and the first actual applications occurred in the early 1970s; Edwards' social value paper appeared in 1971; SJT social policy applications also began in the early 1970s and the 1975 "bullet" study seems to have been SJT's first full-scale application involving both knowledge and value steps; although IIT has no practical applications of social policy, the joint work of Shanteau and Anderson around 1970 moved IIT into the value portion of Fig. 14-1. Because both judgment and decision approaches were now coping with the total decision or policy problem, judgment approaches had to deal with values and decision approaches had to consider knowledge issues more seriously.

What did each basic approach do when faced with new, unfamiliar problems to solve? Each simply transferred as much of its existing methods for one (knowledge or value) into the other. We follow below in more detail exactly what each approach did as it entered new territory.

14.2 DECISION THEORY

The essence of the knowledge step is describing the alternatives on attributes upon which it makes sense to have preferences. DT would most like to have a probability distribution for each option on each attribute, but settles in most applications for point-estimates. How does DT obtain probability distributions or point-estimates? Any way reasonable. Keeney and Sicherman (1976) clearly state the eclectic approach of DT to knowledge questions: The probabilities "may be specified using any combination of analytical models, simulation models, subjective assessments, and data that is available and appropriate" (p. 174). Common methods are the use of simulation models and expert judgment; both are illustrated in a study of fire department operations (Keeney, 1973b; see also Keeney & Raiffa, 1976, Chapter 7) which we describe below.

The fire department problem concerns quantity and quality of equipment, location of equipment, quantity and quality of personnel, etc.—the goal being the most efficient use of available resources. However, these input variables are not very meaningful for measuring fire department efficiency. Fig. 14-2, reproduced from Keeney and Raiffa (1976) shows the steps taken. First, a simulation model developed from available objective data translates locations on the input variables into the somewhat more meaningful attributes of engine and ladder response times (firemen supposedly evaluate everything in terms of response time). That does not solve the knowledge problem, for response times are still one step removed from what the decision maker needs to know to evaluate policy options: number of fatalities and injuries, amount of physical damage, physical and mental fatigue of fire department personnel, and so on.

For various reasons it was not possible to use objective data or existing simulation models to relate response time to the desired attributes, so Keeney turned to expert judgment to supply the missing link. The important

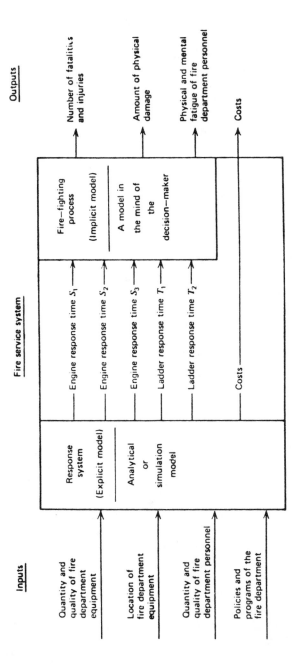

Figure 14-2 Simplified model of a fire department service system. From Keeney & Raiffa, 1976, p. 379. Copyright © John Wiley & Sons, Inc. Reprinted by permission.

methodological point is that *choice* procedures were used to assess the technical expert's *knowledge*. In this case, Keeney measured the deputy fire chief's *preferences* for various engine and ladder response times. Standard DT assessment techniques involving lotteries were used. For example, the deputy chief was indifferent between a 50-50 chance that the first ladder would arrive in either 1 or 5 minutes or that the first ladder would arrive in 3.4 minutes for sure.

Interestingly, the alternatives are never described in terms of the final evaluation attributes (fatalities, etc.). Instead the deputy chief's preferences are substituted as a "proxy" attribute with the presumption that his preferences are based solely on his knowledge of how best to fight fires and his knowledge of what equipment is needed when. This proxy attribute method has the effect of hiding the expert's implicit weighting of fatalities, property damage, fireman fatigue, etc. in his definition of the best way to fight fires. Not everything is hidden, however: the analysis produces a description of the deputy chief's expert judgment policy in terms of function forms and relative weightings for engine and ladder response times as well as specification of the multilinear organizing principle. The important point is that choice methods, originally developed for value problems, were used to measure knowledge. The other examples in Chapter 7 and the Mexico City airport problem in Chapter 8 of Keeney and Raiffa (1976) are similar in their approach to knowledge issues. Two of the examples (7.4 and 7.7.1) involve no choice at all; that is, they are purely knowledge or judgment studies!

14.3 BEHAVIORAL DECISION THEORY (SMART)

Step 8 of the SMART procedure (see Gardiner & Edwards, 1975) is to "measure the location of each entity being evaluated on each dimension," (p. 17) which we consider to be part of the knowledge step. Unfortunately BDT does not have very explicit methods as to how this is to be done. Gardiner and Edwards do distinguish three types of dimensions: (a) purely subjective, (b) partly subjective, and (c) purely objective. There is obviously no problem for the objective case. In the subjective cases knowledge issues are approached by "simply getting an appropriate expert to estimate the position of that entity on that dimension on a 0 to 100 scale" (p. 17). In general, knowledge issues are regarded as not difficult enough to require the complex procedures of DT. For example, Gardiner and Edwards indicate that any disagreements at Step 8 (disagreements about fact) should be resolved by "the simple expedient of asking only the best available expert for each dimension to make [fact] judgments about that dimension" (p. 32). More recent work within BDT has gone beyond this to use more sophisticated solution methods such as simulation models, but in general the BDT methods as represented by SMART pertain mostly to the value step and leave the knowledge step to someone else.

14.4 SOCIAL JUDGMENT THEORY

SJT is a cognitive theory and its methods pertain primarily to the knowledge part of Fig. 14-2. Those methods are designed to assess a person's knowledge in terms of utilization of cue information. But what is to be done when policy choices must be made? For SJT the transition is easy: value judgments are just another type of judgment and the same methodology can be applied. A disadvantage of this facile transfer is that assumptions underlying the knowledge step may be unwittingly transferred to the value arena along with the methods. For example, when Hammond, Mumpower, and Smith (1977) ask the reader to "consider ... a person who must form a judgment about the type of growth *appropriate* for his community" (italics ours, p. 358) it almost seems as if there is a "right" answer to be found. It is clearer that values are involved when they state that "the policy maker's task is ... to integrate information ... into a *judgment that indicates a preference*" (italics ours, p. 358). Notice the reversal from DT: for SJT judgments indicate preferences but for DT preferences indicate judgments. So just as DT moved its choice methods from the value step to the knowledge step of the problem, SJT has moved its judgment methods from the knowledge step to the value step. This is most clearly illustrated in Hammond and Adelman (1976).

14.5 INTEGRATION

For the three approaches which have been applied to social problems (DT, BDT, and SJT), a degree of integration already exists—all would agree that Fig. 14-1 more or less represents the basic structure of policy decisions. An important strategy common to all three approaches is the methodological separation of the knowledge and value portions of Fig. 14-1. The separation is often so complete that judgments or choices made by different people are used in the knowledge and value steps. Such separation is a reflection of the "divide and conquer" strategy which permeates most approaches to judgment and decision making. Hammond and Adelman (1976) also claim an additional advantage: "The separation phase permits elected representatives to function exclusively as policy-makers, and scientists to function exclusively as scientists" (p. 395).

While there is agreement on the global methods for policy and decision problems, we have noted that each approach has had to apply its methods to a new domain in order to solve the complete problem. None of the approaches seems to have given much thought as to whether its transfers are appropriate or whether other, better alternatives exist. One obvious possibility would be to use judgment methods for the knowledge step and choice methods for the value step. A practical assessment of that strategy remains to be done.

A second area of common ground lies in the increasing use of simulation models. In the most recent applications of their methods, DT, BDT, and SJT all seem to be turning whenever possible to the use of simulation models to replace the judgments of technical experts on knowledge issues. With more and more reliance on computer models the question arises as to exactly how human judgment influences model development. Are the judgment aspects hidden in the models? How are such models built; do any of the six approaches have any suggestions for improving them or facilitating their construction?

There are, of course, many methods besides "divide and conquer" for aiding decision makers in complex judgment and decision tasks. Two important classes of such methods are debiasing techniques and consistency-improving techniques. "Debiasing" methods are based on the premise that many "errors of judgment are often systematic rather than random, manifesting bias rather than confusion" (Kahneman & Tversky, in press, p. 1). Conversely, consistency-improving techniques are aimed at reducing random errors of judgment. We refer the reader to Kahneman and Tversky (in press b), Lichtenstein, Slovic, Fischhoff, Layman, and Coombs (1978), and Timmers and Wagenaar (1977) for examples of debiasing methods and to Goldberg (1970, 1976), Dawes (1971), Dawes and Corrigan (1974), and Hammond, Rohrbaugh, Mumpower, and Adelman (1977) for consistency techniques.

Procedure

Chapter 15

Introduction to Procedure

This section describes the procedures used by the six approaches. The appropriate distinction between procedures and methods (discussed in the previous section) is somewhat elusive. Most dictionaries, for example, give almost synonymous definitions of the two terms. We have attempted here to maintain a distinction similar to that between strategy and tactics; whereas the methodology section was concerned with "grand plans" for action, the present section is concerned with specific techniques used to carry out those plans.

Our attempts to contrast and compare the procedures used by the six approaches encountered several difficulties worth mention. First, while proponents' descriptions of their approaches usually discuss at length their theoretical starting points and principles and frequently describe in detail their methodological orientation, neither specific procedures for implementation nor the links between theory, method, and procedure are commonly found in such descriptions. For most approaches, there is no one source that provides a definitive and exhaustive description of its procedures. Since we had little or no direct experience with the procedures of several of the approaches, we therefore had to rely substantially upon review and interpretation of multiple sources in developing descriptions of the approaches' procedures. Obviously, such methods are less than ideal and likely to lead to incompleteness, inaccuracy, and imprecision.

A second problem was that none of the approaches rely exclusively on a single set of procedures. For almost any generalization concerning an approach's procedures, an exception can somewhere be found. If consistency is the hobgoblin of small minds, then (if one looks only to the procedures they use) there are only superior intellects at work on judgment and decision problems. Moreover, the situation is complicated by the fact that the various approaches subsume multiple intended aims and functions. Some of the six approaches are concerned almost exclusively with basic research on judgment and decision processes, some are oriented more toward practical applications, and still others share both aims (see Chapter 5, *Intended Functions*). And, for those approaches with multiple aims and functions, the procedures used in basic research and those used in practical application are not always identical. (The difficulties in this respect were made salient when the authors found that, not infrequently, we disagreed among ourselves concerning the "standard" procedures of those approaches with which we considered ourselves quite familiar.)

Finally, the appropriate criteria for comparing and contrasting procedures are not readily apparent. We might have chosen, for example, congruence with theoretical precepts and methodological principles as the major criterion for comparing procedures. Such congruence would seem to possess considerable validity as a criterion, since coherence among theory, method, and procedure seems necessary for an approach to be described as well-developed. On the other hand, an argument could be made that the most appropriate criteria for comparison and contrast are pragmatic in nature. That is, it could be argued that the comparison should focus on such questions as, say, which procedures are easiest to use or which lead to the most "veridical" descriptions of judgment and decision processes. And, additional candidates for appropriate criteria are easily generated.

Our decision was to make the procedure section as descriptive, neutral, and nonevaluative as possible. We attempt simply to identify and describe as thoroughly as possible similarities and differences among approaches in their procedures. We try to describe the most common procedures in use within an approach. We consider those procedures used in basic research as well as those used in practical application for approaches sharing both intended functions. We try not to speculate about implications of similarities and differences among approaches in procedures.

15.1 PLAN FOR THE PROCEDURE SECTION

The procedure section is organized around the lens model diagram presented in Fig. 15-1. This is a slightly elaborated version of the lens model diagram

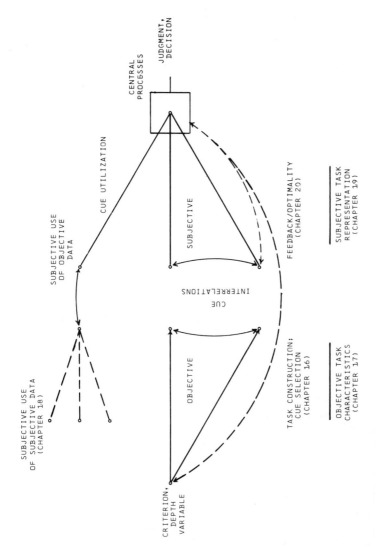

Figure 15-1 Lens Model representation of judgment and decision processes.

173

Table 15-1 Hypothetical Example of Summary Chapter Table

Topic	DT	BDT	PDT	SJT	IIT	AT
15.X Procedural practice						
Practice 1	X^a	X	X			
Practice 2				X	X	X
15.X.X Concept						
Operationalization A	$*^b$	X	X	X		*
Operationalization B				X		X

^{a}Indicates routine use of procedural practice or routine operationalization of concept.
^{b}Indicates occasional use of procedural practice or occasional operationalization of concept.

presented in Fig. 7-1, around which the *Loci of Concepts* chapter was organized.

The procedure section consists of four chapters in addition to this one. Chapter 16 discusses task construction and cue selection. Chapter 17 discusses objective characteristics of judgment and decision tasks. Chapter 18 discusses the subjective use of subjective data. Chapter 19 discusses subjective representations of the task, including (a) subjective representations of observable task element interrelations, (b) the subjective use of objective data, (c) cue utilization, and (d) central processes. Chapter 20 discusses feedback, optimality, and other concepts related to interactions between judges and task. Thus, in general, the procedure section moves from left to right across Fig. 15-1, or from "outside" to "within" the judge.

Each chapter contains a summary table around which the narrative for that chapter is organized. Table 15-1 is a hypothetical example of such a summary table. Each table contains six column headings corresponding to the six approaches. The rows of each table identify either (a) a particular procedural practice or (b) a particular operationalizable concept. An X entered under the appropriate column signifies that the indicated approach (a) routinely follows the procedural practice or (b) commonly operationalizes the concept identified on that row of the table. An asterisk (*) entered under the appropriate column signifies that the indicated approach either (a) sometimes follows the procedural practice or (b) sometimes operationalizes the concept identified on that row of the table. A blank entry signifies that the indicated approach never or almost never follows the identified procedural practice or that it does not contain the identified concept. Related procedural practices and similar concepts are generally grouped together in the summary table under generic headings.

Each chapter concludes with a brief overview.

Chapter 16

Task Construction/ Cue Selection

An appropriate place to begin discussion of procedures is with task construction and cue selection, or the manner in which the judgment or decision analyst proceeds in constructing and presenting a task for the judge or decision maker. It is with respect to this activity that there is perhaps greatest uncertainty as to what constitutes methods and what constitutes procedures. Several of the issues discussed in this chapter are therefore also discussed at greater length in the methodology section, and it is recommended that the reader interested in task construction and cue selection review the method section carefully.

This chapter discusses seven topics concerning task construction and cue selection:

1 Task specification by the judge versus specification by the analyst;
2 Maintenance of the fact/value distinction;
3 The type of response required from the judge;
4 Design of the task;
5 The level of abstraction at which attributes are presented;

6 The metric of the attributes;
7 Iteration.

Major similarities and differences among the approaches with respect to task construction and cue selection are summarized in Table 16-1.

16.1 TASK SPECIFICATION BY JUDGE VERSUS ANALYST

A primary issue is that of who defines the nature of the judgment or decision problem and identifies its dimensions. This issue appears to be resolved primarily on the basis of the intended function of the judgment or decision analysis. If the intended function of the analysis is to aid the judge or decision maker in the context of an applied problem, then the primary responsibility for specifying the task is that of the judge or decision maker (or "client"), while the analyst plays the role of an elicitor or facilitator. If the intended function of the analysis is empirical research on judgment and decision processes, then the analyst or researcher ordinarily specifies the problem, while the judge (or "subject") merely responds to the pre-determined task.

16.1.1 Specification by the Judge

DT's primary function is to aid decision makers with applied decision problems. Almost without exception, therefore, in the DT approach the decision maker defines the problems and its dimensions with the assistance and direction of the analyst. The same holds true for BDT and SJT in their applied versions.

All three approaches are somewhat imprecise concerning procedures for the important step of eliciting specification of the problem and its dimensions from the decision maker. All three seem to view the process as a creative one which is much more an art than a science. There is little likelihood, for example, that proponents of BDT or SJT would disagree with Keeney and Raiffa (1976), when they say:

> The intertwined processes of articulating objectives and identifying attributes are basically creative in nature. Thus, it is not possible to establish a step-by-step procedure that leads one in the end to a meaningful set of objectives and attributes. (p. 64)*

Of the three approaches, DT discusses most extensively procedures for specifying the decision problem and its dimensions (e.g., Keeney & Raiffa,

*Copyright © 1976 John Wiley & Sons, Inc. Reprinted by permission.

Table 16-1 Comparison of Approaches with Respect to Task Construction/Cue Selection

Topics in task construction/cue selection	Approach					
	DT	BDT	PDT	SJT	IIT	AT
16.1 Task construction— task specification by judge versus analyst						
Definition of problem and its dimensions by judge	X^a	X		X		
Definition of problem and its dimensions by analyst		X	X	X	X	X
16.2 Task construction— fact/value distinction						
Distinction maintained	X	X		X		
16.3.1 Task construction— type of response, judgments of preference/utility						
Lotteries	X	X	X			
Direct specification		X		*^{b}		
Wholistic ratings			*	X	X	
16.3.2 Task construction— type of response, judgments of inference						
Choice		X	X			X
Evaluations			*	X	X	X
16.3.3 Task construction— type of response, probability estimation						
Lotteries/probability wheel	X	X	X			
Direct specification	X	X	X			
16.4 Task construction—design						
Within subjects	X	X	X	X	X	
Between subjects		X	X	X	X	X
16.5 Cue selection—level of abstraction						
Objects			X		*	X
Decomposed objects	X	X		X	X	
Variables		X				
16.6 Cue selection—metric						
Qualitative—continuous	X	X	X	X	X	*
Qualitative—discrete	X	X	X	*	X	X
16.7 Iteration						
Iteration practiced	X	X	*	X	*	*

^{a}Indicates that an approach routinely follows procedure or operationalizes concept.
^{b}Indicates that an approach sometimes follows procedure or operationalizes concept.

1976, pp. 31-65). They recommend that the *objectives* defining the decision problem first be identified. Objectives may be identified by examination of the relevant literature and analytical study of the problem, as well as by interaction with the decision maker(s). Questions put to decision makers are of the sort, "What's important?", "Why is it important?", "What else is important?", etc.

The next step is the location of identified objectives within a hierarchical structure. The *hierarchy* establishes the relative importance and generality of objectives. Major objectives are more general and more inclusive than the lower order objectives related to them. The hierarchy is usually established by a trial-and-error procedure involving questions about means-ends relationships. The most general test for whether or not an objective should be included in the hierarchy is whether the decision maker(s) answers affirmatively when asked whether the best imaginable course of action might change if that objective were excluded from the hierarchy.

Finally, *attributes* associated with each objective must be identified. Attributes should be comprehensive and measurable. An attribute is *comprehensive* if particular levels of an attribute clearly indicate the extent to which the associated objective has been achieved. An attribute is *measurable* if it is feasible to obtain estimates of (a) the probability distribution over the possible levels of the attribute for each alternative and (b) the decision maker's preferences for different levels of the attributes. Some attributes are objective, measuring the associated objective directly (e.g., the attribute "dollars" may be associated with the objective *increase profits*). They may also be subjective indices (i.e., measured subjectively), proxy attributes (i.e., measure the objective indirectly), or direct preference measurements. The attributes to be associated with specific objectives are selected on a trial-and-error basis, with the analyst asking questions to insure that the attributes are comprehensive and measurable (e.g., "Is there anything else you would need to know other than the value of attribute x in order to know how well objective X was achieved?"). The decision analyst also questions the decision maker and inspects the final set of attributes in order to determine that the set is complete, operational, decomposable, nonredundant, and minimal.

BDT discusses the step of defining the decision problem and its dimensions less extensively than DT, but more so than SJT. Although the procedures are described in less detail than by DT, they appear to be generally quite similar. BDT (Gardiner & Edwards, 1975) notes, however, that (a) often it is practical and useful to ignore the hierarchical structure of goals or objectives and instead specify a simple list of goals that seem important for the purpose at hand and (b) the number of objectives or goals identified should be kept to a minimum.

SJT does not discuss at length the appropriate procedures for identifying and defining judgment or decison problems, noting (Hammond, Stewart,

Brehmer, & Steinmann, 1975) that the "methods used in this step are highly situation (and investigator) specific" (p. 277). SJT maintains, however, that this step is critical for the success of the analysis and warns that it is important to identify all major cues involved in the problem.

16.1.2 Specification by Analyst

For five of the six approaches, it is sometimes the judgment analyst or researcher rather than the judge or decision maker who defines the problem. DT is the sole exception; its sole intended function is use in applied decision problems, and it conducts little or no basic empirical research on judgment or decision processes. Basic research within DT is ordinarily logical or mathematical in character.

BDT, PDT, SJT, IIT, and AT all conduct basic empirical research concerning human judgment or decision making. In such research the judgment or decision problem and its dimensions are defined by the researcher. The procedures for this step are grist for the philosophy of science mill, and no attempt will be made to describe them here. Suffice it to say that the procedures are perhaps even more situation and investigator specific in basic research than in applied work.

16.2 FACT/VALUE DISTINCTION

In applications, a basic procedural question is "who makes what judgments?" The three approaches actively involved in applications, DT, BDT, and SJT, all seem to agree that (a) policy makers should make judgments about values or preferences and (b) substantive experts should make judgments about facts or inferences about environmental attributes. (See, from DT, Keeney & Raiffa, 1976, pp. 377-390; from BDT, Ford & Gardiner, 1979; from SJT, Hammond, Rohrbaugh, Mumpower, & Adelman, 1977).

The procedures by which particular policy makers and experts are selected to make judgments are not explicitly laid out by any of the approaches, however. In general, the policy makers who make the value judgments are those somehow identified as individuals or groups with a legitimate voice in the decision (e.g., see Hammond & Adelman, 1976). Experts are usually identified on a more ad hoc basis, although they ordinarily possess recognized stature within their discipline (e.g., see Adelman & Mumpower, in press).

16.3 TYPE OF RESPONSE

There exists great variety within and across approaches with respect to the nature of the responses demanded by judgment or decision tasks and the procedures used to elicit them. In this regard, it is useful to distinguish among three different types of judgment or decision tasks.

First, five of the six approaches, DT, BDT, PDT, SJT, and IIT are frequently interested in judgments or decisions related to *preference, value, desirability,* or *utility.* Such tasks require the individual to evaluate a level of an attribute (or a set of attribute levels) with respect to its ·relative desirability or utility (or along some similar dimension). The purpose of eliciting such responses is to obtain information that is either helpful for guiding the judge's choice for action (in DT, and in the applied versions of BDT and SJT) or useful for describing, understanding, or predicting the manner in which the judge uses or integrates multiple pieces of information in making a judgment (in BDT, PDT, SJT, IIT). Such judgments are instances of what was described in Chapter 4, *Scope,* as the single-system case; it is not meaningful to refer to an environmental criterion or correct answer for such judgment or decision problems.

Second, five of the six approaches are frequently involved with *inferences* about states of affairs in the world; these are BDT, PDT, SJT, IIT, and AT. Such inferences may have implications for action or choice, but not necessarily so. In such tasks, the judge is asked to express his or her inference about the "true" state of the world, given certain pieces of information. For instance, the judge may be asked to estimate the value of a distal variable or to make an attribution concerning characteristics of an individual on the basis of a set of cue or attribute values. Paradigmatically, such inferences are instances of the double-system case, since in principle there exists an environmental criterion or "correct answer." Such judgments constitute instances of the single-system case, however, in those frequent cases in which the value of the environmental criterion or correct answer is intrinsically unknown or unknowable.

Finally, and to some extent a special case of the second type of task, three of the six approaches (DT, BDT, and PDT) quite frequently construct tasks in which the judge is required to make *probability estimates.* These may be either estimates of the probability of an event occurring, estimates of the probability of a hypothesis given an event, or estimates of the probability of an event given a hypothesis. Probability estimation tasks can generally be regarded as instances of the double-system case, since a value of the criterion or the correct answer can usually be specified, but they can be distinguished by the manner in which the value of the criterion or correct answer is specified. In judgments of inference in the double-system case, the criterion or correct answer is empirically specified. In probability estimation, it is analytically specified on the basis of normative rules of information processing. Probability estimation tasks appear both in basic research and in practical applications.

In this regard, it should be noted that DT, BDT, and PDT are ordinarily concerned with such "risky" decision making, or decision making under conditions of uncertainty, although DT and BDT are increasingly also concerned with "riskless" decision making, or decision making under conditions of certainty. SJT, IIT, and AT, on the other hand, are ordinarily concerned with riskless decision making, but exceptions can be cited for all three approaches. IIT has devoted substantial attention to risky decision making (e.g., Shanteau, 1975); SJT has occasionally constructed tasks requiring judges to give probability estimates (e.g., Hammond, Stewart, Adelman, & Wascoe, 1975); and, AT appears to be moving toward including tasks involving probability estimation (e.g., Ross, 1977). In terms of procedures, however, it is still more likely to find questions of the sort, "How likely is it that . . . ?", in the first three decision or "probability" theories than in SJT, IIT, or AT.

We now turn to the specific procedures most frequently found in each of the three types of tasks: those involving judgments of preference or utility, those involving judgments of inference, and those involving probability estimation.

16.3.1 Judgments of Preference or Utility

Within DT, the decision maker's responses can take several forms in tasks concerning judgments of preference. Most often they are written or verbal responses to questions about the decision maker's ordinal preferences between pairs of alternatives, particularly alternatives involving lotteries. For instance, decision makers are commonly asked to express their ordinal preferences between two lotteries of the form "receive outcome x_1 with probability p or outcome x_2 with probability $1-p$," or between an option of the form "receive consequence x_c with certainty or receive a lottery offering outcome x_1 with probability p or outcome x_2 with probability $1-p$." The purpose of these questions is to identify pairs to which the decision maker is indifferent. The responses to these questions can then be used in determining whether certain necessary theoretical axioms for DT are satisfied, and, if so, to construct a model of the judge's utility function. The specific procedures used to elicit these responses (and variations in the types of alternatives presented and responses required) are described in greater detail in Chapter 19. The important point here is that the task presented the decision maker requires only the expression of ordinal preferences between alternatives; the parameters of the model of the decision maker's decision processes are then derived from those responses.

The last point is important because BDT differs substantially from DT in the procedures it uses to estimate the parameters of models of decision makers' decision processes. Although DT and BDT share similar theoretical orientations, rather than deriving the parameters of the utility function describing the individual indirectly from expressions of ordinal preference, BDT frequently requires the decision maker to specify directly values of those parameters. That is, the decision maker is asked to indicate directly the relative importance of the various attributes of the decision problem (e.g., by assigning numbers to them in proportion to their relative importance) and to describe directly the shape of the value curves relating levels of attributes to utility (e.g., by drawing a cruve). Such direct specification procedures are used in applications of the BDT approach; basic research within BDT has sometimes relied upon techniques more similar to those described for the DT approach.

PDT relies extensively on the ordinal preference method described above for the DT approach. The judge is most commonly asked to make choices between two lotteries, between a certainty equivalent and a lottery, or between complex combinations of lotteries and/or certainty equivalents (e.g., Kahneman & Tversky, in press [a]). PDT has also at times used procedures involving wholistic ratings of utility or desirability, similar to those described below for SJT (e.g., Slovic & Lichtenstein, 1971).

Within SJT, in tasks involving judgments of preference or desirability the judge is ordinarily required to make wholistic ratings over a series of cases in which the levels of the attributes vary simultaneously. Such ratings are made on interval scales. They are sometimes recorded in written form, although more commonly the series of cases are presented and the judge's responses are recorded via interactive computer graphics techniques. SJT is the only one of the six approaches to rely extensively upon computer graphics technology, although interactive computer programs have recently been developed within the DT approach (e.g., Leal & Pearl, 1977). Occasionally, within SJT judges are requested to specify directly the values of the parameters of models of their judgment processes, in a manner similar to the procedures of BDT. Judges may be asked, for example, to indicate the relative importance of cues by dividing 100 points among them or to indicate the relation between levels of an attribute and desirability by drawing curves.

The IIT approach relies almost entirely upon wholistic ratings of multiple cases in its study of judgments involving preference. The judge responds on what is assumed to be an equal interval scale (that assumption is routinely tested in IIT). Responses are ordinarily recorded by the judge in a paper and pencil format.

16.3.2 Judgments of Inference

All the approaches, with the exception of DT, at times construct tasks in which the judge is required to make inferences about unobservable, distal variables on the basis of observable, proximal information. (DT does occasionally require experts to make subjective evaluations of the levels of attributes on scales such as, say, "quality," but such tasks appear infrequently enough that they are omitted here.)

Tasks from the BDT, PDT, and AT approaches often require the judge to respond to paired choices. For example, in the BDT and PDT approaches, judges are commonly asked questions of the general form, "Given datum x, is event y or event z more likely to occur?" AT tasks are frequently of the form, "Given event x, is cause y or cause z more likely?"

SJT, IIT, and AT frequently (and PDT much less frequently) construct tasks requiring judges to express their inferences in terms of numeric evaluations or ratings. For example, tasks within these approaches frequently ask judges to express on a numeric scale their judgments about the most likely value of some unobservable object or variable on the basis of a set of given cue values. Tasks in which the judge is presented a number of attributes describing an individual and is asked to evaluate that individual on another attribute dimension (i.e., tasks of impression formation) are also common within the IIT and AT approaches.

16.3.3 Probability Estimation

Probability estimation tasks, and the responses required by them, can be roughly subdivided into two categories: (a) those requiring indirect responses and (b) those requiring more or less direct estimation of probability or likelihood.

The indirect procedure ordinarily requires the decision maker to express his or her ordinal preference for alternative lotteries. Subjective probability estimates of events are then derived from these responses. Another common indirect procedure for obtaining probability estimates involves the use of a "probability wheel." The wheel is constructed so that two colors can be adjusted to occupy varying amounts of area. The judge is asked whether he or she prefers a bet in which he or she receives some prize, x_p, if the spinner lands in the target color area, or a bet in which he or she receives the same prize, x_p, if event e occurs. The area of the target color is adjusted until the judge is indifferent between the two bets; the subjective probability estimate, p, for the occurrence of event e is then assumed to be equivalent to the proportion of area covered by the target color. The use of this procedure can therefore be seen to be a special case of the more general lottery techniques.

The lottery procedure is used extensively within the DT approach. It is also found frequently in basic research within BDT, although it appears infrequently, if ever, in practical applications of BDT. In basic research, PDT also frequently employs tasks requiring judges to select among lotteries, although the probability wheel procedure is rarely if ever used.

The second type of task requires the judge or decision maker to express his or her subjective estimates of probability more directly. This type of task is used by all three of the decision approaches, DT, BDT, and PDT. It is also the approach used by IIT in their studies of risky decision making and by SJT in its infrequent studies involving probability estimation. These tasks may require the decision maker to make a statement in terms of numbers between 0 and 1, or to express the odds for various events (e.g., "are the odds for e 100 to 1, 1000 to 1?" or "how much more likely is it that x_1 will occur instead of x_2? Twice as likely? Three times?", etc."), or to construct (with the aid of the decision analyst) a probability distribution. The construction of a probability distribution is usually based on the fractile procedure. The decision maker is first asked a series of questions designed to specify the value of attribute X, x', such that he feels it is equally likely that the obtained value of X will be between x_0 (lowest feasible value) and x' or between x' and x_1 (highest feasible value). This procedure is reiterated for the intervals (x_0, x') and (x', x_1) and so forth, until enough points have been plotted to sketch the distribution. (See Spetzler & Stael von Holstein, 1975, for an extensive discussion of procedures for eliciting probability estimates.)

16.4 DESIGN

The design of studies of judgment and decision making processes was covered extensively in the previous section. Design has direct implications, however, for procedures in so far as it affects the nature of the materials the judge or decision maker sees and the manner in which he or she is required to respond. The most important design factors affecting procedures are related to the idiographic versus nomothetic distinction discussed in Chapter 10 of the Methodology section.

For five of the six approaches, DT, BDT, PDT, SJT, and IIT, their aims are sometimes, if not always, idiographic in orientation. This orientation requires that sufficient data be collected from each judge or decision maker in order to construct a model of that individual's judgment or decision processes. This usually, but not always, entails factorial design in the within-subjects component of the study or analysis. That is, each judge is required to respond to every possible combination of stimulus attributes or to all possible combinations of a finite number of levels of the stimulus attributes. In terms of procedures, this means the judge or decision maker is required to make repeated judgments or decisions.

16.4.1 Decision Theory

The aim of DT is exclusively idiographic. The decision analyst ordinarily constructs tasks containing large numbers of attribute level combinations to which the decision maker will theoretically be asked to respond. The approach can thus be described as factorial, although it is not referred to or described as such by DT. The DT approach usually involves "short cuts," however. For example, instead of asking the decision maker to respond to each of a large number of stimulus attribute combinations, say to indicate his or her preference between attribute combinations (x, y) and (x', y'), over a whole series of values, $Z_{1...n}$, the decision maker may be asked to indicate his or her preference for (x, y) versus (x', y') for z_1, z_2, z_k and z_n, and, as soon as he or she understands the nature of the problem, be asked directly if his or her preference for (x, y) versus (x', y') would change as a function of any plausible value of Z. DT procedures are dynamic, in the sense that the choices presented by the analyst to the decision maker are derived from responses to earlier choices.

16.4.2 Behavioral Decision Theory/Psychological Decision Theory

Although BDT, in its practical applications, is idiographic in orientation, it does not use a within-subjects factorial approach to collect data for the construction of a model representing the decision maker's decision processes. Rather, unlike the procedures of the other approaches, which all involve responses by the judge to a number of questions or trials from which models are derived, the analyst asks the decision maker to indicate directly the characteristics of the model. For instance, decision makers are ordinarily asked to specify the relative importance of attributes by assigning weights on a ratio scale.

In the basic research component of BDT, and in PDT, judges usually respond to each of a pre-established array of stimulus combinations although that array may not be the same for every judge. Judges may or may not see every possible combination of levels of stimulus attributes, but more often they do not. Each combination of stimulus attributes, however, is seen by some judge(s). The primary orientation of basic research in these two approaches is more nomothetic than idiographic. The design of basic research in these two approaches, then, is usually between-subjects factorial. The researcher establishes a set of task materials that include all possible combinations of a number of levels of attributes. Each judge responds only to a set or subset of those combinations; judges often respond to only one instance of any particular judgment or decision problem. Although models may be tested for individual judges, the tests of interest are ordinarily between-subjects.

16.4.3 Social Judgment Theory

In both the applied and basic versions of SJT, the basic orientation is always idiographic. Again, this means that individual models are constructed for each judge and that judges respond to multiple instances of a particular judgment problem. Unlike most other approaches, however, the collection of data for the construction of individual models does not involve factorial design. Because SJT relies extensively on regression techniques in model building, the judge ordinarily responds to only a sample of all possible combinations of cue levels. The analyst or researcher first generates a sample of cue level combinations. The judge then responds to each of the cue level combinations (or *profiles*) in this pre-established set.

Unlike the factorial approaches, in which the stimulus attributes are most always orthogonal, this is frequently not the case in SJT. The SJT approach emphasizes the concept of representative design; that is, that the cue level combinations to which the judge responds should be representative of those in the "real world," preserving cue intercorrelations, ranges and distributions, and other characteristics of the cues in the natural environment. Such characteristics are frequently preserved in the generation of sets of cue level combinations.

Basic research within SJT frequently makes use of between-subjects factorial designs, but only after within-subjects analyses have been conducted.

16.4.4 Information Integration Theory

IIT relies exclusively on factorial design, in which each judge or some group of judges sees each combination of stimulus attribute combinations. In order to keep the total number of cases to a manageable level, either the number of attributes or the number of levels of each attribute is ordinarily small in the typical IIT study. Because of the reliance on factorial design, attributes are ordinarily orthogonal within sets. IIT uses both within-subjects and between-subjects factorial designs. Most often, within-subjects analysis precedes between-subjects analysis.

16.4.5 Attribution Theory

AT is the only of the six approaches that rarely, if ever, constructs models of individual judgment or decision processes. Its primary aim is nomothetic. It therefore uses between-subject factorial designs extensively. In terms of procedures, it first constructs a set of attribute level combinations, which are almost always orthogonal. Most commonly, each judge responds to only one of these combinations (or to only a small subset). Since the approach does not require extensive data from individual judges in order to build models of their judgment or decision processes, it is quite common in AT for judges to respond to a number of different judgment and decision problems within a single study.

16.5 LEVEL OF ABSTRACTION

After the nature of the judgment or decision problem has been established and the structure and dimensions of the task determined, a basic issue is the level of abstraction at which the attributes or cues will be presented to the judge. This issue was discussed at length in the previous section on methodology (Chapter 12), but a brief discussion is also appropriate here.

The level of abstraction at which attributes are presented ranges on a continuum from concrete, realistic *objects* to abstracted *variables.* The approaches using the most concrete (realistic) level of presentation are PDT, IIT (sometimes), and AT. All three approaches sometimes use very detailed verbal descriptions of objects. IIT has used photographs, as has AT, which at times has used recordings or videotapes. The next level of abstraction is that of partially decomposed objects, i.e., real or hypothetical objects, presented in schematic terms. DT, BDT in its research function, SJT, and IIT (usually) fall into this category. BDT, in its applied function, is the only approach to operate procedurally with abstracted variables or dimensions themselves.

The level of abstraction at which variables are presented has greatest implications for procedures with respect to the number of cases that are presented for consideration by individual judges. More abstract level of presentation enable stimulus combinations to be manipulated more easily and require less time for presentation and response. Within-subjects designs are therefore usually characterized by more abstract levels of presentation than are between-subjects designs in which individuals respond to only a few cases.

16.6 CUE METRIC

An issue closely related to that of level of abstraction is the metric in which the attribute levels are presented. In general, the more abstract the level of presentation, the more likely that the attributes will be represented in numerical form. DT, BDT, SJT, and IIT, therefore, more commonly represent levels of attributes by numbers than do PDT and AT.

SJT almost always presents attributes in quantitative form, with an underlying continuous distribution. Such a metric is dictated by the requirements of the regression analysis techniques ordinarily used by SJT. Techniques for application of SJT in nonmetric (i.e., nonnumeric) ecologies have been developed (Bjorkman, 1973; Castellan, 1970), but are not extensively used. DT, BDT, PDT, and IIT all at times present attributes in similar quantitative form; AT rarely, if ever, does so. All of the approaches sometimes present stimulus attributes in discrete forms or in terms of qualitative descriptions, although SJT does so much less commonly than the rest.

16.7 ITERATION

It should be noted that iteration is a procedural mainstay for the three approaches most concerned with aiding decision makers with applied problems; that is, for DT, BDT, and SJT. On the basis of, for example, the judge's expressed dissatisfaction with the analysis, statistical or logical evidence that the model does not describe well the judge or decision maker, or the identification of a previously unrecognized dimension of the problem, some or all of the steps involving task construction or cue selection may be repeated, or efforts may be made to remodel the individual's judgment or decision processes in accord with the procedures described in the following chapters. Iteration of some or all of the steps involved in the process of modeling an individual's judgment or decision processes is more commonly found in the DT, BDT, and SJT approaches than in the other three because satisfactory descriptions of individuals' use of information is essential for adequately aiding with applied problems.

This is not to suggest, however, that iteration is never found in any of the other three approaches. For example, iteration is commonly found in some of the research within IIT that combines some of the features of both applied and basic research (e.g., Shanteau & Phelps, 1977). Moreover, the conduct of any systematic program of basic research on human judgment and decision processes could often be described in terms of incremental iteration. Iteration is therefore sometimes an important procedural component of all six approaches.

16.8 OVERVIEW

The six approaches show considerable diversity in the manner in which they construct tasks and present stimulus, attribute, or cue combinations to judges and decision makers. They also vary greatly in the types of responses they require. Several factors appear to contribute to these differences. One obvious contribution to differences among the approaches is differences in aim or function. The types of procedures employed are affected according to whether basic research or practical application is the intended function and according to whether the aim is more idiographic or more nomothetic. In addition, procedures vary as a function of whether the analysis is concerned with judgments of preference, judgments of inference, or probability estimation. Finally, the differences in theoretical origins and the means of data reduction or data analysis discussed in the Theory and Method sections account for some of the differences among approaches. For example, the type of data most amenable to analysis by Bayes' theorem, regression techniques, and ANOVA techniques vary, and thus the procedures involved in data collection also vary. All six approaches, however, construct tasks which provide data that can be used to construct models of the judgment and decision processes of individuals or of groups of individuals.

Chapter 17

Objective Task Characteristics

The term *objective task characteristics* refers to concepts used to describe the properties of environmental systems with which judges or decision makers interact. Objective task characteristics, therefore, refer to those characteristics of judgment or decision problems which can in principle be objectively measured or manipulated. Objective task characteristics can be contrasted with individuals' subjective representations of task systems. Only the former are of concern in this chapter; subjective representations of judgment and decision tasks will be addressed in Chapter 19.

The approaches differ considerably in the amount of attention they give to objective task characteristics. In general, those approaches more concerned with the double- and n-system cases (including probability estimation problems) pay greater attention to objective task characteristics and contain more and better-developed concepts referring to such characteristics than do the approaches focusing on the single-system case. (See Chapter 4, *Scope,* for a discussion of single- versus double- and n-system cases.) Because of its intensive interest in the double- and n-system cases, SJT pays greater conceptual and procedural attention to objective task characteristics than any of the other approaches. IIT pays perhaps least attention to objective task characteristics, focusing its interests primarily (but not exclusively) on the cognitive systems of judges and decision makers.

This chapter discusses seven topics concerning concepts and procedures related to objective task characteristics:

1 Task elements;
2 Organizing principles;
3 Uncertainty;
4 Cue-criterion relations;
5 Interrelations among observable task elements;
6 Number of task elements;
7 Other task characteristics.

Major similarities and differences among the approaches with respect to their treatment of objective task characteristics are summarized in Table 17-1.

17.1 TASK ELEMENTS

In describing the elements that make up or define judgment or decision problems, it is important to distinguish between the single-system and the double- and n-system cases. In the single-system case either it is not meaningful to refer to an environmental criterion (for judgments of preference, utility, desirability, etc.) or the value of the criterion is intrinsically unknown or unknowable (for certain judgments of inference). Such judgment and decision problems are therefore wholly defined by task elements immediately available to judges or decision makers. These immediately available or observable task elements are described in different terms by the various approaches. They are ordinarily referred to as *data, events,* or *attributes* within DT, BDT and PDT; they are referred to as *cues* within SJT, and sometimes, AT; and, they are referred to as *stimuli* within IIT and, usually AT. These differences among approaches in terminology seem principally to reflect differences in theoretical origins and conceptions of how individuals interact with tasks. Aside from previously discussed differences in level of abstraction and metric, task elements appear to be pretty much procedurally equivalent across approaches. It is relatively easy, for example, to imagine the same task elements being referred to as attributes by DT, BDT, and PDT, as cues by SJT, and as stimuli by IIT and AT.

In addition to those task elements immediately available to individuals, double- and n-system cases (including probability estimation problems) include task elements that are not directly observable or knowable but which must be inferred on the basis of observable task elements. Such task elements are ordinarily referred to by such terms as the *depth variable* or *environmental*

Table 17-1 Comparison of Approaches with Respect to Objective Task Characteristics

Topics in objective task characteristics	DT	BDT	PDT	SJT	IIT	AT
17.1 Task elements						
Datum/events	X[a]	X	X˙			
Cues				X		*[b]
Stimuli					X	X
Depth variables/criterion	X	X	X	X	*	*
17.2 Organizing principles						
Bayes Theorem/normative rules	X	X	X			
Weighted averaging model				X		
17.3 Uncertainty						
Probability	X	X	X	*	*	*
Task uncertainty				X		
Multiple causality					*	*
17.4 Cue-criterion relations						
Ecological validity				X		
Conditional probability	X	X	X			
17.5 Interrelations among observable task elements						
Cue intercorrelations				X		
Conditional dependence/independence	X	X	X			
Redundancy/inconsistency					X	X
17.6 Number of task elements						
Set size	X	X	X	*	X	*

[a]Indicates that an approach routinely follows procedure or operationalizes concept.
[b]Indicates that an approach sometimes follows procedure or operationalizes concept.

criterion in SJT and by such terms as the *criterion* or *correct answer* in the three probability approaches. DT, BDT, PDT, and SJT operationally define or describe such distal or depth task elements much more commonly than do either IIT or AT. Within IIT the correct response to a judgment or decision task is sometimes specified on the basis of normative rules for information integration, and within AT the concept of *cause* is frequently used to refer to task elements which are not directly observable and which must be inferred, but, in general, these latter two approaches focus on single-system problems for which no objectively correct value of the task criterion can be specified.

Although the concepts of depth variable and environmental criterion in SJT and the concepts of criterion and correct answer in the probability approaches are similar, they are ordinarily operationalized in substantially different manners. In basic research on the double- and n-system case within SJT, the value of the depth variable is selected or manipulated so that it is not a wholly predictable function of the values of observable surface cues. Because of such manipulated task uncertainty, the judge cannot always obtain the correct value of the depth variable, even though he or she is responding optimally on the basis of the available surface cues. Within the three probability approaches, the criterion or correct answer is defined solely in terms of the optimal analytical integration of the observable data. If the judge is responding optimally, then he or she will obtain the "correct answer." In short, the criterion value in SJT is defined empirically; the criterion value in the three probability approaches is defined analytically.

17.2 ORGANIZING PRINCIPLES

Also of interest is the manner in which the approaches describe the organization of environmental systems. The organization of environmental systems generally refers to the manner in which observable, known task elements are related to task elements that are not directly observable or knowable. The concept of organizing principles of environmental systems is therefore much more prominent in the four approaches more concerned with double- and n-system cases or with probability estimation (i.e., DT, BDT, PDT, and SJT), than in the approaches more concerned with the single-system case (i.e., IIT and AT).

For the three probability approaches, DT, BDT, and PDT, the environment is often viewed as being organized according to *Bayes' theorem*, which describes the manner in which objective probabilities are optimally revised or combined, or by similar logical or normative rules of organization. In terms of procedures, this means that in tests of optimality with respect to the environmental system, judges will be compared with Bayes' theorem or similar logical or normative rules.

Within the SJT approach, the environment is ordinarily described in terms of a *weighted averaging* model. Such a model assumes that the depth variable or criterion can be best predicted by weighing and combining the information from surface data in a compensatory fashion. The model includes no cross-product products among cues. Procedurally, the weighted averaging model best describing judges' cognitive systems is compared to the weighted averaging model best describing the environmental system in tests of achievement with respect to the environmental system.

For both the three probability approaches and SJT, their assumptions about the nature of the environment have implications for the manner in which they deal with judges' cognitive systems. That is, the models they construct of judges' cognitive systems are similar to the models they assume best describe environmental systems. Implicit in the procedures of all four approaches seems to be the assumption that the organizing principle which describes judges' cognitive systems should correspond to the organizing principle which describes the environment. Tests of congruence or fit between judges and the environmental system, then, are tests of similarity between models of cognitive systems and models of the environment.

IIT and AT do not explicitly postulate an organizing principle for the environment. Both approaches seem to take the position that, at least to some extent, judges "impose" organizing principles on the world in order to make sense of or cope with it. For AT, the organizing principle is frequently that of a *schema* (e.g., Kelley, 1971); for IIT, information integration mechanisms may take a number of forms, including adding, averaging, and multiplying models. One might infer that these two approaches would postulate similar organizing principles within the environment as they do within the individual, but such an inference receives little support from a review of their literature. Neither approach seems to maintain that there is any necessary correspondence between organizing principles within individuals' cognitive systems and organizing principles within the environment. (We should note that while the above statements hold more-or-less true for present day AT, one of its founders, Heider, was quite concerned with the organization of the environmental system. His views were quite similar to those of Brunswik and thus, to those of the SJT approach. Heider's views about the organizing principles of the environment, however, seem to have relatively little impact on current AT procedures.)

17.3 UNCERTAINTY

All six approaches contain concepts referring to uncertainty within the environment; that is, to ambiguity or probabilism intervening among elements of the task environment. Such uncertainty is regarded as intrinsic within the judgment or decision problem; it cannot (at the time the judgment or decision is made, at least) be eliminated, and it exists independently of the judge or decision maker's (or the analyst's) representation of the problem.

Environmental uncertainty is described in several different fashions across the six approaches, including uncertainty about whether an event will occur, uncertainty about the validity of a hypothesis, uncertainty about the consequences or effects of an action, and ambiguity concerning the relations between directly observable, surface events and unobservable or nondirectly observable, depth variables. Again, the concept of uncertainty is more prominent within the four approaches more concerned with the double- and n-system cases (including probability estimation), than within the approaches more concerned with the single-system case. That is, uncertainty is a more prominent concept within DT, BDT, PDT, and SJT than in IIT or AT.

The concept of uncertainty is defined in terms of *probability* by DT, BDT, and PDT. (The same concept appears in IIT in its studies of risky decision making, in a few studies of SJT, and is beginning to appear in the AT approach.) Probability refers to uncertainty about whether an event will occur, about whether a hypothesis is true, or about the consequences of an action. Because of probability, many judgment and decision problems are described as risky; that is, the specific outcomes of possible decisions or courses of action are unknown.

Probability is important within DT, BDT, and PDT primarily because probabilism in the environment must be coped with by the judge or decision maker. In practical applications, objective probabilities usually have no procedural implications since they are unknown. Interest therefore focuses on subjective estimates of such unknown objective probabilities, and procedures are concerned with the elicitation and calibration of individuals' estimates of those probabilities.

For basic research within the BDT and PDT approaches, tasks are constructed so that objective probabilities are known and can be manipulated. The eventual issue of interest in such research is the degree of correspondence between objective probabilities and subjective estimates of them, or the degree to which judges' behavior corresponds with normative prescriptions based upon known objective probabilities.

Within the SJT approach, uncertainty is defined in terms of the concepts of *task uncertainty, surface/depth relations,* or the *zone of ambiguity.* All these concepts refer to the inability for depth or distal variables with which indivduals are ultimately interested to be inferred with certainty on the basis of surface data known to or immediately observable by them. That is, the values of depth variables are ordinarily viewed by SJT as intrinsically unpredictable with perfect certainty. Within SJT, judgments and decisions are not normally considered risky in the sense that the specific outcomes of possible decisions are unknown, as they are in the three probability approaches. Rather, they are "risky" only in the sense that the judge can never be sure that there is a perfect correspondence between his or her judgments and the criterion.

The concept of task uncertainty is important within SJT primarily because of its behavioral implications for individuals who must try to cope with an intrinsically ambiguous environment. In applied decision problems, the concept usually has no effects on procedures, since the value of the environmental criterion, and thus the degree of task uncertainty, is ordinarily not known. In laboratory studies of multiple cue probability learning, however, tasks are (almost) never constructed so that surface/depth relations are certain. That is, the tasks are ordinarily constructed so that the criterion is not perfectly predictable on the basis of the available surface cues, since such task uncertainty is regarded by SJT as typical of the environmental systems with which individuals ordinarily interact. The degree of task uncertainty for such problems is operationalized as the multiple correlation between the criterion and the available surface cues.

The concept of uncertainty is recognized in AT and IIT by the concept of *multiple causality*. Both AT and IIT note that similar events can have different causes and that the same cause can lead to multiple effects. The implication of this concept is that the relation between a possible cause and an effect is uncertain.

Despite its theoretical importance in AT, however, the concept of multiple causality has little impact on procedures. Although AT is quite interested theoretically in the manner in which judges come to understand environmental systems with which they interact, current research in AT rarely involves tasks in which the "right answer" is known and in which the relations between stimulus attributes and criterion can be specified.

Similarly, the concept of multiple causality has little or no effect on procedures in IIT. IIT focuses primarily on the cognitive system of judges, paying relatively little systematic attention to the environmental systems with which they interact. The concept of *probability*, however, sometimes appears in IIT studies of gambling and betting behavior. In this context, it is identical to the concept as it appears in DT, BDT, and PDT.

17.4 CUE–CRITERION RELATIONS

Four of the six approaches contain concepts related to the relationship between observable task elements and the task criterion. This type of concept is most prominent in SJT because of its interest in the double- and n-system case and its concern with the characteristics of environmental systems in general. The relation between a cue and the criterion is described in SJT by the concept of *ecological validity,* which refers to the degree to which the criterion can be predicted by a cue. It is ordinarily operationalized as the simple product-moment correlation between cue and criterion, taking into account any possible curvilinear relation between cue and criterion.

A similar concept in DT, BDT, and PDT is the *conditional probability of the criterion* (hypothesis) given an event (or, some datum), or the *conditional probability of an event* (or, some datum) given a criterion (hypothesis). In DT, the concept has no implications for procedures because of its exclusive concern with practical applications, in which the true probability of a hypothesis given an event (or vice versa) is almost never known. In basic research within BDT and PDT, conditional probabilities concerning cue-criterion relations are known or manipulated by the experimenter.

Neither IIT or AT contain major concepts related to cue-criterion relations. Aside, perhaps, from some of the early work in person perception, environmental relations are usually not known or specified in IIT or AT research and no concepts concerning cue-criterion relations are operationalized.

17.5   INTERRELATIONS AMONG OBSERVABLE
TASK ELEMENTS

The interrelations among observable task elements are of some interest to all six approaches. They have been of particular interest, however, within SJT in which the relevant concept is that of *cue intercorrelation.* This concept is defined as the predictability of one cue from a second cue and is ordinarily operationalized as the product-moment correlation between two cues. Cue intercorrelations are often set in accordance with the magnitude and direction of those believed to characterize the natural environment (representative design), although orthogonal cue sets are also frequently used, particularly for judgments of preference. Basic research on the effects of cue intercorrelations on judgment and decision processes has been commonplace within the SJT approach.

In the DT, BDT, and PDT approaches, the relevant concept is that of *conditional dependence/independence.* This concept is defined and operationalized as the probability of an event (datum) given a second event (datum). It is also referred to by DT as *redundancy.*

Procedurally, both DT and BDT recommend that attributes be defined or constructed so that conditional dependencies among attributes are as low as possible for tasks involving judgments of preference or utility. This procedure avoids "double counting" of attributes within the utility function. Also, for DT, the absence of conditional dependencies among attributes makes it more likely that the independence of utility assumption can be satisfied, which is a necessary condition for construction for each attribute of a single utility function which can be incorporated into some form of a multilinear, multiattribute utility function.

In applications of DT and BDT, conditional independence of attributes is ordinarily not of concern for probability estimation judgments. For such problems, the emphasis is on eliciting and calibrating decision makers' probability estimates, and little attention is given to the characteristics of the environmental data upon which those estimates are based.

Because Bayes' theorem is simpler to apply in such situations, however, basic research by BDT on probability estimation has ordinarily employed tasks with independent attributes. In basic research on probability estimation by PDT, tasks in which elements are independent and tasks in which elements are dependent can each be found. Indeed, much of the recent work in PDT has addressed the hypothesis that individuals do not take into proper account conditional dependence and independence in estimating probabilities.

In IIT, the major concept concerning interrelations among observable task elements is that of *redundancy.* This concept refers to the degree to which stimuli or task elements provide the same information. Such redundancy is usually self-evident or "apparent" and is not measured in terms of empirical correlations or probabilities. For example, the statements "Mr. A is kind" and "Mr. A is kind to Mr. B" are obviously (logically) redundant. The counterpart to redundancy in IIT is *inconsistency*. Wyer (1970) defined and operationalized inconsistency as the degree to which the joint probability of two stimuli are less than the product of their unconditional probabilities. A number of empirical studies on the effects of redundancy and inconsistency on information integration processes have been performed within IIT.

Within AT, a concept similar to the redundancy concept of IIT is that of *consistency,* or the degree to which behavior over time and modality is similar or identical. As with the concept of redundancy in IIT, consistency is usually operationally defined in terms of self-evident or logical consistency (e.g., "Ms. A was kind to Ms. B this morning," and "Ms. A was kind to Ms. C this afternoon." There is no clear counterpart in AT to IIT's concept of inconsistency, however, although the importance of this idea is clearly recognized. Kelley (1971) noted, for instance, that "conflicting or ambiguous cues may evoke schemata that lead to contradictory inferences" (p. 173). Moreover, there has been a substantial amount of research within AT on the effects of "mixed" sets of adjectives on impression formation.

17.6 NUMBER OF TASK ELEMENTS

There has been some empirical work across the six approaches on the effects of the number of attributes within a task on judgment and decision processes. The IIT approach is perhaps most prominent in this regard. Numerous studies involving tests of averaging versus summative models as descriptions of information integration processes have varied the number of items of information presented judges. Within BDT, research on conservatism in probability estimation has varied sample size as a simple means of varying diagnosticity. Within PDT, the effects of number of cues on individuals' internal consistency and their confidence in their judgments have been investigated.

Although it is not clear to what extent results from basic research motivate it, all approaches seem to assume, explicitly or implicitly, that cognitive limitations make it difficult for judges to deal simultaneously and effectively with large numbers of items of information. Procedurally, this means that limits are placed on the number of items of information contained in a task. For instance, DT explicitly advocates that the number of attributes be as small as possible, analyses within SJT usually limit the number of cues presented at one time to a judge to 5-8 or so, and BDT also advocates a small number of attributes, although setting a more generous upper limit than most of the other approaches. BDT suggests that 8 attributes are enough, whereas 15 are too many. If all the important dimensions of a problem cannot be described within such limits, as frequently occurs in applications, the generally accepted procedure across approaches is to subdivide the judgment or decision problem into multiple tasks.

17.7 OTHER TASK CHARACTERISTICS

A number of other concepts related to task characteristics have been omitted from this discussion, either because they have no direct impacts on procedures or because they affect procedures for only a small fraction of the work within an approach. For instance, the importance of *cue variability* and *cue range* is explicitly recognized within the SJT approach. SJT warns that the results of any judgment analysis are theoretically generalizable only to cue sets exhibiting the same formal characteristics as those of the cue sets with which the analysis was conducted. (DT offers a similar procedural admonition, warning against attempts to assess the relative importance of attributes independently of their range.) Similarly, *ecological reliability* and *cue intersubstitutability* are important concepts in SJT, but they rarely, if ever, have direct impacts on procedures.

Consierable work has been done within IIT and AT on *order effects*. But although the order in which items of information are presented is an important procedural feature of many specific studies, it is not an important procedural consideration in the majority of work within these approaches; therefore, it is omitted here.

17.8 OVERVIEW

Although they vary considerably in the degree of attention they accord it, all six approaches attend to some extent to the properties of environmental systems with which judges or decision makers interact. SJT pays perhaps greatest attention to objective task characteristics because it deals more extensively with double- and n-system cases than do any of the other approaches. In double- and n-system cases, the existence of an environmental criterion requires that task characteristics concerning interrelations between observable task elements and the criterion be considered, in addition to interrelations among the observable task elements themselves. Because of their interest in probability estimation tasks, in which there exists a correct response or criterion, the three probability approaches also give considerable attention to objective task characteristics. IIT and AT give perhaps least extensive coverage to the objective task characteristics of tasks, because they focus primarily upon the single-system case in which there exists no environmental criterion or correct answer and in which observable task elements wholly define the problem. Concepts and procedures within these latter two approaches thus focus solely on the nature and interrelations of observable task elements.

Chapter 18

Subjective Use
of Subjective Data

All six approaches are concerned with judges' use of subjective data, or data which is not readily observable by or known to the judgment or decision analyst. The approaches differ, however, in the extent to and manner in which they address this issue. Furthermore, their treatment of the subjective use of subjective data differs depending on whether the judgment problem is one of preference or inference, or one of probability estimation.

This chapter discusses two topics concerned with the subjective use of subjective data:

1 Subjective data in judgments of preference or inference;
2 Subjective data in probability estimation.

Major similarities and differences among the approaches with respect to their treatment of the subjective use of subjective data are summarized in Table 18-1.

Table 18-1 Comparison of Approaches with Respect to Subjective Use
of Subjective Data

Topics in subjective use of subjective data	DT	BDT	PDT	SJT	IIT	AT
18.1 Subjective data in judgments of preference or inference						
Subjective data transformed into objective metric	X[a]	X	X	X	*[b]	*
18.2 Subjective data in probability estimation						
Calibration/lotteries	X	X	X			
Direct estimation	X	X	X			
Fractile procedure	X	*				

[a]Indicates that an approach routinely follows procedure or operationalizes concept.
[b]Indicates that an approach sometimes follows procedure or operationalizes concept.

18.1 SUBJECTIVE DATA IN JUDGMENTS OF PREFERENCE OR INFERENCE

The primary procedural differences among the approaches with respect to their treatment of the subjective use of subjective data in judgments of preference or inference are concerned with the extent to which they ordinarily try to objectify such "soft" data into "hard" data before describing or modeling individuals' judgment processes.

For DT, BDT, PDT, and SJT, their standard methods of data analysis and model construction are best suited for use when the cues, stimuli, or attributes are described or specified in terms of a numeric (or at least an ordinal) scale. They therefore ordinarily transform subjective data into ordinal or interval scales of measurement, prior to data analysis. For example, if a judgment or decision problem included an attribute such as *aesthetics,* the analyst might first have an "expert" (or perhaps the judge him or herself) rate each alternative on a one-to-ten scale of, say, beauty. The analysis would then model the relation between the individual's responses and the levels of the transformed attributes. Judges might still respond to more complex, wholistic objects, but the analysis would be based upon the transformed data. Any effects of judges' responses to data available from the complex, wholistic objects but not captured by their description in terms of the transformed attributes is ordinarily treated as error. Within PDT, however, such "error" sometimes serves as a basis for inferring the presence of psychological biases in the use of subjective data.

Although they too sometimes transform "soft" data into more objective forms, IIT and AT can deal more readily with responses to complex, wholistic objects; that is, with situations in which the information being attended to by the judge is not known by the analyst. IIT and AT are better able to deal with such problems because of their use of ANOVA methods for data analysis. For example, if the judgment problem involved job preferences (a topic that has received considerable attention within IIT), the use of ANOVA techniques would permit analysis of judges' use of complex, multidimensional stimuli such as city names, simply by treating each city name as a particular level of a factor. In the other four approaches, each city would probably first be transformed into some common dimension such as "desirability," before the analysis.

(The interested reader is referred to Chapter 12, *Stimulus-Object Decomposition*, which treats more extensively many of the issues discussed here concerning the manner in which cues, attributes, stimuli, etc. are described or dimensionalized for the purposes of data analysis and model construction.)

18.2 SUBJECTIVE DATA IN PROBABILITY ESTIMATION

In tasks of probability estimation, the precise nature of the data being used by judges is ordinarily not of concern. Instead a major component of DT and BDT, and to a lesser extent, PDT is the refinement, or *calibration*, of subjective hunches, impressions, or intuitions into subjective judgmental probabilities. The procedures for such calibration ordinarily involve lotteries or imaginary bets. With DT and BDT, such calibration is based upon the decision maker adopting two principles of consistent behavior: (a) transitivity of preferences and (b) substitutability of indifferent consequences in a lottery. Internal consistency is thus the criterion for admitting subjective estimates of probability into the decision analysis. PDT often uses the lottery procedures in basic research, but without requiring individuals to adopt the above two principles of consistent behavior.

In particular, the procedures for assessing subjective probabilities involve the decision maker making a series of choices in which he or she indicates his or her ordinal preference between alternative lotteries. The procedures are based on an "if you had to bet" approach. For instance, the decision maker might be asked to indicate his or her preference for the following choice: "Do you prefer a lottery offering prize W if it rains tomorrow and L if it doesn't, or a lottery offering prize W with a probability of .20 and L with a probability of .80?" Probability wheels (see 16.3.3) are frequently used in this step to define the objective probabilities against which the subjective probability of events are compared and contrasted.

Formally, judgmental probability can be defined as follows: If E is an uncertain event in the real world and the decision maker is indifferent between a lottery that results in consequence x_c if E occurs and consequence y_c if E does not occur and a lottery that gives an objective probability p of consequence x_c and a complementary probability of l-p of consequence y_c, then the judgmental probability of E is p. During the calibration task, the DT or BDT decision analyst attempts to identify and compensate for any cognitive or motivational biases on the part of the decision maker, e.g., personal biases, anchoring, unstated assumptions, conservatism, or inability to conceptualize independence. Much of the research by PDT involving the use of lottery procedures is concerned with the specification and further description of such biases.

BDT ordinarily, and DT and PDT sometimes, relies on more direct methods for eliciting point estimates of probability. Most commonly, the decision maker is asked to estimate the subjective probability of an event by specifying a number between 0 and 1, by indicating his or her estimate of the likelihood or odds (or log odds) of an event's occurrence, or by indicating which of two events he or she considers more likely. (SJT has relied on direct point estimates in its infrequent treatment of probability estimation problems; objective probabilities are ordinarily specified for the judge in IIT's study of risky decision making.)

In addition to the above procedures for eliciting point estimates of probability, DT has developed procedures for eliciting subjective probability distributions. The most common of these is based upon the fractile procedure. First, the lowest plausible value of an attribute X, x_0, and the highest plausible value, x_1, are identified. Next, the decision maker is asked to express his or her preferences for a series of alternatives of the form: "Do you prefer a lottery offering prize W if the value of X is between x_0 and x' and L if the value of X is between x' and x_1 or a lottery offering prize W with $p = .50$ and L with $p = .50$?" The purpose of these questions is to find a value x' such that the decision maker is indifferent between the two lotteries. The intervals (x_0, x') and (x', x_1) are then divided using the same type of procedure and this process is iterated until a sufficient number of points have been plotted to permit description of the distribution. The fractile procedure is also sometimes used within applications of BDT.

18.3 OVERVIEW

Although all six approaches are concerned with the manner in which judges make use of subjective data, procedurally, most approaches "objectify" the subjective data used in judgments of preferences or inference. That is, subjective data is usually transformed into ordinal or interval scales for the formal judgment or decision analysis. This practice is less pronounced in IIT and AT, in which the uses of ANOVA techniques makes it easier to analyze responses based upon complex, multidimensional objects for which the precise nature of the information being attended to by the judge is not known. The procedures used in probability estimation tasks are ordinarily not concerned with the nature or values of the subjective, personal, and nonexplicit data used by judges.

Chapter 19

Subjective Task Representations

All six approaches are intensely interested in subjective representations of judgment and decision tasks; that is, in the manner in which individuals organize and use data or information in making judgments or decisions. Indeed, such concerns are at the core of all six approaches. This chapter is therefore by far the lengthiest of the five chapters dealing with procedures.

This chapter addresses the following four topics concerning subjective task representations:

1 Subjective interrelations among observable task elements;
2 Subjective use of objective data;
3 Cue utilization;
4 Central processes.

Major similarities and differences among the approaches with respect to procedures for dealing with subjective task representations are indicated in Table 19-1.

Table 19-1   Comparison of Approaches with Respect to Subjective Task Representations

Topics in subjective task representations	DT	BDT	PDT	SJT	IIT	AT
19.1 Subjective interrelations among observable task elements						
Subjective representations of cue intercorrelations/associative bonds			X^a	X		
Preference and utility independence/ dependence	X	$*^b$			*	
19.2 Subjective use of objective data						
Value/utility	X	X	X			
Function form				X		
Scale values					X	
Directionality						X
19.3 Cue utilization						
Weights/scaling constants	X	X	X	X	X	*
Subjective probability	X	X				
19.4.1 Central processes—organizing principles						
Bayes' Theorem	X	X	X			
Expected utility/value	X	X	X		*	
Multilinear model	X					
Additive/weighted averaging models	X	X		X	X	
Multiplicative model	X			*	X	
Subtracting models					X	
Noncompensatory models			*	*		
Schemata						X
19.4.2 Central processes—psychological and cognitive factors						
Biases	*	X	X			X
Cognitive control				X		

^{a}Indicates that an approach routinely follows procedure or operationalizes concept.
^{b}Indicates that an approach sometimes follows procedure or operationalizes concept.

19.1   SUBJECTIVE INTERRELATIONS AMONG OBSERVABLE TASK ELEMENTS

Two types of interrelations among observable task elements can be distinguished. The first is that of subjective representations of environmental interrelations among observable cues, attributes, stimuli, etc. The second is that of dependencies in the utility, value, or desirability of levels of an attribute as a function of the levels of other attributes. Each is discussed in turn.

19.1.1 Subjective Representations of Objective Interrelations

SJT and PDT have been the two approaches most interested in judges' subjective representations of the interrelations among observable task elements. That is, both approaches are interested in the subjective counterpart to objective intercorrelations among task elements.

In SJT the relevant concept is that of *subjective representations* of *ecological intercorrelations* among cues. Procedurally, such representations are generally assessed by having the judge predict levels of cue X, given levels of cue Y (Knowles, Hammond, Stewart & Summers, 1971, 1972). A similar concept in PDT is that of *associative bonds*. This concept has its basis in the work of Chapman and Chapman (1967, 1969) on "illusory correlation." It is generally assessed by having the judge predict or try to recall the level of an attribute X, given a particular level of attribute Y.

Individuals' representations of environmental interrelations among task elements are rarely, if ever, directly assessed by the other four approaches. Both DT and BDT emphasize that in practical applications environmental dependencies among attributes should be held to zero in order to minimize possible "double-counting" of attributes, but no formal procedures for assessing subjective representations of environmental dependencies are found within either approach. Within IIT, the behavioral effects of environmental redundancy are taken into account by concepts such as *discounting,* but the magnitude of subjective representations of redundancy is rarely, if ever, measured directly. In AT, there are no procedures directly addressing the idea of subjective representations of environmental intercorrelations or dependencies.

19.1.2 Preferential and Utility Independence/Dependence

The concepts of preferential and utility independence/dependence refer to whether the utility, value, or desirability of levels of an attribute change as a function of levels of other attributes. These concepts are of major importance in DT, and procedures have been developed within this approach for routine tests of both preferential and utility independence. The importance of these concepts is also explicitly recognized by BDT and IIT, but they are not routinely addressed by either. These concepts are rarely, if ever, operationally addressed by PDT, SJT, and AT.

Within the DT approach, preferential independence is necessary for the creation of an additive or multiplicative utility function (see 19.2.1 for discussion of utility functions). The basic idea of *preferential independence* is that preferences among levels of an attribute X do not depend upon the level of some attribute Y. Preferential independence is thus *order* preserving. The extension of this concept to more than two attributes is that of *conditional preferential independence.* This means that preferences among levels of an attribute X do not depend upon the level of some attribute Y, given some level of an attribute Z. The presence or absence of preferential independence is established via a series of questions involving choices among paired comparisons. This procedure is similar to that described immediately below for the assessment of utility independence.

Utility independence is necessary for the creation of multilinear utility functions. It allows the creation of utility functions for each attribute without reference to levels of other attributes. The basic idea of *utility independence* is that the utility of any level of an attribute X does not depend upon the level of some attribute Y. In other words, the utility of any level x_i does not change as a function of y_1, y_k, y_n, etc. Utility independence is thus *interval* preserving. The extension of this concept to the case of more than two attributes is that of *conditional utility independence.* This means that the utility associated with any level of an attribute X does not change as attribute Y varies, holding constant attribute Z at various levels.

The presence or absence of utility independence is established by a series of questions involving paired comparisons. For example, to check whether X is utility independent of Y, attribute Y is set at some level, y_i and the analyst asks the decision maker to make a series of choices between a 50-50 lottery (involving x values) and either a second 50-50 lottery (involving different x values) or a particular level of X. The procedure is then repeated with Y set at level y_j and then further reiterated. If the paired comparisons are not affected by the particular levels of Y, X is utility independent of Y.

The assessment of conditional utility independence involves a simple extension of this procedure. Attribute X is conditionally independent of attribute Y (although not necessarily vice versa), if the preference order for lotteries involving changes in X does not depend on the level of Y, when Z is fixed at any level.

If utility independence does not obtain, the decision analyst may take any of several actions, among them transformation of the attributes, direct assessment of the utilities of a number of multiattribute outcomes followed by extrapolation to the entire outcome space, or the use of other forms of utility functions. Since it appears to be most often the case that the independence of utility axiom is satisfied, we comment no further on these alternative techniques.

BDT acknowledges the theoretical validity of the preferential and utility independence assumptions, but, at least in its applied function, does not test them. BDT relies on the robustness of linear models to accommodate any violations of these assumptions. There are thus no procedures within BDT for testing these assumptions.

IIT also recognizes the importance of independence assumptions. It ordinarily assumes that the scale and weight values of attributes are not dependent on the levels of other attributes, but models involving variable weights and/or scale values have at times been tested. Tests of independence assumptions within IIT are not common, but would take the form of tests of goodness of fit for constant versus variable weight models. As noted previously, concepts related to preferential and utility independency/dependence are neither conceptually nor procedurally prominent in PDT, SJT, or IIT.

19.1.3 Overview

This section was concerned with subjective representations of the interrelations among observable task elements. Two types of interrelations were identified: (a) subjective representations of environmental interrelations among cues, attributes, stimuli, etc., and (b) dependencies in the utility, value, or desirability of levels of an attribute as a function of the levels of other attributes. Of the six approaches, SJT and PDT are most concerned with the former issues, as indicated by their use and operationalization of concepts such as cue intercorrelation and associative bonds. DT is most concerned with preference and utility dependency/independence; it is the only approach containing procedures routinely used to address this issue, although BDT and IIT also explicitly acknowledge its importance.

19.2 SUBJECTIVE USE OF OBJECTIVE DATA

All six approaches contain concepts referring to functional relationships between cue, attribute, or stimuli levels and individuals' judgments or decisions. These concepts may apply to judgments of preference—in DT, BDT, and PDT; to judgments of inference—in AT; or, to both—in SJT and IIT. Within the three probability approaches the relevant concept is that of *value* or *utility*, with SJT it is *function form*, within IIT it is *scale value*, and within AT it can be referred to as *directionality*.

The procedures of each approach for operationalizing these concepts are discussed in turn.

19.2.1 Decision Theory

For DT, the concepts of interest are those of *value* or *utility;* they are relevant only to judgments of preference. A *value function* represents a formalization of an individual's value or preference structure for decision problems under conditions of certainty; it serves to compare various levels of different attributes indirectly. In particular, a value function v associates a real number $v(x)$ to each point in an evaluation space, provided that, if the decision maker prefers x_i to x_j (is indifferent between them), then he prefers $v(x_i)$ to $v(x_j)$ (is indifferent between them). In essence, what the value function does is to rescale the objective values of an attribute X. A graphical representation of the v-function plots the X values, using the natural units of the attribute, on the ordinate and the $v(x)$ values, ranging from 0 to 1, on the abscissa.

In terms of procedures, after the range of the attribute is established, the fractile method described earlier is used to find the value x' such that the decision maker is indifferent between receiving a 50-50 lottery offering x_0 or x_1, or receiving x' for sure. This mid-value splitting technique is iterated until sufficient points have been established to enable plotting of the function. If the preferential independence assumption is met (see Chapter 19.1.2), this same procedure can be extended to the n-attribute case.

Utility functions are not identical to value functions; a utility function is a value function, although the converse is not necessarily true. Utility functions are appropriate for the assessment of preferences under conditions of uncertainty. They are more complex to assess than value functions, since the decision maker's risk preferences must be taken into account.

The procedures for assigning utility functions to probabilistic alternatives are described below. We begin with the procedures for alternatives evaluated in terms of one attribute X. First, the range of the attribute scale, from the minimum possible to the maximum possible value, is defined. The decision analyst then identifies certain relevant qualitative characteristics of the utility function. He or she determines if the u-function is monotonic; whether for x_i, $1, \ldots n$, it is always the case that x_j is preferred to (not preferred to) x_i, where $j > i$. The analyst also determines the decision maker's attitude toward risk; i.e., the analyst asks the decision maker if he or she prefers the certainty option offering x_i or a 50-50 lottery offering x_{i+k} or x_{i-k} for a number of different levels of both x_i and k. The point here is to identify the general form of the utility function; the form of the function will be concave if the decision maker is risk averse and convex if he or she is risk prone.

Next, the quantitative characteristics of the utility function are determined in an analogous fashion to that which was done with value functions. A few points on the utility function are fixed using the fractile technique. That is, the procedure starts by identifying the certainty equivalent x' such that the decision maker is indifferent between it and a 50-50 lottery offering x_0 and x_1 (the worst and best possible outcomes). The procedure is iterated until a sufficient number of points have been fixed to plot a straight line describing the function, or to fit a parametric curve, if the decision maker is risk prone or risk averse.

In the extension to the n-attribute case, the analyst is dealing with vectors rather than scalars. Utility must therefore be assessed over a multi-attribute consequence space. The procedures are essentially the same as above, however, if the utility independence assumption is satisfied for all pairs of attributes. If the utility independence assumption is not satisfied, the analyst will ordinarily attempt to redefine the attributes so they are utility independent or directly assess preferences within the multiattribute consequence space.

19.2.2 Behavioral Decision Theory

For BDT, the concept of interest is that of the *value curve*. Although they share similar theoretical origins, DT and BDT differ considerably in their procedures for assessing value curves. Although BDT occasionally uses similar techniques to those of DT in basic research, within its practical applications it routinely assesses value curves in a much more direct manner.

The concept of value curve in BDT refers to an individual's value or preference structure for each dimension of value used in evaluating the relative desirability or utility of competing alternatives. The value curve, then, represents the functional relationship between an attribute value and judgments of desirability. In graphic terms, the x-axis represents the *plausible* range of a dimension (which is not necessarily numeric, e.g., it may range from "poor" to "excellent"), while the y-axis represents desirability (with the same metric for each dimension).

Procedurally, the first steps in BDT involve the identification of the appropriate decision maker(s), the alternatives to be evaluated, and the relevant dimensions of value. Also, the relative weights associated with each dimension are ordinarily identified (see 19.3.2) prior to specification of the value curves.

Value curves are ordinarily assessed by one of two methods. If the utility associated with an underlying dimension is conditionally monotonic, the BDT analyst often approximates the value curve by drawing a straight line. The justification for this simplified procedure for defining value curves is the robustness of linear approximation after aggregation across attributes. If the utility associated with an underlying dimension is not monotonic, or if the decision maker emphasizes the nonlinearity of the value function, the usual procedure is simply to ask the respondent to draw a graph describing his or her value curve for that dimension.

19.2.3 Psychological Decision Theory

PDT conceptualizes value and utility in a somewhat different fashion from DT or BDT. In prospect theory (Kahneman & Tversky, 1979), the carriers of value in problems of risky decision making are changes in wealth or welfare, rather than final states, and value is treated as a function of (a) the asset position that serves as a reference point and (b) the magnitude of the change (positive or negative) from that reference point. PDT, like IIT below, attends more closely than DT or BDT to the "psychological meaning" of value or utility. In general, the value function, v, is concave for gains and convex for losses and is steeper for losses than for gains. In terms of procedures, the value curve for an individual is constructed on the basis of his or her choices among risky prospects of the form "receive x with probability p, y with probability q, and (if $p + q < 1$), nothing with probability 1-p-q."

19.2.4 Social Judgment Theory

In SJT, the concept of *function form* refers to the functional relationship between the values of a cue and either an individual's ratings of desirability or his or her inferences concerning the value of a criterion. The function form relates values of an attribute (in terms of the ranges appearing in the task) to values of the judgment (made on an interval scale); graphically, it appears similar to the concepts of value or utility in DT or BDT. Unlike DT or BDT, however, the function forms associated with each dimension are ordinarily all assessed simultaneously, along with the weights associated with each dimension, on the basis of wholistic ratings of a number of profiles or cases.

Procedurally, the judgment problem and its relevant dimensions are first identified, and the ranges for each cue are established by the judge and/or analyst. A number of hypothetical profiles or cases are then constructed (or, a number of real profiles selected). These profiles contain different combinations of the values of the cues and are presented sequentially to the judge, frequently via interactive computer techniques. The judge rates the desirability of each or estimates the value of the criterion, responding on an interval scale.

The relationship between judgments and cue values are then described by multiple regression statistical techniques. The basic model within SJT is a weighted averaging model which includes both the natural cue values and the squared deviation of each cue value from the cue mean. Inclusion of the squared terms permits the specification of U and inverted-U shaped function forms or any cue-judgment function that can be approximated by some portion of a parabola, as well as linear function forms. Function forms share a common range and are ordinarily displayed graphically (along with relative weights) via interactive computer graphics techniques. Judges are sometimes asked simply to draw the desired function form for a cue, especially after a preliminary analysis based upon their wholistic ratings of multiple cases.

19.2.5 Information Integration Theory

IIT can be distinguished from DT, BDT, and SJT by its concern with the subjective rescaling of attributes. That is, rather than relating judgments to the natural metric of the dimensions, IIT relates judgments to the subjective metrics of the dimensions; objective values are thus translated into *scale values.*

The primary concerns of IIT are with the algebraic models that best describe human information integration and with substantive theory. Scales are of secondary interest insofar as the functional scale values of stimuli are dependent upon the model best describing the judge's information integration processes. The central issue in IIT theory, then, is the test of the goodness of fit of a model to the data. Such a test provides joint validation of the model and the response scale. In other words, the scale value of stimuli can only be discussed in terms of an integration model with good fit to the data.

Procedurally, the judgment analyst first constructs stimulus combinations, using factorial design. The judge then rates each combination, on a scale assumed to possess interval properties; this assumption is tested within the course of IIT procedures. The judge may express his or her rating in terms of numbers, lengths of lines, graphs, and so forth.

A test of the goodness of fit of the model to the data is then performed. For example, if the hypothesized model were an averaging model, the test of goodness of fit would require no significant interactions in an analysis of variance and parallelism when levels of each stimulus were plotted as a function of the levels of each other stimulus. If the goodness of fit test is passed, the response scale is validated as an interval scale. Satisfactory fit testifies to the adequacy of the response measure, and such validation of the model thus provides a functional scaling of the response. Observed row means then provide estimates on an interval scale of the scale values of the row stimuli.

The same general procedure is followed for the tests of adding, subtracting, or multiplying models. If the model satisfactorily passes the appropriate goodness of fit test, then row means can be interpreted as scale values of the stimuli. Many IIT studies, however, provide little information concerning scale values because of the small number of factorial levels involved in the design. For example, a 2×2 ANOVA design provides essentially no information on the stimulus scale, since the 0 and 1 points on a scale are arbitrary.

19.2.6 Attribution Theory

Only a weak form of a concept of functional relationship is found in the AT approach, that of *directionality*. Directionality indicates the general nature of the relationship between levels of stimuli and levels of judgment. Within AT, these descriptions are usually nomothetic and are frequently based upon the results from analyses of data from ANOVA designs. For example, it is common to encounter statements of the form: "Low levels of attribute X are associated with judgments that the level of variable Y is low, while high levels of attribute X are associated with judgments that the level of variable Y is high."

Procedurally, a number of stimulus combinations are first generated, usually in a factorial design and frequently involving only two levels of each attribute. Judges then rate some or all of the attribute combinations; usually, each judge responds to only one or a small subset of all possible combinations. Data is ordinarily aggregated across judges; for those attributes that statistical analyses (usually, ANOVA) indicate have a significant effect on judgments, the direction of the effect is reported.

19.2.7 Overview

All six approaches contain some concept related to the functional relations between attributes and judgments, although there exists considerable variation in both the nature of these concepts and, particularly, in the procedures by which they operationalize those concepts. The end output of the procedures of DT, BDT, and PDT, and SJT, however, seem much the same. Each of those approaches generates a description of the relationships between attribute levels and individuals' judgments of desirability (or of the value of a criterion) and this description is frequently represented in graphic form. AT also commonly describes such relationships between attribute levels and judgments, although in less specific form and usually in reference to groups of judges rather than individuals. IIT takes the most divergent approach to this issue, rescaling objective attribute levels into psychological scale values.

The major procedural difference among the approaches is probably the manner in which they elicit responses from judges in order to identify utility or value functions, function forms, or scale values. The procedures can be divided into three general categories. First, DT and PDT (and, occasionally, BDT) rely upon procedures involving indication of preference among lotteries, bets, or other risky choices. Second, BDT usually relies upon more direct procedures, approximating value curves with straight lines or simply having the judge draw the value curve; occasionally SJT also makes use of this procedure. Finally, SJT, IIT, and AT customarily require judges to make wholistic ratings of profiles or objects.

Two issues concerning the relative merit of the various procedures for identifying functional relationships between attribute levels and individuals' judgments are deserving of brief note. The first of these is the issue of ease of use and practicality. Under this heading would also fall such considerations as user satisfaction and time required for conduct of the procedures. Although empirical tests are required to establish the facts of the matter, DT's procedures appear to rate lowest in this respect because of the number of questions to which the decision maker must respond and the amount of time required for the specification of value or utility curves. On their face, the direct specification procedures used by BDT appear to be simplest and least time consuming.

The second issue is the type of error to which procedures are most prone or resistant. In particular the error associated with any procedure can be divided into two components: errors of estimation and errors of elicitation. Estimation error is error associated with imprecision of procedures from a theoretical standpoint; these can be described as "errors in principle." Elicitation error is error associated with psychological factors, such as fatigue, boredom, or inattention; these can be described as "errors in practice." DT with its rigorous, exhaustive procedures for testing independence assumptions and constructing value or utility functions would seem to be on one end of the continuum, insofar as it employs procedures that are designed to minimize errors of measurement. BDT with its simple and direct procedures appears to be on the other end of the continuum, with procedures designed to minimize errors of elicitation. Which type of error is more important in the analysis of judgment or decision processes is, of course, a topic for empirical research.

19.3 CUE UTILIZATION

All six approaches contain some concept related to cue utilization. In particular, all six approaches make use of the concept of *weight*, or the importance of a piece of information to individuals' judgments of preference or inferences about states of the world. We discuss in turn the procedures used by each approach in operationalizing the concept of weight.

19.3.1 Decision Theory

DT has two concepts related to weight. The first is that of *scaling constants* which are used to weight the various unidimensional value or utility functions that enter a multidimensional utility function. The second is that of *subjective probability* which is used to weight the utility of an outcome when making a decision under conditions of uncertainty.

Scaling Constants We turn first to the procedures for assessing scaling constants for multiattribute value functions under conditions of certainty. We start with the simplest case, that involving only two attributes. After the unidimensional value functions for two attributes X and Y are obtained using the procedures described above (19.2.1), the analyst asks the respondent to make a series of choices between alternatives in order to obtain information for identifying the two scaling constants k_x and k_y. The purpose of these choices is to identify two pairs of X, Y values to which the decision maker is indifferent.

The analyst begins by asking the decision maker which of the pairs (x_0, y_1) and (x_1, y_0) is preferred, where x_0 and y_0 are the worst levels of those attributes and x_1 and y_1 are the best. The decision maker can indicate that he or she is either indifferent, prefers the option with the highest X value (x_1, y_0), or prefers the option with the highest Y value (x_0, y_1). If he or she is indifferent, then, $k_x = k_y = .5$; if the option with the highest X value is preferred, then, $k_x > k_y$; and, if the option with the highest Y value is preferred, then $k_y > k_x$. Supposing that (x_1, y_0) is preferred to (x_0, y_1), the analyst then asks the decision maker a series of questions designed to identify a value, x_i, such that he or she is indifferent between (x_i, y_0) and (x_0, y_1). Knowing the value x_i, and given that

$$\sum_{i=1}^{n} k_i = 1$$

then k_x and k_y can be derived using simple algebra. This procedure can easily be generalized to the case of more than two attributes.

We now turn to the procedures for assessing scaling constants for multiattribute utility functions under conditions of uncertainty. Again, we deal with the case of two attributes. The form of a multiattribute utility function can be specified in terms of (a) conditional utility functions over the attributes and (b) scaling constants. For example, a multilinear utility function with two attributes can be specified as

$$u(y, z) = k_y u_y(y) + k_z u_z(z) + k_{yz} u_y(y) u_z(z) \tag{19.1}$$

where there is one conditional utility function each for Y and Z, and three scaling constants: k_y, k_z, k_{yz}. The two utility functions u_y and u_z are scaled from 0 to 1.

The basic idea underlying the procedures is to obtain a set of three independent equations with three unkowns, which are then solved to find the ks. The procedures for generating these equations may involve either certainty comparisons or probabilistic techniques. A typical set of procedures might involve the following steps:

If we assume that preferences are a monotonically increasing function of Y, Z, and (Y, Z), then the first equation can be easily generated; for (Y_1, Z_1):

$$1 = k_y + k_z + k_{yz} \tag{19.2}$$

Then, using the techniques described above for the estimation of scaling constants under certainty, if the decision maker's preferences indicate that $k_y > k_z$, a value of Y, (y_i) can be identified such that the decision maker is indifferent between (y_i, z_0) and (y_0, z_1). The second equation can thus be written as

$$k_z = k_y u_y (y_i) \tag{19.3}$$

Next, using probabilistic scaling techniques, a third equation can be generated via a series of questions designed to find the probability, (p_y) such that the decision maker is indifferent between the consequence (y_i, z_0) for sure and a lottery offering consequence (y_1, z_1) with probability, p, and consequence (y_0, z_0) with probability $1\text{-}p$. The third equation, then, can be written as

$$k_y = p_y \tag{19.4}$$

These three equations can then be solved for the values of the scaling constants.

These procedures can be generalized to the case of more than two attributes. In the n-attribute case, the rank order of the values of the ks are ordinarily first determined in order to guide the process of eliciting estimates of their relative magnitude. The customary procedure for this ranking involves setting the values of each attribute at their lowest levels. The analyst then asks the decision maker to indicate which of the attributes he or she would move to its highest level, if he or she could move only one. Then, the decision maker is asked which of the remaining attributes he or she would raise to its highest level, and so on, until the rank order of the importance of each attribute has been established.

Subjective Probability   The second concept in DT that sometimes serves as a weighting factor is that of subjective probability, the assessment of which we have already described in 18.2. In evaluating multiattribute utility functions under uncertainty, the utilities of probabilistic alternatives must be transformed into subjective expected utilities in order to make final evaluations of each alternative. This transformation is accomplished by weighting utility by the subjective probability of the event. If the estimate of probability is a point estimate, the procedure for calculating subjective expected utility is given by the formula

$$SEU_i = p_i U_i \tag{19.5}$$

where SEU is the subjective expected utility of an alternative, p_i is its probability, and U_i is its utility. If the subjective probability of an alternative is expressed in terms of a probability distribution, the procedure for determining its subjective expected utility is given by the formula

$$SEU_i = \int p_i (U_i) \tag{19.6}$$

where $\int p_i$ indicates integration over the probability distribution for the ith alternative.

19.3.2 Behavioral Decision Theory

Within BDT, there also exists two concepts related to weight. The first is that of *weight*, which refers to the relative importance the judge assigns to relevant dimensions in evaluating preference for multiattribute alternatives. After the entities to be evaluated and the relevant dimensions of value have been identified, the judge ranks the dimensions in order of importance. The judge then rates the dimensions in order of importance, preserving ratios, with the least important dimension assigned a rating of 10. The ratings are then summed and each is divided by the sum in order to establish a measure of the relative importance of each dimension; relative weights, therefore, sum to one. The relative weights are then entered into the following formula

$$V_j = \sum_{i=1}^{n} w_i v_i (x_{ij}) \tag{19.7}$$

where V_j is the overall value of the jth entity, w_i is the relative weight associated with the ith attribute, v_i is the value curve associated with the ith attribute, and x_{ij} is the level on the ith attribute for the jth entity. Thus, for each alternative, its overall utility is the weighted sum of the utility of each attribute level for that alternative.

The second concept is that of *subjective probability*. In basic research in BDT, it is sometimes used in the same manner as in DT to calculate the subjective expected utility of probabilistic options or alternatives.

19.3.3 Psychological Decision Theory

In PDT, the concept of *decision weight* replaces that of subjective probability in the analysis of decision making under risk. According to prospect theory, risky options are evaluated by the formula

$$SEV_i = w\ (p_i)V_i \tag{19.8}$$

where SEV_i is the subjective expected value for the ith alternative, the decision weight $w\ (p_i)$ replaces the probability p_i used in DT and BDT, and the value of an alternative V_i is determined by the value function, v, as assessed by the procedures described in 19.2.3. Decision weights are generally lower than the corresponding probabilities, except in the range of low probabilities. Decision weights for certain quantities are also generally higher than for uncertain quantities with the same expected value.

Decision weights are assessed by the same type of procedures used by DT or BDT to assess subjective probabilities. That is, they are inferred from preferences between risky options, or *prospects*. Decision weights are not required to obey the probability axioms, however, nor do they provide an adequate measure of degree of belief.

19.3.4 Social Judgment Theory

In SJT, the concept of *weight* refers to the relative importance judges place on cues in making judgments of preference or inference. The procedures involved in assessing weights are identical to those described for assessing function forms, since the two are assessed simultaneously. In particular, the procedures are based on wholistic ratings of a number of hypothetical (or real) profiles. A weighted averaging model describing the judges' use of information is then developed on the basis of regression analyses. Relative weights for each cue are computed by dividing the beta weight for each cue by the sum of the beta weights for all cues; relative weights thus sum to one. Relative weights are ordinarily displayed graphically in terms of bar graphs, the relative lengths of which indicate the importance of each dimension, as well as by a numeric value between 0 and 1. Relative weights are combined with function forms to evaluate individual profiles or alternatives in terms of the formula

$$Y_j = \sum_{i=1}^{n} w_i f_i(x_{ij}) \tag{19.9}$$

where, Y_j is the judgment for the jth profile, w_i is the relative weight associated with the ith cue, f_i is the function form associated with the ith cue, and x_{ij} is the level on the ith cue for the jth profile.

19.3.5 Information Integration Theory

In IIT, the concept of *weight* refers to the salience or importance of the information contained by a stimulus item. It may be regarded as the amount of information in the stimulus. The concept of weight is operationalized in IIT differently from the other approaches. All the other approaches derive weights from the data; they normally make no a priori assumptions about the values of weights, other than restrictions such as that the weights must sum to 1. IIT, however, ordinarily specifies weights a priori on the basis of substantive theory and the particular model of the information integration process to be tested. Weights are frequently assumed to be equal across stimuli, unless there are good theoretical reasons to set them otherwise a priori. For example, stimuli might be assigned greater or lesser weight according to their serial position in a sequence. Relative weights can be manipulated by varying the number of equivalent stimuli in a subset, or by manipulating the reliability of a piece of information. Specific procedures for estimating differential weights are fairly complex and nongeneral and will not be discussed here (the interested reader is referred to Anderson, 1972; Norman, 1976).

In IIT studies of risky decision making, the probability of events is assumed to modify value in determining the subjective utility of bets. Such probabilities, therefore, can also be thought of as weighting factors. The treatment of probabilities by IIT is similar to the decision weight concept of PDT's prospect theory. The weight associated with a probability is not a direct function of its magnitude but of its subjective scale value for an individual.

19.3.6 Attribution Theory

AT contains no well-developed concept of weight, particularly with respect to individual judges. A related idea appears, however, in nomothetic statements concerning the judgment processes of groups of judges. This idea is usually presented in a dichotomous yes/no form and is based upon standard tests of *statistical significance.* In particular, statements of the type "attribute X significantly affects (does not significantly affect) judgments about variable Y" are frequently found within AT.

19.3.7 Overview

All six approaches contain concepts referring to the importance of particular attributes in judgments of preference or inference. A major topic over the past few years has been which set of procedures leads to the most accurate descriptions of such weights. Recently, however, a number of theoretical and empirical studies (Dawes & Corrigan, 1974; Einhorn & Hogarth, 1975; Schmidt, 1971; Wainer, 1976) have demonstrated that in many instances all possible sets of weights produce essentially the same results. The conclusion suggested by such research is that the establishment of differential weights is often unnecessary; equal weights will serve just as well. Recent theoretical research by McClelland (1978) and others, however, has suggested that the determination of optimal differential weights in multiattribute decisions is more commonly important than the results of the above studies had indicated. Nonoptimal weights can give quite erroneous results when attributes or cues are negatively intercorrelated, and McClelland has argued that such negative intercorrelations are characteristic of many interesting or difficult decision problems. In any case, there appears to be no empirical evidence to indicate that any one of the six approaches' procedures is significantly better than any other in eliciting optimal weights.

The major issue concerning the relative merit of various procedures for eliciting weights, therefore, may not be their relative accuracy, but rather more practical and psychological issues such as ease of use, user satisfaction, and time required. Again, the DT approach appears to be the most complex and time consuming when a large number of scaling constants must be assessed. They appear to be relatively simple and quick, however, when only a small number of attributes are involved in the multiattribute utility function. There do not appear to be great differences among the other approaches with respect to ease of use, satisfaction, time required and so forth. Empirical research is necessary, of course, to provide reliable evidence concerning these issues.

19.4 CENTRAL PROCESSES

Two separate topics are discussed under the heading of central processes. The first is that of *organizing principle,* which refers to the manner in which information is organized or integrated into a judgment or decision. The second is that of *psychological and cognitive factors,* which refer to processes which bias or otherwise influence individuals' judgments or decisions. Each is discussed in turn.

19.4.1 Organizing Principles

The concept of organizing principle refers to the manner in which information or data is combined into a judgment or decision. In general, organizing principles may be distinguished according to whether they are intended to be *prescriptive,* dictating the manner in which information is to be combined into a judgment, as is most often the case in DT and BDT, or *descriptive,* describing the cognitive processes by which individuals combine information into judgments, as in IIT or AT. In point of fact, the distinction between prescriptive and descriptive organizing principles does not hold up well under close scrutiny. For example, DT has been identified as an approach which is solely concerned with applied judgment and decision problems and which is not concerned with basic research on human cognitive processes. It might be expected, therefore, that organizing principles within DT could be regarded as purely prescriptive. With respect to multiattribute utility functions, however, the validity of such a conclusion is far from clear.

The multiattribute utility function that is fitted to a particular judgment or decision problem is indeed regarded within DT as the appropriate means for combining information concerning (a) the utility of particular levels of each attribute, (b) the relative importance of each attribute, and (c) the specific levels of an alternative on an attribute into an overall evaluation of the utility of that alternative. In that sense, multiattribute utility functions are thus prescriptive. But multiattribute utility functions can take a number of forms, including additive, multiplicative, and multilinear ones, and the appropriate utility function for use with a particular problem is selected on the basis of the individual's expressions of ordinal preferences among lotteries or other options. DT's selection of an organizing principle for use in evaluating alternatives thus also contains a descriptive component; the type of multiattribute utility function which best fits or describes certain ordinal preferences of the individual is used in prescribing the overall utility of alternatives for him or her.

Although the distinction between prescriptive and descriptive organizing principles is therefore sometimes problematic, it is nonetheless generally useful for clarifying the intended function of organizing principles across approaches. The organizing principles commonly found within each of the six approaches will now be considered; each will be distinguished according to whether it is better characterized as descriptive or prescriptive.

Decision Theory The first type of organizing principle within DT is that of *Bayes' Theorem*, which specifies the optimal means of revising objective probabilities. Bayes' Theorem states that

$$P(H_i/D) = \frac{P(D/H_i)\,P(H_i)}{\Sigma\,[P(D/H_i)\,P(H_i)]}$$ (19.10)

where $P(H_i/D)$ is the probability that some hypothesis H_i is true, $P(D/H_i)$ is the conditional probability that the datum D would be observed if H_i were true, and $P(H_i)$ is the prior probability of hypothesis H_i. Bayes' Theorem is regarded by DT as the appropriate means for revising subjective probabilities, and it is used prescriptively when applicable to practical decision problems in which subjective estimates of probability must be revised or integrated. Other logical rules for the revision or integration of probabilities are also used when appropriate.

The second organizing principle is that of *expected utility*. Within DT, it is prescribed that alternatives with greater expected utility should be preferred to those with lesser expected utility; where expected utility is defined by the formula

$$EU_i = p_i u_i$$ (19.11)

and where EU_i is the expected utility of alternative i, p_i is its probability, and u_i is its utility. If the probability of an event is subjectively estimated rather than objectively known, the expected utility of an alternative is referred to an *subjective expected utility*. The maximization of expected utility or subjective expected utility is also prescribed by DT.

The final type of organizing principle is that of multiattribute utility functions. The most general form of such utility functions is the *multilinear* model. The multilinear model (for two variables) can be described by the following formula

$$u\,(y,\,z) = k_y u_y\,(y) + k_z u_z\,(z) + k_{yz} u_y\,(y)\,u_z\,(z) \qquad (19.12)$$

which states that the utility of an alternative for particular levels of Y and Z, $[u\,(y,\,z)]$, is a function of the scaling constant for Y, times the utility for·the particular level of Y, $[(k_y u_y\,(y)]$; plus the scaling constant for Z, times the utility for the particular level of Z, $[k_z u_z\,(z)]$; plus the weighted utility of the joint levels for Y and Z, $[k_{yz} u_y\,(y)u_z\,(z)]$.

The multilinear model can be shown to subsume both *additive* models

$$u\,(y,\,z) = k_y u_y\,(y) + k_y u_y\,(x) \qquad (19.13)$$

and *multiplicative* models

$$u\,(y,\,z) = u_y\,(y)\,u_z\,(z) \qquad (19.14)$$

Both additive and multiplicative, as well as multilinear, utility functions are frequently used within DT (although since the so-called additive model is constrained for $\Sigma k_i = 1$, it would be more accurately described as a weighted averaging model). The organizing principles specified by the above multiattribute utility functions can generally be regarded as prescriptive, although selection of the particular type of utility function for use in a problem is based upon descriptive information regarding the individual's preference structure, as noted earlier.

Behavior Decision Theory Bayes' Theorem and similar logical rules for the integration of probabilities frequently serve as prescriptive organizing principles for BDT. For applied problems such rules are used prescriptively wherever appropriate to the nature of the problem.

BDT has also made extensive use of Bayes' Theorem in basic research. Much of this research has involved tests of the adequacy of the theorem as a descriptive model of individuals' revisions of subjective estimates of probability. In terms of procedures, such tests have customarily involved the elicitation of subjective probability estimates or revisions on the basis of a given set of information. Such estimates are then compared to those yielded by Bayes' Theorem; the degree of congruence between the estimates elicited from individuals and those generated by Bayes' Theorem indicate the adequacy of the theorem as a descriptive model of individuals' organizing principles.

Also found in BDT are *subjective expected utility models.* Subjective expected utility is used within DT as a prescriptive model for ordering the desirability of uncertain alternatives, events, or actions. In general, maximization of subjective expected utility can be regarded as a basic prescriptive principle of BDT.

Finally, within BDT the following organizing principle is provided for evaluating the relative desirability of competing multiattribute alternatives under conditions of certainty:

$$V_j = \sum_{i=1}^{n} w_i v_i (x_{ij}) \tag{19.15}$$

where V_j is the overall value of the jth alternative, w_i is the relative weight and v_i is the value curve associated with the $i$the attribute, x_{ij} is the level on the ith attribute for the jth alternative, and where the relative weights are constrained to sum to 1. BDT thus relies on *weighted averaging* organizing principles in practical applications. BDT justifies its exclusive use of weighted averaging models, in contrast to multiplicative and multilinear models, on the grounds that even when the assumptions for such models are not satisfied they ordinarily provide good approximations to the solutions yielded by more complex models involving multiplicative terms.

Psychological Decision Theory PDT frequently makes use of Bayes' Theorem as well as other logical or normative rules of information use in its basic research. Although such organizing principles are not used prescriptively, neither can their use be considered descriptive. Rather, they are used as standards against which individuals' behavior is contrasted. Deviations from the responses prescribed by such models serve as data for use in developing and testing hypotheses concerning the influence of psychological factors and biases on information processing.

Also found within the prospect theory component of PDT is the concept of *subjective expected value,* as defined by the following formula:

$$SEV_i = w (p_i) V_i \tag{19.16}$$

where SEV_i is the subjective expected value of an alternative, the decision weight, $w (p_i)$, is a measure of the subjective weight associated with a given probability, and the value of an alternative, V_i, reflects the change in wealth or welfare afforded by the alternative. This formula is identical to that for subjective expected value (or utility) within DT or BDT, with the exceptions that (a) the subjective probability term is replaced by its decision weight and (b) the value function is based upon subjective evaluations of changes in wealth and welfare. As thus modified, the above formula for subjective expected value is proposed as descriptive of individuals' decision making concerning probabilistic options or alternatives.

Social Judgment Theory The mainstay of SJT is the following *weighted averaging model*

$$Y_j = \sum_{i=1}^{n} w_i f_i (x_{ij}) \tag{19.17}$$

where Y_j is the judgment for the jth profile, w_i is the relative weight and f_i is the function form associated with the ith cue, x_{ij} is the level of the ith cue for the jth profile, and relative weights are constrained to sum to 1. Such models provide descriptions of the *judgment policies* which individuals bring to particular judgment or decision problems.

SJT is perhaps the best example of an approach in which concepts concerning the objective characteristics of the task environment affect the concepts and procedures associated with a judge's organizing principles. SJT holds that environmental task systems can ordinarily best be described in terms of a weighted averaging model that involve the association of relative weights and function forms with each cue; parallel concepts are used to describe the organizing principles of individual judges.' In SJT, weighted averaging models may be used either to describe individuals' judgment or decision processes or to evaluate competing alternatives; that is, they may serve either descriptive or (weakly) prescriptive functions.

SJT explicitly acknowledges the descriptive validity of other organizing principles, such as multiplicative and noncompensatory models. Such models are rarely found within SJT, however, with the occasional exception of *noncompensatory models* involving cut-off rules which yield extreme (minimum or maximum) judgments for certain levels of particular cues.

Information Integration Theory IIT is almost exclusively concerned with the development of *descriptions* of the organizing principles used in information integration processes. Moreover, the nature of organizing principles hypothesized as descriptive of individuals' information integration processes is theoretically and substantively based. Substantive theories of judgments have thus been tested which have involved a variety of simple algebraic models, including *adding, averaging, multiplying,* and *subtracting* models. Much of the work within IIT has involved tests of the adequacy of adding versus averaging models and multiplicative versus linear models (i.e., adding, averaging, and subtracting models) for describing information integration processes in the context of specific problems.

As an example, the averaging model in IIT can be described in the following manner:

$$R = C + \frac{\sum\limits_{i=0}^{n} w_i s_i}{\sum\limits_{i=0}^{n} w_i} \qquad (19.18)$$

where R is the individual's response, C allows for an arbitrary zero in the response scale, w_i is the weights associated with each stimulus, and s_i is the scale value for each level of the stimuli, with s_0 as an internal organismic variable. A formulation of the additive model in IIT can be obtained by omitting the denominator term in Equation 19.18.

Attribution Theory   The most prominent organizing principle within AT is that of *schemata.* According to Kelley (1973), schemata are "assumed patterns of data in a complete analysis of variance framework" (115). These schemata can be interpreted as a repertoire of abstract ideas about the operation and interaction of causal factors. The individual uses these schemata to fit bits and pieces of relevant information into an interpretable framework and, thus, to reach (usually reasonably good) causal attributions.

Two major principles guide the attributional analysis, as well as the construction of causal schemata. These are the covariation and discounting principles. The *covariation* principle states that an effect is attributed to the one of its plausible causes with which it covaries over time. The *discounting* principle states that the role of a given cause in producing an effect is discounted if other plausible causes are also present.

In short, causal schemata are conceptions of the manner in which two or more causal factors interact in relation to a particular kind of effect. They can be described as similar to an analysis of variance layout; the individual may "fill in the cells" either by observation or by "thought experiments." The judge relies upon these schemata in organizing information into inferences about the causes of events.

Procedurally, the adequacy of schemata as models of individuals' organizing principles is tested via traditional hypothetico-deductive techniques. Predictions of judges' inferences are derived from these models and the responses from judges are tested against those predictions. Congruence between predictions and responses is interpreted as confirmation in support of the models as a description of the organizing principles used by judges in making inferences.

19.4.2 Psychological and Cognitive Factors

Most of the approaches contain concepts referring to psychological or cognitive factors that bias or otherwise influence judgment or decision making processes. Psychological factors are most prominent within PDT and AT; cognitive factors are most prominent within SJT.

Psychological Biases PDT gives greater attention to psychological factors biasing or influencing judgment and decision processes than do any of the other approaches. Indeed, the investigation of such biases is the focal point of PDT. Included in PDT are such concepts as *representativeness, availability, anchoring, causality,* and *diagnosticity,* all of which refer to factors that bias or distort judgment and decision making processes and lead to less than optimal performance. A similar concept within BDT is that of *conservatism* which refers to individuals' frequent failure to revise probabilities upon the receipt of new information as much as they should in comparison with optimal models. AT also contains a number of concepts referring to psychological biases, for example, the so-called *attribution error,* which refers to the tendency for individuals to overattribute effects to personological versus environmental causes.

Concepts concerning psychological biases do not ordinarily affect procedures directly. Rather, they are the subject matter of basic research, particularly within PDT, BDT, and AT. PDT, however, has specified corrective procedures for such biases in applied decision making settings (Kahneman & Tversky, in press, and DT and BDT analysts frequently attempt to prevent such biases from affecting their applied decision analyses.

Cognitive Factors Several of the approaches appear to recognize implicitly or explicitly the potential effects of cognitive limitations or other cognitive factors on judgment and decision problems. For example, all the approaches seem to recognize limitations in the number of items of information which individuals can process simultaneously, and limit to a fairly small number the items of information presented for consideration at one time.

SJT, however, is the only approach to operationalize and measure routinely a concept related to cognitive factors. *Cognitive control* is a major concept within SJT; it can be operationalized as the multiple correlation coefficient between cues and observed judgments or as the correlation between observed judgments and those predicted by a given model. More specifically, it can be interpreted as variance in judgments "around" a given model. If the given model is an optimal model of an individual's judgment processes, cognitive control can be interpreted as a measure of the individuals' ability to exercise or apply a given judgment policy consistently, without error.

Less than perfect correlation between predicted and observed judgments can be indicative of an ill-fitting model as well as of less than perfect cognitive control. The correlation across judgments on repeated trials is indicative of the source of error. To the extent the test-retest correlation between repeated trials, or *consistency,* is high, a less than optimal model is indicated. To the extent consistency is low, less than perfect cognitive control is indicated as the source of error.

19.4.3 Overview

This section was concerned with central processes involved in judgment and decision processes. Two types of central processes were distinguished: (a) those related to the manner in which data or information is organized into a judgment or decision and (b) those related to psychological or cognitive factors that influence judgment or decision processes.

Organizing principles were distinguished according to whether they were descriptive or prescriptive. Although this distinction is sometimes less than clear-cut, the organizing principles postulated within PDT, SJT, IIT, and AT are generally descriptive; the organizing principles postulated within DT and BDT are generally prescriptive.

A variety of organizing principles were found both across and within approaches. These organizing principles can be grouped into three major categories. The first category is represented by Bayes' Theorem and the expected utility and expected value models. These models specify optimal responses on logical or normative grounds and are normally prescriptive, although they sometimes serve merely as a criterion against which the results of descriptive basic research are contrasted. Instances of this category of organizing principles are found within the DT, BDT, PDT, and occasionally, IIT approaches.

The second category is that of algebraic models, including multilinear, adding, averaging, multiplicative, and subtracting models. Instances of such models are commonly found in DT and BDT (in their applied versions), SJT, and IIT. Several forms of such algebraic models are to be found in DT and IIT; the weighted averaging model is the only model in this category to be found in BDT, and it is by far the most common in SJT. Such models normally serve descriptive purposes in IIT and SJT. They are used prescriptively in DT and BDT, and to a lesser degree in applications of SJT.

The final category is found in AT, that of *schemata*. These models are exclusively descriptive and are generally not as precisely or quantitatively formulated as models in the former two categories.

With respect to psychological and cognitive factors, psychological biases which lead to less than optimal performance were identified as important concepts particularly within PDT, but also within BDT and AT. Procedures developed by PDT for attempting to prevent such biases from affecting applied decision analyses are sometimes used in DT and BDT. SJT's concept of cognitive control is the only concept concerning cognitive factors that influence judgment and decision processes to be routinely operationalized and measured.

Chapter 20

Feedback/Optimality

We turn finally to those procedures and concepts related to feedback, optimality, and other aspects of the interaction between judges and the task environment. Such concepts are generally most applicable to the double-system case, in which there exists an environmental criterion or correct answer and in which it is thus possible for learning to take place. Such concepts are therefore most prominent in SJT, with its theoretical emphasis on the double-system case, and in DT, BDT, and PDT, with their emphasis on probability estimation problems. Such concepts assume little or no importance for IIT and AT.

This chapter addresses the following three topics concerning feedback and optimality:

1 Feedback;
2 Feedforward;
3 Optimality.

Major similarities and differences among the approaches with respect to concepts and procedures for dealing with issues of feedback and optimality are indicated in Table 20-1.

Table 20-1 Comparison of Approaches with Respect to Feedback/Optimality

Topics in feedback/optimality	DT	BDT	PDT	SJT	IIT	AT
20.1 Feedback						
Outcome		X^a		X		
Cognitive				X		
20.2 Feedforward						
Feedforward				X		
20.3.1 Optimality-analytically defined						
Internal consistency	X	X	X			
Cognitive control				X		
Accuracy (of probability estimates)		X	X			
Maximization of expected utility		X	X		X	
20.3.2 Optimality-empirically defined						
Achievement				X		
Accuracy				X		

[a] Indicates that an approach routinely follows procedure or operationalizes concept.

20.1 FEEDBACK

The concept of feedback refers to information provided about the accuracy or quality of one's inferences. Of the six approaches, the concept of feedback is commonly operationalized only within BDT and SJT.

BDT has conducted probability estimation studies in which the effects of feedback on judge's accuracy have been investigated. Procedurally, after the judge makes a probability estimate he or she is told the (stochastically) correct answer. SJT has also made use of this type of procedure, describing it as *outcome feedback*. That is, after every inference about the value of a criterion, the judge is given the correct answer.

SJT distinguishes between outcome feedback and *cognitive feedback*. Cognitive feedback differs from outcome feedback in that it provides more than yes/no or correct/incorrect information to the judge. In particular, it consists of information describing the relationships between (a) cues and the criterion, between (b) cues and the judge's inferences, or (c) both. That is, the judge is shown graphic models describing for the environmental system, (a) the weights associated with each attribute, (b) the function forms between attributes and the criterion, and (c) the degree of task uncertainty within the system; and/or, the judge is shown for him or herself, a model describing (a) the weights he or she associates with each attribute, (b) the function forms between attributes and his or her judgments, and (c) his or her degree of cognitive control. The judge is thus given information about the congruence between his or her cognitive system and the environmental system with which he or she is interacting. SJT has conducted numerous studies comparing the effects of outcome versus cognitive feedback on learning; the conclusion has been that cognitive feedback is generally superior in facilitating learning (see Hammond et al., 1975).

20.2 FEEDFORWARD

The concept of feedforward is unique to the SJT approach. Feedforward consists of information describing the relationships between task attributes and the task criterion, which is given the judge before he or she interacts with the task. Feedforward is usually displayed in the same manner as the cognitive feedback described immediately above. Studies conducted by SJT of the effects of feedforward on learning indicate that it facilitates learning of cue-criterion relations (Deane, Hammond, & Summers, 1972; Hammond & Summers, 1965; Summers & Hammond, 1966).

20.3 OPTIMALITY

Concepts concerning the quality of individuals' judgments or decisions generally involve the idea of optimality. Two types of optimality can be distinguished; those which are defined analytically and those which are defined empirically. Each is discussed in turn.

20.3.1 Analytically Defined Optimality

Analytically defined optimality refers to optimality with respect to (a) relations between individuals' judgments or decisions and observable task elements, or (b) relations between judgments or decisions and criteria that can be analytically inferred from such observable task elements. It is thus applicable to all three types of judgment tasks previously identified in the procedure section: judgments of preference, judgments of inference, and probability estimation judgments.

One of the major analytically defined concepts of optimality is that of *internal consistency.* Internal consistency applies primarily to judgments of preference, although it is also applicable to inference problems in which the true value of the environmental criterion is unknown or intrinsically unknowable. Internal consistency is usually defined in terms of adherence to or violations of principles of logic. It is an important concept within DT, BDT, and PDT. Most commonly, internal consistency refers to transitivity or intransitivity among preferences or choices. Preferences are *transitive* if A is preferred to B, B is preferred to C, and A is preferred to C; if A is preferred to B, B is preferred to C, and C is preferred to A, then the individual's preferences are *intransitive.* Within DT, this issue is ordinarily addressed by first explicitly identifying and resolving any such inconsistencies, and then formalizing decision makers' preference and utility structures (as corrected for inconsistency) and using the resultant formal models to evaluate multiple alternatives. This procedure thus assures that the overall evaluations of alternatives are logically consistent. In practical applications, BDT does not usually address the inconsistency issue directly, arguing that any logical inconsistencies inadvertently incorporated into formal models of individuals' utility structures ordinarily have little effect. PDT, and to a lesser extent BDT, have conducted basic research directed toward discovering and describing the psychological factors that lead to logical inconsistencies in choices among risky options.

A related analytically defined concept of optimality applicable to judgments of preference or inference is that of *cognitive control,* which is found in SJT. Cognitive control refers to the degree to which individuals are consistent in applying a given judgment policy to a particular judgment or decision task. It is operationally defined as the multiple correlation coefficient between cues and observed judgments or as the correlation between observed judgments and those predicted by the best-fitting model of the individuals' judgment processes.

Although, cognitive control was previously discussed in section 19.4, it is also relevant here, not only because it refers to the consistency with which individuals integrate information into judgments, but also because a significant amount of the basic research within SJT has been concerned with discovering the effects of objective task characteristics (e.g., degree of task uncertainty, ecological validity of cues) on individuals' degree of cognitive control. The concept of cognitive control is thus quite closely tied to the objective characteristics of the environmental systems with which judges interact. In practical applications, SJT often replaces judges with their own models, both for judgments of preference and inference, thereby ensuring that alternatives are evaluated optimally; i.e., that individuals' judgment policies are applied to the alternatives with perfect cognitive control.

A third analytically defined concept of optimality is that of *accuracy* with respect to probability estimation. The optimal analytical revision and integration of objective probabilities is specified by Bayes' Theorem or other logical principles. Both BDT and PDT have conducted basic research concerning the accuracy with which individuals estimate or revise probability estimates with respect to the optimal estimate or revision specified by Bayes' Theorem or similar logical principles. That is, individuals' responses are compared to the correct answer, as analytically derived from observable task elements.

The fourth and final analytically defined concept related to optimality is the *maximization of expected utility.* For example, in studies of betting and gambling behavior conducted by BDT, PDT, and IIT, the optimality or suboptimality of individuals' choices or behaviors have been assessed by comparison with the analytically computed expected value of those courses of action. Achievement of such optimality is often tied to the concept of *accuracy*, since maximizing expected value among risky options is often dependent upon the individuals' ability to estimate accurately the probabilities entailed by complex options.

20.3.2 Empirically Defined Optimality

Empirically defined optimality refers to optimality with respect to relations between individuals' judgments and depth variables in the environment which are not directly observable but which must be inferred on the basis of observable task elements. SJT is the only one of the six approaches in which such concepts are prominent, again, as a result of its greater interest in the double- and n-system cases.

The optimality of the judges' responses with respect to the depth variable or environmental criterion is described in SJT by two concepts: *achievement* and *knowledge*. The relation between these two concepts is described by the following formula:

$$r_a = G R_s R_e \qquad\qquad (20.1)$$

where r_a is achievement, G is knowledge, R_s is cognitive control, and R_e is task uncertainty.

Achievement, or r_a, is operationally defined as the correlation between the individual's responses and the values of the criterion. Achievement thus refers to the congruence between the individual's estimates and the true values of the environmental criterion.

Achivement can be a misleading index of optimality, however. Achievement may be less than perfect (i.e., $r_a < 1.0$) not because of suboptimal performance by the judge, but because the task is intrinsically unpredictable with perfect certainty (i.e., there exists task uncertainty within the system, or $R_e < 1.0$). Moreover, the individuals' achievement may be less than optimal not because his or her judgment policy does not correspond perfectly to the environmental system, but because he or she applies the judgment policy with less than perfect cognitive control (i.e., $R_s < 1.0$). A more general index of optimality within SJT, therefore, is knowledge, or G, which refers to correspondence between the predictable components of the environmental system and the judge's cognitive system. Knowledge is operationally defined as the correlation between those values of the environmental criterion and those values of the judge's responses predicted by the models best describing each. Achievement is therefore a function of cognitive control and task uncertainty, as well as the judge's knowledge about the environmental system.

20.4 OVERVIEW

This section was concerned with concepts and procedures related to feedback, optimality, and other aspects of the interaction between judges and the task environment. The concept of feedback, or information about the quality of one's inferences, is found in SJT and BDT; the concept of feedforward is found in SJT.

A number of different concepts of optimality with respect to judges' interactions with task systems were identified. Optimality can be distinguished according to whether it is analytically or empirically defined. Concepts of analytically defined optimality are most prominent in the three probability approaches, SJT, and, to a lesser extent, IIT. SJT is the only approach for which empirically defined concepts of optimality are important.

References

Adelman, L. *Information about task properties. A necessary, but not a sufficient condition for high levels of achievement in multiple-cue probability learning tasks.* (Center for Research on Judgment and Policy Report No. 199). Boulder: Institute of Behavioral Science, University of Colorado, 1977.

Adelman, L., & Mumpower, J. The analysis of expert judgment. *Technological Forecasting and Social Change,* in press.

Anderson, N. H. Averaging versus adding as a stimulus-combination rule in impression formation. *Journal of Experimental Psychology,* 1965, *70,* 394-400.

Anderson, N. H. Functional measurement and psychophysical judgment. *Psychological Review,* 1970, *77*(3), 153-170.

Anderson, N. H. *Information integration theory: A brief survey.* (Center for Human Information Processing Report No. 24). La Jolla: University of California, San Diego, 1972.

Anderson, N. H. Information integration theory applied to attitudes about U.S. Presidents. *Journal of Educational Psychology,* 1973, *64*(1), 1-8.

Anderson, N. Cognitive algebra: Integration theory applied to social attribution. In L. Berkowitz (Ed.), *Advances in experimental social psychology* (Vol. 7). New York: Academic Press, 1974.

Anderson, N. H., & Alexander, G. R. Choice test of the averaging hypothesis for information integration. *Cognitive Psychology,* 1971, *2*(3), 313-324.

Anderson, N. H., & Shanteau, J. Weak inference with linear models. *Psychological Bulletin,* 1977, *84*(6), 1155-1170.

Arrow, K. J. *Social choice and individual values* (2nd ed.). New York: Wiley, 1963.

Balke, W. M., Hammond, K. R., & Meyer, G. D. An alternative approach to labor-management relations. *Administrative Science Quarterly,* 1973, *18,* 311-327.

Berlin, Isaiah. *Russian thinkers.* New York: Viking Press, 1978.

Björkman, M. Inference behavior in nonmetric ecologies. In L. Rappoport & D. A. Summers (Eds.), *Human judgment and social interaction.* New York: Holt, Rinehart & Winston, 1973.

Bock, R. D., & Jones, L. V. *The measurement and prediction of judgment and choice.* San Francisco: Holden-Day, 1968.

Brehmer, B. Cognitive dependence on additive and configural cue-criterion relations. *American Journal of Psychology,* 1969, *82,* 490-503.

Brehmer, B. Hypotheses about relations between scaled variables in the learning of probabilistic inference tasks. *Organizational Behavior and Human Performance,* 1974, *11*(1), 1-27.

Brehmer, B. Policy conflict and policy change as a function of task characteristics. IV. The effect of cue intercorrelations. *Scandinavian Journal of Psychology,* 1975, *16,* 85-96.

Brehmer, B., & Hammond, K. R. Cognitive sources of interpersonal conflict: Analysis of interactions between linear and nonlinear cognitive systems. *Organizational Behavior and Human Performance,* 1973, *10,* 290-313.

Brehmer, B., & Hammond, K. R. Cognitive factors in interpersonal conflict. In D. Druckman (Ed.), *Negotiations: Social-Psychological perspectives.* Beverly Hills/London: Sage Publications, Inc., 1977.

Bruner, J. S., Goodnow, J. J., & Austin, G. A. *A study of thinking.* New York: Wiley, 1956.

Brunswik, E. *Wahrnehmung und gegenstandswelt: grundlegung einer psychologie vom gegenstand her* (Perception and the world of objects: the foundations of a psychology in terms of objects). Leipzig und Wien: Deuticke, 1934.

Brunswik, E. The conceptual framework of psychology. In *International encyclopedia of unified science* (Vol. 1, No. 10). Chicago: University of Chicago Press, 1952.

Brunswik, E. Representative design and probabilistic theory in a functional psychology. *Psychological Review,* 1955, *62*(3), 193-217.

Brunswik, E. *Perception and the representative design of psychological experiments* (2nd ed.). Berkeley: University of California Press, 1956.

Brunswik, E. Scope and aspects of the cognitive problem. In H. Gruber, K. R. Hammond & R. Jessor, (Eds.), *Contemporary approaches to cognition: A symposium held at the University of Colorado.* Cambridge: Harvard University Press, 1957.

Campbell, D., & Fiske, D. Convergent and discrimination validation by the multitrait-multimethod matrix. *Psychological Bulletin,* 1959, *56*(2), 81.

Castellan, N. J. Determination of joint distributions from marginal distributions in dichotomous systems. *Psychometrika,* 1970, *35*(4), 439-454.

Chapman, L. J., & Chapman, J. P. Genesis of popular but erroneous psychodiagnostic observation. *Journal of Abnormal Psychology,* 1967, *72,* 193-207.

Chapman, L. J., & Chapman, J. P. Illusory correlation as an obstacle to the use of valid psychodiagnostic signs. *Journal of Abnormal Psychology,* 1969, *74,* 271-280.

Cliff, N. Adverbs as multipliers. *Psychological Review,* 1959, *66*(1), 27-44.

Cochrane, J. L., & Zeleny, M. (Eds.). *Multiple criteria decision making.* Columbia: University of South Carolina Press, 1973.

Cook, R. L., & Stewart, T. R. A comparison of seven methods for obtaining subjective descriptions of judgmental policy. *Organizational Behavior and Human Performance,* 1975, *13,* 31-45.

Coombs, C. H. *A theory of data.* New York: Wiley, 1964.

Coombs, C. H., & Bowen, J. Additivity of risk in portfolios. *Perception and Psychophysics,* 1971, *10,* 43-46.

Coombs, L. C., Coombs, C. H., & McClelland, G. H. Preference scales for number and sex of children. *Population Studies,* 1975, *29*(2), 273-298.

Crow, W. J., & Hammond, K. R. The generality of accuracy and response sets in interpersonal perception. *Journal of Abnormal Social Psychology,* 1957, *54*(3), 384-390.

Davidson, D., Suppes, P., & Siegel, S. *Decision-making: An experimental approach.* Stanford: Stanford University Press, 1957.

Dawes, R. M. A case study of graduate admissions: Application of three principles of human decision making. *American Psychologist,* 1971, *26,* 180-188.

Dawes, R. M. The mind, the model, and the task. In F. Restle, R. M. Shiffrin, N. J. Castellan, H. R. Lindman, & D. P. Pisoni (Eds.), *Cognitive theory* (Vol. 1). Hillsdale, N. J.: Erlbaum, 1975.

Dawes, R. M., & Corrigan, B. Linear models in decision making. *Psychological Bulletin,* 1974, *81*(2), 95-106.

Deane, D. H., Hammond, K. R., & Summers, D. A. Acquisition and application of knowledge in complex inference tasks. *Journal of Experimental Psychology,* 1972, *92,* 20-26.

de Neufville, R., & Keeney, R. L. Use of decision analysis in airport development for Mexico City. In A. W. Drake, R. L. Keeney & P. M. Morse (Eds.), *Analysis of public systems.* Cambridge, Mass.: M.I.T. Press, 1972.

Druckman, D. *Negotiations.* Beverly Hills: Sage Publications, 1977.

Edwards, W. Probability-preferences in gambling. *American Journal of Psychology,* 1953, *66,* 349-364.

Edwards, W. The theory of decision making. *Psychological Bulletin,* 1954, *51*(4), 380-417.

Edwards, W. Behavioral decision theory. *Annual Review of Psychology,* 1961, *12,* 473-498.

Edwards, W. Social utilities. *The Engineering Economist,* Summer Symposium Series, 1971, *6.*

Edwards, W. *Application of research on cognition to man-machine system design.* (Engineering Psychology Laboratory Report No. 010342-1-F). Ann Arbor: University of Michigan, 1972.

Edwards, W. Technology for Director Dubious: Evaluation and decision in public context. In K. R. Hammond (Ed.), *Judgment and decision in public policy formation.* Boulder: Westview Press, 1978.

Edwards, W., & Tversky, A. *Decision making: Selected readings.* Middlesex, England: Penguin Books, Ltd., 1967.

Einhorn, H. J., & Hogarth, R. M. Unit weighting schemes for decision making. *Organizational Behavior and Human Performance*, 1975, *13*, 171-192.

Einhorn, H. J., & Hogarth, R. M. Confidence in judgment: Persistence of the illusion of validity. *Psychological Review*, 1978, *85*, 395-416.

Einhorn, H. J., Kleinmuntz, B., & Kleinmuntz, D. N. Linear regression and process-tracing models of judgment. *Psychological Review*, 1979, *86*, 465-485.

Fischer, G. W. Convergent validation of decomposed multi-attribute utility assessment procedures for risky and riskless decisions. *Organizational Behavior and Human Performance*, 1977, *18*(2), 295-315.

Fischhoff, B. Attribution theory and judgment under uncertainty. In J. H. Harvey, W. J. Ickes, & R. F. Kidd (Eds.), *New directions in attribution research* (Vol. 1). Hillsdale, N.J.: Erlbaum, 1976.

Fischhoff, B. *Decision analysis: Clinical art or clinical science?* Paper presented at the Sixth Research Conference on Subjective Probability, Utility and Decision Making, Warsaw, 1977.

Fishbein, M., & Ajzen, I. *Belief, attitude, intention, and behavior: An introduction to theory and research.* Reading, Mass.: Addison-Wesley Publishing Co., 1975.

Fishburn, P. C. Interdependent preferences on finite sets. *Journal of Mathematical Psychology*, 1972, *9*(2), 225-236.

Ford, A., & Gardiner, P. C. A new measure of sensitivity for social system simulation models. *IEEE Transaction on Systems, Man, and Cybernetics*, 1979, *9*, 105-114.

Frieze, I. H. The role of information processing in making causal attributions for success and failure. In J. S. Carroll & J. W. Payne (Eds.), *Cognition and Social Behavior.* Hillsdale, N.J.: Erlbaum, 1976.

Frieze, I. H., Bar-Tal, D., & Carroll, J. S. (Eds.). *New approaches to social problems: Applications of attribution theory.* San Francisco: Jossey-Bass, 1979.

Frieze, I., & Weiner, B. Cue utilization and attributional judgments for success and failure. *Journal of Personality*, 1971, *39*, 591-605.

Fryback, D. G. *Use of radiologists' subjective probability estimates in a medical decision making problem.* (Michigan Mathematical Psychology Program Report No. 74-14). Ann Arbor: University of Michigan, 1974.

Gardiner, P. C., & Edwards, W. Public values: Multiattribute-utility measurement for social decision making. In M. F. Kaplan & S. Schwartz (Eds.), *Human judgment and decision processes.* New York: Academic Press, 1975.

Gillis, J. S. Effects of chlorpromazine and thiothixene on acute schizophrenic patients. In K. R. Hammond & C. R. B. Joyce (Eds.), *Psychoactive drugs and social judgment: Theory and research.* New York: Wiley, 1975.

Goldberg, L. R. Man versus model of man: A rationale, plus some evidence, for a method of improving on clinical inferences. *Psychological Bulletin,* 1970, *73*(6), 422-432.

Goldberg, L. R. Man versus model of man: Just how conflicting is that evidence? *Organizational Behavior and Human Performance,* 1976, *16*(1), 13-22.

Grether, D. M., & Plott, C. R. Economic theory of choice and the preference reversal phenomenon. *American Economic Review,* 1979, *69,* 623-638.

Hamilos, C. A., & Pitz, G. F. The encoding and recognition of probabilistic information in a decision task. *Organizational Behavior and Human Performance,* 1977, *20*(2), 184-202.

Hammond, K. R. Probabilistic functioning and the clinical method. *Psychological Review,* 1955, *62*(4), 255-262.

Hammond, K. R. *The psychology of Egon Brunswik.* New York: Holt, Rinehart, & Winston, 1966.

Hammond, K. R. Computer graphics as an aid to learning. *Science,* 1971, *172,* 903-908.

Hammond, K. R. Toward increasing competence of thought in public policy formation. In K. R. Hammond (Ed.), *Judgment and decision in public policy formation.* Boulder: Westview Press, 1978.

Hammond, K. R., & Adelman, L. Science, values, and human judgment. *Science,* 1976, *194,* 389-396.

Hammond, K. R., & Brehmer, B. Quasi-Rationality and distrust: Implications for international conflict. In L. Rappoport & D. A. Summers (Eds.), *Human judgment and social interaction.* New York: Holt, Rinehart and Winston, 1973.

Hammond, K. R., & Joyce, C. R. B. (Eds.), *Psychoactive drugs and social judgment: Theory and research.* New York: Wiley, 1975.

Hammond, K. R., & Kern, F. *Teaching comprehensive medical care: A psychological study of a change in medical education.* Cambridge, Mass.: Harvard University Press, 1959.

Hammond, K. R., Klitz, J. K., & Cook, R. L. How systems analysts can provide more effective assistance to the policy maker. *Journal of Applied Systems Analysis,* 1978, *5*(2), 111-136.

Hammond, K. R., Mumpower, J. L., & Smith, T. H. Linking environmental models with models of human judgment: A symmetrical decision aid. *IEEE Transactions on Systems, Man, and Cybernetics,* 1977, *SMC-7*(5), 358-367.

Hammond, K. R., Rohrbaugh, J., Mumpower, J., & Adelman, L. Social judgment theory: Applications in policy formation. In M. F. Kaplan & S. Schwartz (Eds.), *Human judgment and decision processes in applied settings.* New York: Academic Press, 1977.

Hammond, K. R., Stewart, T. R., Adelman, L., & Wascoe, N. E. *Report to the Denver city council and mayor regarding the choice of handgun ammunition for the Denver police department.* (Center for Research on Judgment and Policy Report No. 179). Boulder: Institute of Behavioral Science, University of Colorado, 1975.

Hammond, K. R., Stewart, T. R., Brehmer, B., & Steinmann, D. Social judgment theory. In M. Kaplan & S. Schwartz (Eds.), *Human judgment and decision processes.* New York: Academic Press, 1975.

Hammond, K. R., & Summers, D. A. Cognitive dependence on linear and nonlinear cues. *Psychological Review,* 1965, *72,* 215-224.

Hammond, K. R., Summers, D. A., & Deane, D. H. Negative effects of outcome-feedback in multiple-cue probability learning. *Organizational Behavior and Human Performance,* 1973, *9*(1), 30-34.

Harsanyi, J. C. Nonlinear social welfare functions. Do welfare economists have a special exemption from Bayesian rationality? *Theory and Decision,* 1974, *6*(3), 311-332.

Harvey, J. H., Ickes, W. J., & Kidd, R. F. (Eds.). *New directions in attribution research.* Hillsdale, N.J.: Erlbaum, 1976.

Hawkins, D. *The science and ethics of equality.* New York: Basic Books, 1977.

Heider, F. Ding und Medium. *Symposion,* 1926, *1,* 109-157.

Heider, F. *The psychology of interpersonal relations.* New York: Wiley, 1958.

Heider, F. On perception, event structure, and psychological environment. *Psychological Issues,* 1959, *3,* 1-23.

Holton, G. *Thematic origins of scientific thought: Kepler to Einstein.* Cambridge, Mass.: Harvard University Press, 1973.

Jensen, F. A., & Peterson, C. R. Psychological effects of proper scoring rules. *Organizational Behavior and Human Performance,* 1973, *9,* 307-317.

Jones, E. E. The rocky road from acts to dispositions. *American Psychologist,* 1979, *34,* 107-117.

Jones, E. E., & Davis, K. E. From acts to dispositions: The attribution process in person perception. In L. Berkowitz (Ed.), *Advances in experimental social psychology* (Vol. 2). New York: Academic Press, 1965.

Jones, E. E., Davis, K. E., & Gergen, K. J. Role playing variations and their informational value for person perception. *Journal of Abnormal and Social Psychology,* 1961, *63,* 302-310.

Jones, E. E., & Goethals, C. R. Order effects in impression formation: Attribution context and the nature of the entity. In E. E. Jones, D. E. Kanouse, H. H. Kelley, R. E. Nisbett, S. Valins, & B. Weiner (Eds.), *Attribution: Perceiving the causes of behavior.* Morristown, N.J.: General Learning Press, 1971, 1972.

Jones, E. E., Kanouse, D. E., Kelley, H. H., Nisbett, R. E., Valins, S., & Weiner, B. *Attribution: Perceiving the causes of behavior.* Morristown, N.J.: General Learning Press, 1971, 1972.

Jones, E. E., & McGillis, D. Correspondent inferences and the attribution cube: a comparative reappraisal. In J. H. Harvey, W. J. Ickes, & R. F. Kidd (Eds.), *New directions in attribution research* (Vol. 1). Hillsdale, N.J.: Erlbaum, 1976.

Kahneman, D., & Tversky, A. Subjective probability: A judgment of representativeness. *Cognitive Psychology,* 1972, *3,* 430-454.

Kahneman, D., & Tversky, A. On the psychology of prediction. *Psychological Review,* 1973, *80*(4), 237-251.

Kahneman, D., & Tversky, A. Prospect theory. *Econometrica,* 1979, *47,* 263-291.

Kahneman, D., & Tversky, A. Intuitive predictions: Biases and corrective procedures. In S. G. Makridakis (Ed.), special issue of *Management Science,* in press.

Kaplan, M. F., & Schersching, G. Juror deliberation: An information integration analysis. In B. D. Sales (Ed.), *Perspectives in law and psychology.* Volume II: *The jury, judicial, and trial process.* New York: Plenum, 1978.

Kaplan, M. F., & Schwartz, S. (Eds.). *Human judgment and decision processes.* New York: Academic Press, 1975.

Keeney, R. L. A decision analysis with multiple objectives: The Mexico City airport. *Bell Journal of F-onomics and Management Science,* 1973, *4,* 101-117. (a)

Keeney, R. L. A utility function for the response times of engines and ladders to fires. *Urban Analysis,* 1973, *1,* 209-222. (b)

Keeney, R. L. *Preference models of environment impact.* (International Institute for Applied Systems Analysis Research Memorandum RM-76-4). Laxenburg, Austria: IIASA, 1976.

Keeney, R. L. The art of assessing multiattribute utility functions. *Organizational Behavior and Human Performance,* 1977, *19*(2), 267-310.

Keeney, R. L., & Kirkwood, C. W. Group decision making using cardinal social welfare functions. *Management Science,* 1975, *22*(4), 430-437.

Keeney, R. L., & Raiffa, H. *Decisions with multiple objectives: Preferences and value tradeoffs.* New York: Wiley, 1976.

Keeney, R. L., & Sicherman, A. Assessing and analyzing preferences concerning multiple objectives: An interactive computer program. *Behavioral Sciences,* 1976, *21*(3), 173-182.

Kelley, H. H. Attribution theory in social psychology. In D. Levine (Ed.), Nebraska symposium on motivation, 1967 (Vol. 15). Lincoln: University of Nebraska Press, 1967.

Kelley, H. H. Causal schemata and the attribution processes. In E. E. Jones, D. E. Kanouse, H. H. Kelley, R. E. Nisbett, S. Valins, & B. Weiner (Eds.), *Attribution: Perceiving the causes of behavior.* New York: General Learning Press, 1971, 1972.

Kelley, H. H. The processes of causal attribution. *American Psychologist,* 1973, *28*(2), 107-128.

Knowles, B. A., Hammond, K. R., Stewart, T. R., & Summers, D. A. Positive and negative redundancy in multiple cue probability tasks. *Journal of Experimental Psychology,* 1971, *90,* 157-159.

Knowles, B. A., Hammond, K. R., Stewart, T. R., & Summers, D. A. Detection of redundancy in multiple cue probability tasks. *Journal of Experimental Psychology,* 1972, *93,* 425-427.

Krantz, D. H., Luce, R. D., Suppes, P., & Tversky, A. *Foundations of measurement.* Volume I: *Additive and polynomial representations.* New York: Academic Press, 1971.

Krantz, D. H., & Tversky, A. Conjoint-Measurement analysis of composition rules in psychology. *Psychological Review,* 1971, *78*(2), 151-169.

Krech, D. Discussion: Theory and reductionism. *Psychological Review,* 1955, *62*(3), 229-230.

Kukla, A. Foundations of an attributional theory of performance. *Psychological Review*, 1972, *79*(6), 454-470.

Lampel, A. K., Anderson, N. H. Combining visual and verbal information in an impression-formation task. *Journal of Personality and Social Psychology*, 1968, *9*(1), 1-6.

Leal, L., & Pearl, J. An interactive program for conversational elicitation of decision structures. *IEEE Transactions on Systems, Man, and Cybernetics*, 1977, *SMC-7*(5), 368-376.

Lichtenstein, S., Earle, T. C., & Slovic, P. Cue utilization in a numerical prediction task. *Journal of Experimental Psychology: Human Perception and Performance*, 1975, *104*, 77-85.

Lichtenstein, S. C., & Slovic, P. Reversals of preference between bids and choices in gambling decisions. *Journal of Experimental Psychology*, 1971, *89*(1), 46-55.

Lichtenstein, S., Slovic, P., Fischhoff, B., Layman, M., & Coombs, B. Judged frequency of lethal events. *Journal of Experimental Psychology: Human Learning and Memory*, 1978, *4*, 551-578.

Lindell, M. K., & Stewart, T. R. The effects of redundancy in multiple-cue probability learning. *American Journal of Psychology*, 1974, *87*(3), 393-398.

Lopes, L. L. Model-based decision and inference in stud poker. *Journal of Experimental Psychology*, 1976, *105*, 217-239.

Luce, R. D. *Individual choice behavior*. New York: Wiley, 1959.

Luce, R. D., & Raiffa, H. *Games and decisions*. New York: Wiley, 1957.

Massaro, D. W., & Anderson, N. H. Judgmental model of the Ebbinghaus illusion. *Journal of Experimental Psychology*, 1971, *89*, 147-151.

McArthur, L. A. The how and what of why: Some determinants and consequences of causal attribution. *Journal of Personality and Social Psychology*, 1972, *22*, 171-193.

McClelland, G. H. *Psychological processing of evaluative meaning of adverb-adjective combinations*. (Michigan Mathematical Psychology Program Technical Report 1974-11). Ann Arbor: University of Michigan, 1974.

McClelland, G. H. *Equal versus differential weighting for multiattribute decisions: There are no free lunches*. (Center for Research on Judgment and Policy Report No. 207). Boulder: Institute of Behavioral Science, University of Colorado, 1978.

McClelland, G., & Rohrbaugh, J. Who accepts the Pareto axiom? The role of utility and equity in arbitration decisions. *Behavioral Science*, 1978, *23*, 446-456.

McClelland, L., & Auslander, N. Perceptions of crowding and pleasantness in public settings. *Environment and Behavior*, 1978, *10*, 535-553.

McClintock, C. G. Social motivation in settings of outcome interdependence. In D. Druckman (Ed.), *Negotiations: Social-psychological perspectives*. Beverly Hills: Sage Publications, 1977.

Mosteller, F., & Nogee, P. An experimental measurement of utility. *Journal of Political Economy*, 1951, *59*(5), 371-404.

Mumpower, J. *A comparison of attribution, social learning, and social judgment theories*. (Center for Research on Judgment and Policy Report

No. 208). Boulder: Institute of Behavioral Science, University of Colorado, 1976.

Mumpower, J. L., & Hammond, K. R. Entangled task-dimensions: An impediment to interpersonal learning. *Organizational Behavior and Human Performance*, 1974, *11*(3), 377-389.

Mumpower, J., Veirs, V., & Hammond, K. R. Scientific information, social values, and policy formation: The application of simulation models and judgment analysis to the Denver regional air pollution problem. *IEEE Transactions on Systems, Man, and Cybernetics*, 1979, *SMC-9*(9), 464-476.

Nisbett, R. E. Taste, deprivation and weight determinants of eating behavior. *Journal of Personality and Social Psychology*, 1968, *10*, 107-116.

Nisbett, R. E. & Borgida, E. Attribution and the psychology of prediction. *Journal of Personality and Social Psychology*, 1975, *32*, 932-943.

Nisbett, R. E., & Wilson, T. D. Telling more than we can know: Verbal reports on mental processes. *Psychological Review*, 1977, *84*(3), 231-259.

Norman, K. L. A solution for weights and scale values in functional measurement. *Psychological Review*, 1976, *83*(1), 80-84.

Ostrom, T. M., Werner, C., & Saks, M. J. An integration theory analysis of jurors' presumptions of guilt. *Journal of Personality and Social Psychology*, 1978, *36*, 436-450.

Pepper, Stephen. *World hypotheses*. Berkeley: University of California, 1948.

Peterson, C. R., DuCharme, W. M., & Edwards, W. Sampling distributions and probability revisions. *Journal of Experimental Psychology*, 1968, *76*, 236-243.

Phelps, R. H., & Shanteau, J. Livestock judges: How much information can an expert use? *Organizational Behavior and Human Performance*, 1978, *21*(2), 209-219.

Phillips, L. D., & Edwards, W. Conservatism in a simple probability inference task. *Journal of Experimental Psychology*, 1966, *72*(3), 346-354.

Raiffa, H. *Decision analysis: Introductory lectures on choices under uncertainty*. Reading, Mass.: Addison-Wesley, 1968.

Raiffa, H. *Preferences for multi-attributed alternatives*. (RM-5868-DOT/RC). Santa Monica: The Rand Corporation, 1969.

Rapoport, A. (Ed.). *Game theory as a theory of conflict resolution*. Dordrecht, Holland: D. Reidel Publishing Co., 1974.

Rappoport, L., & Summers, D. A. (Eds.). *Human judgment and social interaction*. New York: Holt, Rinehart & Winston, 1973.

Rawls, J. *A theory of justice*. Cambridge, Mass.: Harvard University Press, 1971.

Reeder, G., & Brewer, M. A schematic model of dispositional attribution in interpersonal perception. *Psychological Review*, 1979, *86*(1), 61-79.

Roche, J. G. *Preference tradeoffs among instructional programs: An investigation of cost-benefit and decision analysis techniques in local educational decision making*. Unpublished doctoral dissertation, Graduate School of Business Administration, Harvard University, 1971.

Rohrbaugh, J. Cognitive maps: Describing the policy ecology of a community. *Great Plains-Rocky Mountain Geographical Journal*, 1977, *6*(1), 64-73.

Ross, L. The intuitive psychologist and his shortcomings: Distortions in the attribution process. In L. Berkowitz (Ed.), *Advances in experimental social psychology* (Vol. 10). New York: Academic Press, 1977.

Schmidt, F. L. The relative efficiency of regression and simple unit predictor weights in applied differential psychology. *Educational and Psychological Measurement,* 1971, *31*(3), 699-714.

Shanteau, J. C. An additive model for sequential decision making. *Journal of Experimental Psychology,* 1970, *85*(2), 181-191.

Shanteau, J. Descriptive versus normative models of sequential inference judgment. *Journal of Experimental Psychology,* 1972, *93*(1), 63-68.

Shanteau, J. An information-integration analysis of risky decision making. In M. F. Kaplan & S. Schwartz (Eds.), *Human judgment and decision processes.* New York: Academic Press, 1975.

Shanteau, J. C., & Anderson, N. H. Test of a conflict model for preference judgment. *Journal of Mathematical Psychology,* 1969, *6*(2), 312-325.

Shanteau, J., & Nagy, G. Decisions made about other people: A human judgment analysis of dating choice. In J. Carroll & J. Payne (Eds.), *Cognition and social behavior.* Hillsdale, N.J.: Erlbaum, 1976.

Shanteau, J., & Phelps, R. H. Judgment and Swine: Approaches and issues in applied judgment analysis. In M. F. Kaplan & S. Schwartz (Eds.), *Human judgment and decision processes in applied settings.* New York: Academic Press, 1977.

Shaver, K. *An introduction to attribution processes.* Cambridge, Mass.: Winthrop, 1975.

Shephard, R. N. *Use of judgments in making optional decisions.* Paper presented at the meeting of the American Association for the Advancement of Science, 1962.

Slovic, P. Towards understanding and improving decisions. In E. I. Salkovitz (Ed.), *Science, technology, and the modern Navy: Thirtieth anniversary 1946-1976.* Arlington, Va.: Department of the Navy, Office of Naval Research, 1976.

Slovic, P., Fischhoff, B., & Lichtenstein, S. Behavioral decision theory. In *Annual Review of Psychology,* 1977, *28*, 1-39.

Slovic, P., & Lichtenstein, S. C. Importance of variance preferences in gambling decisions. *Journal of Experimental Psychology,* 1968, *78*(4), 646-654.

Slovic, P., & Lichtenstein, S. Comparison of Bayesian and regression approaches to the study of information processing in judgment. *Organizational Behavior and Human Performance,* 1971, *6*, 649-744.

Slovic, P., & Lichtenstein, S. Comparison of Bayesian and regression approaches to the study of information processing in judgment. In L. Rappoport & D. Summers (Eds.), *Human judgment and social interaction.* New York: Holt, Rinehart, and Winston, 1973.

Spetzler, C. S., & Stael von Holstein, C.-A. Probability encoding in decision analysis. *Management Science,* 1975, *22*(3), 340-358.

Starr, M. K., & Zeleny, M., MCDM—State and future of the arts. *TIMS Studies in the Management Sciences,* 1977, *6*, 5-29.

Stewart, T. R., Joyce, C. R. B., & Lindell, M. K. New analyses: Application of judgment theory to physicians' judgments of drug effects. In K. R. Hammond & C. R. B. Joyce (Eds.), *Psychoactive drugs and social judgment: Theory and research.* New York: Wiley, 1975.

Storms, M. D., & Nisbett, R. E. Insomnia and the attribution process. *Journal of Personality and Social Psychology,* 1970, *16,* 319-328.

Summers, D. A., & Hammond, K. R. Inference behavior in multiple-cue tasks involving both linear and nonlinear relations. In C. P. Duncan (Ed.), *Thinking: Current experimental studies.* Philadelphia: Lippincott, 1967. (Reprinted from *Journal of Experimental Psychology,* 1966, *71.*)

Thrall, R. M., Coombs, C. H., & Davis, R. L. (Eds.). *Decision processes.* New York: Wiley, 1954.

Timmers, H., & Wagenaar, W. A. Inverse statistics and misperception of exponential growth. *Perception and Psychophysics,* 1977, *21*(6), 558-562.

Tversky, A. Additivity, utility and subjective probability. *Journal of Mathematical Psychology,* 1967, *4*(2), 175-201.

Tversky, A. Intransitivity of preferences. *Psychological Review,* 1969, *76*(1), 31-48.

Tversky, A. Elimination by aspects: A theory of choice. *Psychological Review,* 1972, *79*(4), 281-299. (a)

Tversky, A. Choice by elimination. *Journal of Mathematical Psychology,* 1972, *9*(4), 341-367. (b)

Tversky, A. Features of similarity. *Psychological Review,* 1977, *84*(4), 327-352.

Tversky, A. Addendum to K. R. Hammond, G. H. McClelland, & J. Mumpower, *The Colorado report on the integration of approaches to judgment and decision making.* (Center for Research on Judgment and Policy Report No. 213). Boulder: Institute of Behavioral Science, University of Colorado, 1978.

Tversky, A., & Kahneman, D. Belief in the law of small numbers. *Psychological Bulletin,* 1971, *76*(2), 105-110.

Tversky, A., & Kahneman, D. Availability: A heuristic for judging frequency and probability. *Cognitive Psychology,* 1973, *5,* 207-232.

Tversky, A., & Kahneman, D. Judgment under uncertainty: Heuristics and biases. *Science,* 1974, *185,* 1124-1131.

Tversky, A., & Kahneman, D. Causal schemas in judgments under uncertainty. In M. Fishbein (Ed.), *Progress in social psychology,* Hillsdale, N.J.: Erlbaum, 1979.

Urdang, L. (Ed.). *Random House dictionary* (college edition). New York: Random House, 1968.

Valins, S., & Nisbett, R. E. Attribution processes in the development and treatment of emotional disorder. In E. E. Jones, D. E. Kanouse, H. H. Kelley, R. E. Nisbett, S. Valins, & B. Weiner (Eds.), *Attribution: Perceiving the causes of behavior.* New York: General Learning Press, 1971, 1972.

von Neumann, J., & Morgenstern, O. *Theory of games and economic behavior* (2nd ed.). Princeton, N.J.: Princeton University, 1947.

Wainer, H. Estimating coefficients in linear models: It don't make no nevermind. *Psychological Bulletin,* 1976, *83*(2), 213-217.

Weiner, B., & Kukla, A. An attributional analysis of achievement motivation. *Journal of Personality and Social Psychology,* 1970, *15*(1), 1-20.

Wortman, C. Causal attributions and personal control. In J. Harvey, J. Ickes, & R. Kidd (Eds.), *New directions in attribution research* (Vol. 1). Hillsdale, N.J.: Erlbaum, 1976.

Wyer, R. S. Information redundancy, inconsistency, and novelty and their role in impression formation. *Journal of Experimental Social Psychology,* 1970, *6,* 111-127.

Zeleny, M. On the inadequacy of the regression paradigm used in the study of human judgment. *Theory and Decision,* 1976, *7,* 57-65.

Zeleny, M. Adaptive displacement of preferences in decision making. *TIMS Studies in the Management Sciences,* 1977, *6,* 147-157.

Author Index

245

Subject Index